GETTING GOOD PEOPLE AND KEEPING THEM

A Manager's Guide

Originally published as Your Team of Tigers

Craig S. Rice

amacom
American Management Associations

This book is available at a special
discount when ordered in bulk quantities.
For information, contact Special Sales Department,
American Management Associations, Publications Group,
135 West 50th Street, New York, NY 10020.

Library of Congress Cataloging in Publication Data

Rice, Craig S.
    Getting good people and keeping them.

    Originally published as: Your team of tigers. © *1982.*
    Includes index.
    1. Personnel management. 2. Executive ability.
I. American Management Associations. II. Title.
HF5549.R4868 1984   658.3   83-25685
ISBN 08144-5605-7
ISBN 0-8144-7614-7   pbk

Printing number

10 9 8 7 6 5 4 3 2

Preface

Psychologists generally agree that if you work with above-average people, you are almost certain to be, or to want to be, a high producer yourself. Thus, while this book concentrates on one idea, above-average people, it serves you in two closely related and parallel ways: in helping you to work more effectively with high achievers and in helping you become a top achiever yourself.

Why are top-quality achievers so important? For at least three reasons. First, they can greatly increase total team output through their own efforts. Second, they can and usually do stimulate others to improve the quality and quantity of their performance, so again total team output increases. Third, and perhaps most important, the above-average employee can generate a remarkably large output per dollar of wages or for each hour you invest in guiding the employee. A tiger can give you a high ROI, or return on investment, for your time and effort.

The book is divided into two parts. The first part is designed for managers who want to get better results from their employee groups, units, teams, or departments. It outlines proven procedures for finding, attracting, selecting, supervising, maintaining, motivating, and retaining high-performing employees. The second part focuses on managers themselves as high-achievers—how they can become top performers and stay that way.

The techniques described in these pages are based on the successful experiences of dozens of managers, each of whom built at least one winning team of tigers. They are also founded on actual practice in over 80 of America's best-known, most successful companies. It took each of those executives and companies years of trial and error, retrial and revision, to build a productive system. With this book you now have a pretested, streamlined, workable program in your hands that you can put to use today.

The book offers a fresh, unique approach to management. To begin with, it is aimed only at excellence—at the above-average employee, the winning player, the tiger. Unlike other books on managing people, very little space is devoted to the average employee and almost none to the below-average performer. The book focuses on high-quality, high-performing, high-producing people—getting them, using them, rewarding them, and holding them. Second, the book is dedicated to the proposition that high performers *can* be found and recruited and that, if handled properly, they will pay off big dividends compared with their salaries. (Many experienced managers still think that good people are either totally unavailable or too expensive.) Third, the book tunes into today's people and today's attitudes—the differences in how employers and employees look at things today compared with just a few years ago. The book parts company with old myths and outdated ideas about people's potential and focuses on finding, selecting, training, and supervising the high achiever for maximum benefit to both the employee and the company.

Every idea suggested has been tested, not just once but many times. Methods that did not work well were dropped. Only the good, productive systems were retained, and were often expanded and improved. Each technique is accompanied by one or more case histories of specific companies that illustrate how the method is applied. The cases demonstrate that the techniques really do work and show you what you can expect to gain for yourself. Each chapter ends with ten short commandments, or golden rules, that summarize the techniques presented. These rules are boiled down still further into an OBI, or "one best idea," for you to use in applying the techniques to the world of management.

Start today to build your own team of tigers—and to become a tiger yourself. And once you have your team assembled, *hold that tiger!*

Craig S. Rice

Contents

PART ONE
Finding and Employing the High Achiever

Tigers! Above-average employees! These people can multiply your power, profits, productivity, prestige, and even your pay. But, as reported recently in the Kiplinger Newsletter, *"Getting and keeping good employees is our country's No. 1 labor problem. That's what we found in talks with executives in a variety of lines across the country."*

What does it take to effectively recruit, select, train, motivate, and supervise a winning team of tigers? This part of the book gives you the tools and techniques you need. It starts with a chapter on the importance of high producers and what they can do for you. Then follows a series of chapters on the techniques you need to find high-producing tigers, get them to apply to you, screen them, and sell them on your firm.

Chapter 4 introduces an ingeniously practical chart called "Circles and Xs" that has worked beautifully for many companies in helping them screen and select the best candidates. Later chapters give dozens of effective methods and professional secrets for training, supervising, motivating, and retaining your tiger team. Throughout, you'll see how these techniques have been used successfully by some of the nation's largest and best-known corporations, including U.S. Steel, General Foods, Colgate, Standard Oil, General Electric, Chrysler, Revlon, and American Home. All key points are recapped in the Ten Commandments section at the end of each chapter.

The part closes with a chapter called "Hold That Tiger," which introduces some of the most important techniques you'll need— techniques that can help you challenge, reward, and promote your high producers so that you will hold on to your winning team.

CHAPTER 1
Seeing People as the Heart of Business Success

Leo Burnett liked to say, "People are the heart of our business." He would go on to explain that their ideas and their actions are the key causes of success in most companies. This is especially noticeable where products are designed, produced, or purchased for resale, and where "people" services are provided to customers. Leo started a little ad agency in Chicago a few years before World War II. He began with some used furniture and five *above*-average people. Now that company is approaching $1 billion in billing. Apparently Leo's feeling about the importance of people was right on target.

The objective of this chapter is to take a look at working people in general and above-average people in particular. We will review many typical situations and suggest some methods for finding and using high-caliber people. High producers are readily available today—the quality of business training has vastly improved, and the number of professionally educated people has greatly increased. America's better managers recognize, evaluate, find, use, and keep these tigers to help improve company profits and their own personal income as well.

PEOPLE ARE VALUABLE

"My dumbest mistake was corrected when we learned to recognize and value the human resource," said Len W., a VP of a famous corporation. "We did this by taking three fairly simple steps. First, we quit depending exclusively on cash, technical systems, and machines. As you and I know, the thought that all we need to do is plug in some procedure at one end and wait for the profits to come out at the other end gets to be very sexy to a manager. Everything is pure mechanics, right? If only it were so! How simple life would be. The plain fact is that none of these machines or systems functions until someone—a person—designs them, builds them, starts them, runs them, uses them, fixes them, and shuts them off at night. The human is the key.

"Second, we realized that human beings as a species get more valuable with each passing month and year," Len continued. "At one time, we could afford to have hundreds, even millions, of nameless, faceless, unidentifiable humans toiling at almost prehistoric tasks like ditch digging. Today, those same people, or rather their children, have technical educations, homes, cars, hopes, dreams, opinions, and insight into the way the world should be run. They have the skill to design, build, and operate power shovels that do the digging. Obviously, people become more valuable every year.

"Third, we eliminated preconceptions about which of our people might be high producers or leaders. We opened our eyes to the fact that some of our best people might have been working for many years, totally unrecognized." It was once commonly believed that only the banker's son or that rare "college man" would ever amount to much. Today we realize that any employee is a potential high producer.

Human Insight at Columbia Broadcasting System

Gus J., a manager for an award-winning CBS production group, felt that NBC and ABC were doing a better job with some of their techniques and programs. He called a meeting of the group and announced that they were missing a great opportunity. He told managers, "We have not been recognizing that the key to our future success is better use of quality people." The managers shifted their emphasis, dropping some preconceptions about who was and who was not a potential high producer. The managers changed their hiring and promotion policies and brought in some above-average people. Along with Gus, they ended up winning some of the top company and industry awards for excellence in broadcast production.

EXPECTING EXCELLENCE

"My next worst mistake was eliminated when we took three more simple steps," said Len, the corporate VP quoted earlier. "First, we improved human communications with a better exchange of information, of ideas, and of feelings. Second, we cut down on the use of abrasive or offensive directives. And third, we began to expect—and yes, even demand—more from each person. We expressed the belief that each was really able to perform at a higher level. The result, to our amazement, was that most did even better than we had dared hope!" Consider this: Most people can do twice the quantity and quality they think they can, and three times what they are presently doing—if they are allowed, encouraged, and, in fact, *expected* to perform and bloom. Experts say we use only about one-fifth of our brain's potential.

Tripling Output at Colgate

Ory D., a division manager at Colgate-Palmolive, saw his small department sinking, with sales and profits declining, and he was worried. He needed some constructive, even dramatic, action. Where to look? Ory decided to begin with what he had. He increased and improved his lines of communication to his people. Told them the whole problem, warts and all. He was not tough about it. He didn't need to be, because the facts spoke for themselves. His people got the message. Then Ory expressed great confidence in them and raised the individual objectives. Within just a few months, the sales and profit picture had more than tripled. Ory had developed some homemade high producers using communication, reasonable relations, and increased expectations. Like the CBS managers, the Colgate executive had once again demonstrated that people are the heart of the operation.

THE ABCs OF PEOPLE

"We start staffing by reviewing the basic ABCs of people," said Sid V., a successful food company executive. Regrettably, the human equation is sometimes lost in our haste to get things done—to produce, sell, and deliver those goods and services and make a profit. In the shuffle, we often forget that we are dealing with individuals. Sometimes we even ignore what our common sense and experience have taught us: If we are going to maximize people's performance, we must have insight into their ABCs—their makeups, ideas, capabilities, feelings, attitudes, hopes, dreams, and goals. Some individuals are unrecognized jewels that we hold right in our hands, while others are undiscovered gems waiting to be found elsewhere. But once we fix our jeweler's glass to our eye and start taking a real look at potential producers, then we begin to get a better insight into the surprising sparkle of basic people—particularly the vibrance of the atypical, above-average employee. After our insight comes our objective. When we can distinguish glass from zircon from diamond, we can now decide what we want to meet our team-staffing needs: how much, how many, how good, how big. We set our own standards after reviewing the ABCs of people's feelings, structures, makeups, and abilities.

Johnson & Johnson Strikes Gold

Cal G., a J&J executive, had several department managers, each doing a fairly good job, although one group was lagging. He visited with Roy, the manager of that group, on various occasions and frankly could not seem to find anything wrong. Everything was being done by the book. Then Cal suggested that Roy think a little more about his people—what made them tick and what made them stop ticking. Their situations, problems, and opportunities. Their personal and business goals. Their feelings. Nothing complex. Just a little simple thought, consideration, analysis, and insight into the human equation. With a certain reluctance, Roy finally gave it a try. He got some unexpected results. Roy found that two of his group were really unpolished nuggets of gold. One wanted to handle a larger workload of his present duties. The other sought increased authority and responsibility and was more than willing to really put forth the necessary effort. In both cases, no one had ever questioned the employees or even bothered to understand them as people. A simple look at the ABCs had struck gold and as a result, everyone gained.

IDENTIFYING TIGERS

We looked at what makes tigers tick, and especially how they differ from ordinary, average employees," said Abe D., a skilled team builder. And so Abe did two important things: He bothered to look, and since he kept his eyes open, he saw that above-average people are, indeed, a little different. If they weren't, they wouldn't be tigers. To review and understand quality people, you might use the five Ws below. The answers you get will vary from place to place and person to person, but the questions touch on some basics that generally apply.

1. *Who* are they, these tigers? They are usually the high producers or the potential high producers. They are either willing and able, or they can be made willing and able.

2. *What* makes tigers run? Usually money, but in addition, other things, such as feelings. Feelings of importance, authority, responsibility, of doing something worthwhile.

3. *Where* are they? Perhaps right in your own organization, hiding or camouflaged, or working for someone else (or looking for another job).

4. *When* do you need them? When your team performance is not what it should be or what you want it to be.

5. *Why* do they respond? Because man does not live by bread alone. Tigers are looking for other stimulation and motivation that you can easily provide.

AT&T Identifies High Performer

Hud J., a unit manager at AT&T, had long been disappointed with results from one of his groups. Hud recognized that people, not machines, were his most valuable asset. He improved his communications, set higher goals, and reviewed the basic ABCs of people, focusing on the caliber of person he wanted to fill an opening in the group. Then Hud went through the five Ws with each of several promising employees and job applicants. He discovered that a minority woman applicant, to whom he had not given much thought earlier, fit the department needs almost perfectly. She was hired and became supervisor of what was soon his top-producing team. The results did not stop there, because the department became pacesetter—an inspiration to other groups, which also improved their performance. Hud had looked for a dynamic person, found her, used the five Ws to understand what made her tick, and put her ability to work for the benefit of everyone, including himself.

WHAT TIGERS CAN DO

Get a measure of what an above-average person can do, because only then will you have a feel for the surprising value of a high producer for you and your group. Some managers use the "triple-double" formula to estimate producer power: High producers can usually solve twice the problems, handle twice the load, and get twice the results. Sometimes a lot more. Occasionally one high producer can replace several average employees.

Then we come to "quality," something not easily measured. What is it worth to you to have your biggest customer or your boss say, "I had no idea you and your group could produce such fine work, or that you had such terrific people. You're setting a great example for our entire organization!"?

Procter & Gamble Knows People Power

P&G had been struggling to build the Joy dishwashing detergent market share. Percentage of market had been creeping up, but only

slowly. Then P&G switched the product over to an aggressive advertising group, led by a true high producer. He studied the situation
. . . set dramatic new goals, and the group took dynamic action. The
brand share increased sharply. During the annual meeting, a major
stockholder said, "I would like to know which manager found and
assigned that new team to the Joy brand. We need more executives
like him." (His name was provided and was later made available for
discussions with the board of directors.)

GET READY FOR A TIGER RIDE

Brace yourself—mentally and emotionally. The extra high producer is a different breed of horse from the average or below-
average employee, who may require prodding, needling, or stern
handling. Some horses need the stick. Others respond readily to a
word or a touch. If either of these techniques is mixed up and used
on the wrong horse, the results can be poor. Effective managers
wisely shift gears according to the kind of employee involved. They
recognize that above-average people are different in some key ways.
They like a fast track. They are aggressive, willing, able, confident,
and dynamic. They are out to win races, not graze in the pasture. If
you look at the high producers with that sort of upbeat appreciation
and expectation, then you will be ready to use their full potential for
the good of your company, yourself, and the individual employees.

7-UP Takes a New View

At one time, 7-UP was a small company, headed by a few able
managers. But they had mostly average producers as department
heads. The difficulty of competing with Coke, Pepsi, and other
brands became increasingly evident and burdensome. Clearly the
company needed some high-producing department leaders. One top
manager said, "Well, if we're really going to go out and seek driving,
determined individuals, then we'll have to switch our own thinking a
little, too. Things will never be quite the same." And he was right:
Things never were the same again. Top management had found its
rocket but it was ready for the ride. The corporate atmosphere

changed. Things started to happen. 7-UP became "the UN-Cola"—a
viable alternative beverage. Awareness, image, and market share
greatly improved, largely because top management was ready for
the high producers and knew how to put their talents to good use.

GUARD AGAINST TIGER TROUBLE

You can prevent tiger problems by anticipating tigers' probable
actions and by recognizing their limitations. They tend to be highly
self-confident, self-assured, dynamic, pushy, challengers, movers.
To protect yourself, as well as to fully utilize this energy, a good first
step is to direct it toward your most serious problems. These will
soak up some of the tigers' drive and apply it in a constructive way.
Second, be sure the high-quality persons not only understand the
situation but are also aware of its probable cause. Third, give them
room to study, check, plan, set goals, and take action. Fourth, establish reasonable guidelines, but don't tie their hands any more
than necessary. Retain maximum feasible flexibility. Fifth, try to
avoid oversupervising or breathing down their necks to the extent
that they feel their every move is being watched, questioned,
doubted, or second-guessed. Under these enlightened, flexible, and
progressive conditions, a high producer will often plow the whole
field—while others are still hitching up the tractor.

Kraft Sets Guidelines That Protect Everyone

Van Y., the manager of a Kraft foods division, had just hired several
dynamic new employees and moved up two previously unrecognized high producers. These changes had been arranged in early
December and were to take effect January 2. Van realized that he
could look forward to big results during the next calendar year. But
he also took some wise precautions to avoid trouble. Van not only
prepared himself and his people for this change, he went a step
further, establishing reasonable, usable, practical descriptions and
guidelines for these new positions. Van outlined problems to be
tackled, focused on one or two key ones in each department . . .

came flat out and said that everyone would have fairly broad freedom to operate, with him as general reviewer and adviser. Van took two extra steps. He made sure that all principal managers and supervisors agreed on these guidelines, and then he provided them to all employees—so that everyone was singing from the same song sheet. And it worked beautifully. Output, production, and profits improved in each profit center, and every key problem was either solved or reduced in size.

RECOGNIZE THE REVISED DYNAMICS

Set a clear policy for yourself. First, see the changed structure as a new ball game, with increased capabilities to handle tougher situations and achieve higher goals—even in totally different areas of operation, such as a new business. Second, load on the problems. Well-burdened producers tend to work best (as long as they are not totally swamped). In fact, they are accustomed to large assignment loads and, if not given enough work, tend to take on or volunteer for extra projects. Your best-quality people will have a "hidden agenda"—a list of projects they personally want to accomplish with their department when opportunity, extra staff, or extra time permits. Third, encourage innovation, creativity, fresh approaches, new directions. This will not only stimulate the high producers but will utilize their abilities more fully and, most important, provide maximum benefits for you and your organization.

Ford's Escort—a Tough, Serious Innovation

Most major managers at Ford recognized that the small car market needed a breakthrough from Ford. Without this, there would be trouble, both with dealers and with the consumer market. Next, the managers loaded this whole project on a few high producers. The problem was complex, with hundreds of elements. And third, Ford managers not only encouraged but insisted on the best possible creative thinking that would still be compatible with the real world of finite resources. Result: the eminently successful Ford Escort, "The

World Car." This didn't "just happen." It occurred because the Ford managers recognized the human element, the abilities of above-average people. Ford prepared mentally, set guidelines, established a basic policy of appreciating the whole revised dynamics of a new ball game. Management loaded those high producers. Challenged them. Ford demanded creativity—and got it!

SELL YOUR EMPLOYEES ON HIGH PRODUCERS

Convince employees and supervisors, who may dislike—even fear—the high producer. Three simple selling steps nearly always work well: First, show them that the above-average employee will help the entire team make better progress—"you know, the thing the boss has been bugging us about." Second, note that a high producer will bring credit to everyone, "which is nice to know when the time comes for upper management to hand out the raises, bonuses, and promotions." Third, point out that a high producer accomplishes a lot and takes some of the load off everyone. "We will be working smarter, not harder. Maybe a bit easier, in fact!" As a fourth point (an extra if you need it), you might mention that above-average performers become that way partly because they know how to get along with people, "so this cat will be a good guy to work with." For supervisors, you can make a final point: "You will be in control. This fellow knows how to take orders and follow through on them. You'll enjoy supervising him."

Proper Preparation Produces Extra Performance for Marlboro

The Marlboro brand had not been doing well. The supervisor, Ben J., was upset and critical. "We'd better make some progress around here, or heads will roll!" Then the VP met with Ben to tell him they had found a young woman candidate to fill the position the supervisor had outlined for product brand assistant. The VP wisely took the time to demonstrate to Ben that this was an ideal person to help them make progress, bring credit to the team, and take the load off the supervisor. He also pointed out that she had a pleasant personality and a history of following orders very well. Ben interviewed the candidate along with several alternates. He agreed with the VP's assessment, hired the woman, and made nearly the same comments to his brand group as the VP had made to him. The team accepted her with little trouble, but—more important—her performance set a challenging example and brought out undeveloped ambitions and latent talent among two other team members. The brand position improved, and sure enough, some promotions were handed out— largely because both the VP and Ben had known how to sell the team on using a high producer.

AIM FOR THE TOP PERFORMER

If it is true that people are the heart of a business, then it is also true that a strong heart is better than a weak one. As a team-building objective, set high standards for your next candidates, at least to start with. You can always reduce your quality specs. It is harder to raise them. Reach for the stars. You are likely to capture a few if you try. You may amaze yourself at how many top-quality people are available or out there looking. But you are not likely to get them if you don't begin with high objectives, set your sights for high producers, and open the door for them. This is certainly worth trying a few times. Done right, the results can be dramatic, as demonstrated by this Procter & Gamble brand group's experience.

Secret Deodorant Brand Group Reaches for High Producer

The Secret brand was facing a new and effective competitor that was badly eroding its market share. The situation was serious. The supervisor decided to look for a seasoned, proven successful, highly aggressive advertising agency assistant group manager. He raised his sights and standards far above his earlier ones. "You'll never find a person like that!" one team member said. "Maybe not," replied the supervisor, "but what can we lose by trying? We might surprise ourselves." They did try—and they did get surprised. The new superquality person brought enormous insight into the problem, since he just happened to be the brand manager of their major competitive product! He had been having trouble with his own supervisor for years. Moving him over to the Secret brand brought the team just what it wanted . . . and eliminated its most formidable threat—all in one action.

TEN COMMANDMENTS FOR LOOKING AT ABOVE-AVERAGE EMPLOYEES

1. Recognize the potential of the human resource.
2. Communicate effectively to spark top performance.
3. Start with the ABCs of human feelings.
4. Take a good look at what makes tigers tick.
5. Measure the real advantage of high producers.
6. Prepare mentally and emotionally for high-quality people.
7. Guard against tiger trouble by staying flexible.
8. Set clear ground rules.
9. Sell high achievers to employees and supervisors.
10. Aim for top-performing employees.

The OBI (one best idea) for looking at tigers is to see, appreciate, and apply the power potential of high producers.

CHAPTER 2
How You Can Find Above-Average People

Managers in Japan find high-quality people by seeking advice from schoolteachers. The program is described in a phrase that, freely translated, means "Grow your own high producers, but start with proven seedlings." Most employees join a company right out of high school or college and spend many years or a lifetime with that firm. When you "marry" for life, you select with care. So the Japanese manager consults the people who have checked, measured, and tested each young person for many years—his or her teachers. A recommendation is made to the company. And this is not done lightly, since the student's reputation—as well as that of the teachers, the school, the manager, and the company—now ride on a successful outcome. This system rarely fails.

Most managers feel that either they can't locate above-average people, or if they do find them, they will cost too much. And they're right—sometimes, but not always. Ideal candidates are often available at a very low cost. But finding them is a little like two silent people groping for each other in the dark. To speed things up, someone has got to make a squeak or light a match.

ESTABLISH YOUR "IDEAL" CRITERIA

Begin with your own criteria, your "ideal" specifications. True, you might not find this ideal, but you'll never know how close your candidate is unless you have some sort of standard. And it doesn't hurt to reach for the stars—you won't get them all, but you might surprise yourself and capture a few.

A good basic approach to setting up criteria is to start with the job description. Ask yourself just what are the five or six major prerequisites of the perfect candidate, in education, work experience, and even personality. Label these as "requirements" or "must haves." Then refine this a bit by adding five or six preferences— extras you'd like to find but don't consider absolutely essential.

Now you have a practical, usable set of criteria and guidelines. You have a track to run on. You know almost precisely what and who you are looking for.

Royal Crown Uses a "Wish List"

Scott R., president of a large Royal Crown Cola bottling plant, said, "I have a confession. At one time, we tried to make do with just about any sort of employee. You know, average and below. We honestly didn't think we could find any other kind. But we were wrong. We discovered our mistake after we decided to list about ten ways we might locate better quality people. We tried all ten methods. Some didn't help us a whole lot, but others got surprising results.

"One of our new approaches was to make a list of the specifications that an ideal candidate should have—before we started looking. We began with sort of a "wish list" of top-priority characteristics. To these we added some qualities we hoped for but did not regard as essential. That way, we felt we would recognize a true winner if we ever saw one. In the end, we were surprised to find several outstanding candidates who not only fit our specs almost exactly, but who subsequently became the major contributors to the dramatic growth in our success. Good people are out there all right, but to find them, you've got to know a few secrets about how to look for them."

START BY LOOKING AT HOME

Look out, you may be standing on a tiger's tail! Your best source for that ideal candidate may be right under your nose. And yet, most of us fail to fully recognize the value of what we have immediately at hand, especially if talents are hidden, unused, or unrequested. We usually find it expedient to label, pigeonhole, and stereotype people. "Sam's a talker, but I've never seen him do any planning. Susie's the quiet, studious type. She couldn't handle a sales position." We just might be surprised at what people can do if we give them the opportunity.

How do you know you've got a live one? There is one very simple clue: if he or she shows any indication of wanting added responsibility. A simple way to discover that is to give every person on your team or in your group a little extra burden and authority once in a while, perhaps something quite small. Then watch carefully. If one of them gobbles it up, does the job, and comes back for more, you probably have a tiger you didn't recognize.

Unexpected Potential at Procter & Gamble

Sam was the shipping clerk at a P&G soap plant. He had quite a reputation for glib chatter with the women on the packing line. Then, late last year, P&G's production planner was taken out of action for some weeks because of stomach surgery. "We're in a bad spot," said the plant manager. "We simply must have careful production schedules. Sam? Oh, he's just a mouthy guy. I doubt he could do much planning." But after some open-minded thought, the plant manager realized that, in fact, Sam's present duties included some fairly complex shipping schedules. They called for understanding volume, capacity, storage, movement and time coordination—all key elements of production planning. Sam was given a chance to fill in on the plans desk and did a superlative job. When the previous planner returned and was promoted, Sam took over permanently.

CONSULT YOUR OTHER HIGH PRODUCERS

It often takes one to know one, and above-average people tend to associate with other high achievers. Or they know where to look. For every ten departments, there are usually a few top-quality people who are ready for promotion but who cannot be moved up in their unit because the next higher position is filled. Such high achievers are bumping their heads on the ceiling and may be getting frustrated and angry. They are usually ripe for the picking.

Lever Brothers High Producer Provides Lead on Top Candidate

A Lever Brothers accounting department manager lost her key assistant, and no one in the department was anywhere near qualified for the job. She asked one of her best employees if he knew of anyone. "Yes, I do. He's well trained, with lots of experience and a fine reputation, but he has no way to move up. Shall I ask him to phone you?" Naturally, the department manager agreed and ended up hiring a far-above-average executive.

USE THE COMPANY EMPLOYMENT OFFICE

Some companies operate only a small personnel group that handles employee records, while other firms have large staffs to help find new employees. Where appropriate, give the employment group your job description, candidate specifications, and your approximate time frame. Allow it enough lead time to check its sources, run ads, screen candidates, contact references, and review current as well as past applications. The office will often have records on candidates who are willing, able, and qualified, and who at least appear to be above-average. Some companies have reciprocal agreements with other firms. Company A may receive many excellent applications for one job opening. If its personnel office has been told that noncompetitive Company B is looking for the same kind of candidate, then some applicants may be encouraged to contact Company B. Company B does the same for Company A, and everybody gains, including the candidates.

Armour Employment Office Tracks Down Skilled Technician

A division of Armour and Company had introduced a successful new scientific product and needed a highly skilled quality control technician for the new production. The employment office was contacted. While they had no applicants of that type, they were testing an informal reciprocal arrangement for referrals with a noncompetitive company, an electronics firm. Sure enough, it had several such applicants, three of whom were contacted. One was unavailable, but the other two were interviewed. The result: An excellent employee was brought on board. She was later promoted to quality control chief.

LISTEN FOR REPUTATIONS

As we all know, people talk a lot about others in their trade. This is a rich source of information, if you stay alert and use it— even keep a little list of high-quality people you hear about. Managers who get together at conferences, exhibitions, industrial shows, and sales and training events are often candid, outspoken, or simply off-guard. They will discuss their successes and their frustrations, their searches and their finds, or people they feel are terrible or terrific. The trade press is usually full of stories about promotions and above-average performers. Your own suppliers of goods and services often have firsthand knowledge of outstanding achievers. Suppliers usually feel it's to their advantage to help high producers, because those people will then be in an even better position to reciprocate the assistance in various ways.

Reynolds Metals Hires Division President

Dan B., a top executive for a division of the Reynolds Metals Company, paid a courtesy call on Ted W., the plant manager of a major food canner to which Reynolds supplied aluminum. "Ted, you sure have been doing a super job with your food product sales, and we appreciate the business," Dan said. "Thanks, Dan. We try awfully hard. But as you may have heard, we're being bought, so I might be looking for another job pretty soon." The Reynolds supplier took careful note of this and passed Ted's name along to the group head, who happened to be searching for a candidate to become president of a smaller company Reynolds owned. Interviews were held, and eventually Ted was hired to head up the subsidiary. His reputation as a plant manager was recognized, and he continued to show out-standing performance in his new assignment.

WATCH OTHER ORGANIZATIONS

People at the better companies—especially successful com-petitors—usually not only (1) know your field, but (2) have learned many good methods, and (3) have a track record of proven perform-ance and results, plus (4)—here's a surprise—rather than being wed-ded to these other groups forever, above-average people are often very much ready to leave. Why? Many reasons. There may be no room for them to advance. Or following a major success, they may have been given overly ambitious goals or just loaded with the most difficult problems to solve. Sometimes, in poor companies, super-visors feel jealous, uneasy, or (rightly or wrongly) even threatened by high-performing subordinates. Success in such cases can be a mixed blessing. (Like Gresham's law, bad companies have even been known to drive away good people.)

There are many ways to stay informed about other companies' staffs. These three work especially well: (1) Maintain contact with people you like who leave your firm and join others. Maybe have lunch occasionally. (2) Watch your industry trade journals for an-nouncements of important new products, plant or office openings or closings, or individual personal awards. (3) Be alert for news of major staff reorganizations. All these are symptoms of substantial shifts in assignments. Good people may be available. If you don't want to make direct contact, you can always ask a third party to place a few discreet phone calls to appropriate officers of the firm.

Major New York Advertising Agency Wins Top Awards

Early last year, one of the ad agency's creative groups (composed of four people) took a sick, failing, nearly bankrupt brand and built a dramatic new advertising-marketing program for it. The campaign proved so successful that within a year the sales decline was totally reversed. The product moved up into a high-profit position and be-came second in a giant industry, with the group capturing national recognition both for marketing expertise and for advertising creativity. But within a few months of the award date, two members of the creative group were let go. As one of their colleagues said, "Well, today's hero is tomorrow's bum." A couple of months later, the other two members left voluntarily. All four were offered positions of greater responsibility and higher compensation with other advertising firms. Prospective employers had kept their eyes open for above-average people.

CHECK YOUR LOCAL EMPLOYMENT AGENCIES

Use the local agencies just as you did your company employment office, but be sure to coordinate this with your employment people so you are not both contacting the same agency. Get a firm agreement with each agency on fees; give its representatives the job description and candidate specs plus adequate lead time and a thorough understanding that you want only "above-average" people. Make it clear what you mean by that term and that you will consider no other caliber of candidate. Some agencies think they must arrange interviews for all candidates just to prove to both the applicants and the company client that they are doing something. It's called "trotting out the bodies," and that is all some clients expect. Let each agency know you're different.

Some agencies will be a little bit shocked (since they aren't used to such talk) and may try to convince you that you are asking too much. You aren't—at least not on the first try. Finding high achievers takes more work than finding average people. The natural tendency for some agencies is to convince you to set low standards and high wages, so their job is easy and their commission is nice and fat. Set high standards, insist on them, and instead of wasting your time with a lot of unqualified candidates, you will probably end up with a top-quality person. Although they are high producers, such people don't always know how to aggressively promote themselves or don't like to do this. Knowing that agencies have scores of computerized contacts, they may register with an agency or two and hope for good luck so they can get back quickly to the thing they do best.

Kellogg Finds a Publicity Officer

The problem was pretty clear-cut: A division of Kellogg was authorized to hire a publicity officer, yet a study of the local staff showed that nearly all had either production or accounting backgrounds. None even came close to the job specs. Leo R., the division manager, made a careful check among high producers, his plant employment office, and other nearby organizations but turned up no leads. So he gave the specs to a local employment agency. "Leo, we appreciate this challenge," they told him. "We don't get many job orders for management people, but we'll give your request a major effort. We know exactly what you want. Finding him or her may take a while." It did. The agency looked for many months, screened out lots of "close, but no cigar" contenders, and finally found just three that looked very near to specs. So close that Leo had a task choosing between them. He selected a bright, well-trained, dynamic young woman. She proved to be a real winner, who dramatically exceeded their highest publicity goals.

TOUCH BASE WITH COMMERCIAL GROUPS

Commercial groups and people you trust can be another source of leads. These might include officers or associates in your local chamber of commerce; local or national trade associations; and civic, service, or social clubs, like Rotary, Shriners, Lions, Kiwanis, Elks, Optomists, and others. Or even athletic and country clubs or community associations, such as the symphony, theater, museum, or governmental groups.

Your best approach with these organizations is rarely through any sort of mass public announcement but rather through selective contacts and inquiries. These professional-civic-social contacts are not famous for fabulous results, but gold is where you find it. You should leave no stone unturned, because these sources can and have produced good results with little or no cost or effort. Just take advice from such contacts with some care, reservation, and a grain of salt. While these people may be well meaning, they are rarely professional personnel specialists and sometimes have their own amateur ax to grind. Your best value from such groups is quite often simply a matter of picking up a good lead to be checked out carefully. But pay special attention to the pros and cons of political and social relations and to any "strings attached" in accepting or rejecting a candidate from these sources.

Textron Division Finds a Winner

An executive for a Textron division had been looking for an attorney in a specialized field, but without much luck. "Joe," the executive told a friend and officer at the chamber of commerce, "If you happen to hear of a young lawyer with a scientific background, we'd sure like his name." Joe answered, "Well, I have some good news and some bad news for you. The bad news is that I can't assist you much if you want *his* name. The good news is that I can help if you'll accept *her* name. My daughter Nancy has a degree in organic chemistry and is just graduating with honors from law school. She told me she'd love to work for your company, especially because of the location." Nancy was interviewed, screened, and given a fine job offer. In a strange turn of events, however, Nancy ended up declining the offer in favor of a better opportunity. Textron had found a winner, but she slipped away.

CHECK WITH OUTSIDE SERVICE PROFESSIONALS

Consider contacting selected professional outside service people you employ, such as your management consultant, CPA, auditor, market researcher, exporters, commercial banker, or law firm. They usually have friends at many companies and, informally, may know of people who are looking for better positions. Sometimes an above-average person is unhappy or in a division about to be closed, and a consultant you employ may even have been asked to help relocate that person. Or would like to do him or her a favor as well as help a client like you to find a high-quality employee. In such cases, word is passed discreetly, with the professional actually playing no active role other than giving a name to a company, for its management to pursue. But nothing at all might have happened if you had not made a few quiet inquiries.

Borden Locates a Top Billing Department Manager

Borden had just opened a new plant, and staffing had moved along smoothly, except that the company still needed a first-rate billing department manager. A check of all Borden's normal sources had brought in some possibilities, but none was very much above-average. One relatively good candidate had been considering Borden's offer, but then took another job instead, leaving matters in a discouraging state. Borden's auditor mentioned to the plant manager that "one of our clients is moving its operation out West to the sunbelt, and its excellent billing manager wants to remain in this area. Would you like his phone number?" The plant manager accepted, phoned his prospect, interviewed him, and ended up hiring one of Borden's finest department managers ever. He not only introduced many profitable innovations but was later promoted to a major position at a corporate headquarters office.

SERIOUSLY CONSIDER RECRUITERS

Recruiters, or so-called head hunters, may be an especially good source when you are looking for above-average people—high producers who must fill unusual job specifications or have a unique combination of skills or training. Recruiters are usually quite accustomed to such requests. They know where and when to look, how to advertise, interview, reference check, analyze, and test candidates, because they do it often for many clients.

How to use recruiters? Essentially, your approach might be similar to that used with a high-quality personnel employment agency, with these modifications: (1) Your procedure and theirs should be unusually professional. (2) You should work in a very thorough manner. Provide them with complete data, job description, and job specs. (3) This source is best used for middle-level jobs and above—almost never for clerks. (4) Set a somewhat longer time schedule. (5) Expect to pay a higher fee. (Discuss this fully.) Your best plan is to get recruiters referred to you by other managers, so you can learn something about their track record before hand. Also, visit with two or three before you start working with one. Then stay put and give the firm your total cooperation.

In short, demands for high-quality people do not frighten recruiters but instead offer them a challenge and an opportunity to serve clients and place above-average people in suitable and profitable positions. Successful completion of such projects often leads to additional assignments for the recruiter. High achievers tend to want more of this same type in their organizations. Also, top people in the firm are frequently surprised to make such rare finds and encourage the recruiter to "Play it again, Sam!"

Union Carbide Hires a High-Quality Engineer

Union Carbide's problem was threefold: The candidate had to have an engineering degree, be highly skilled at handling difficult human relations situations, and be a very high producer—a truly above-average and specialized person. "You are looking for a rare individual" said Jim W., the company recruiter. "But we have the job description and specifications. We've done similar searches in the past with excellent results, so there's every reason to believe we can do it again. We mainly need your support, patience, and cooperation, with perhaps an open mind and a degree of flexibility." Said Max B., the client, "No problem, Jim. Have at it. Just keep me informed every week, and let me know how we can help." Jim went to work. The search took some months, and in the end, Jim came up with only one candidate who fit all the criteria. The person was a foreign-trained minority (a recently naturalized Japanese immigrant). He turned out to have far greater technical skills than expected, plus human relations abilities (he was a fine speaker and a troubleshooter with a keen sense of humor), plus a high-volume production track record. Said Max, "Look no further. We don't need to comparison-shop. You've found our tiger. Let's close the deal."

TEN COMMANDMENTS FOR FINDING
ABOVE-AVERAGE PEOPLE

1. Begin with ideal specs for the person you want.
2. Look in your own company first.
3. Talk with your other high producers.
4. Check with your company employment office.
5. Listen for reputations and leads and get the word out.
6. Watch other firms, especially competitors.
7. Check your local employment agencies.
8. Touch base with selected commercial or civic groups.
9. Contact your key outside service people.
10. Talk it over with professional personnel recruiters.

The OBI (one best idea) for finding above-average people is simply this: Start with clear, ideal criteria and then check the entire range of your best business sources to track down the person who most closely matches those specifications. Gold is where you find it— even in unexpected places—so use your resources and leave no stone unturned!

CHAPTER 3
Ten Best Ways to Get High Producers Applying to You

Japanese firms attract high-quality applicants with a system that works astonishingly well. The heart of their plan is simple: reputation. Major Japanese companies are past masters of effective public relations. And some of their best PR people are their own employees. The message they send out to everyone is: "Here is a solid company of high-quality people, products, and services you can be proud of, that provides a good, secure future for both the business and the individual. A company of great respect for (and high morale among) the employees." These company attributes are communicated through good policies, civic involvement, advertising, and trade shows. Result: High producers, above-average people, apply in large numbers to these Japanese companies, which can then take their pick.

Ralston Purina, Campbell Soup, Kodak, and United Airlines are all good examples of companies that usually have many high-quality applicants—often more than are required. The same is true with the better local firms in nearly every city. They frequently get more above-average people than they need, because they know how to attract the high achievers. Our objective here is to look at ways to spark the attention and interest of top producers. Rather than having you searching for them, these methods get them looking for you. This has many advantages. It saves you a lot of time, expense, and work and is far more efficient than those perennial panics to beat the hot, dusty bushes on a tiger hunt. High-quality applications simply flow in, and you make your own selection. Here's how to do it.

HAVE SOMETHING TO OFFER

Don't make the mistake of saying: "The employees should be damn glad to work for our company." That may be 100 percent true, but your job is to make *them* realize that. Show your applicants and your employees alike what you have to trade, to offer. Show them the attraction and make them want it so bad that they can almost taste it. Find out what it was that attracted the top-quality people you now have. Or what it is that most interests your highest-caliber candidates. What do they know about your company, like best about it, and find most attractive in other prospective employers? A survey may be in order. You will locate the "on" button in their minds and discover the inherent drama in your own company. Then, play precisely that tune, their song, in a way that builds their attention, interest, and desire—and invites their action. Don't expect something for nothing. You must generate the attraction and trade it for their overt commitment and you've won big.

Ralston Purina Takes Its Pick of Top Producers

The Ralston Purina Company has built a reputation for quality, leadership, and prestige among both the public and business community in general and the farming industry in particular. Ralston Purina products, packaging, promotions, and publicity all sing this song and reflect this strength. There is a feeling of pride among most of the company's key managers that is contagious. This attracts many above-average achievers who want some of this prestige and pride to rub off on them. Result: As supervisory, executive, and managerial positions open up at Ralston Purina, it is not at all uncommon for several exceptional people to apply for the same job. Ralston Purina can then select the very best of the best. The firm has much to attract top producers—and it knows how to prove it.

SHOW A SOLID CORPORATE FUTURE

Because above-average people are often more concerned with the near-term future and just beyond than with the immediate situation, you will have to offer them the potential for a good future with the company. This doesn't mean that the future must be all star-studded—with rockets, big promises, pie in the sky, we'll all be rich tomorrow. In fact, some of the gung ho entrepreneurial spirit and surge that brought the company from youth to adulthood may have lessened and matured into calm, steady progress, but the promise of better things, or at least the realistic hope, should be there. The company should clearly exhibit at least moderate optimism for the future by demonstrating that (1) the firm has done well with what it had to work with in the past, and (2) it has some positive plans and opportunity to apply this ability in the future. This should be expressed in terms of expansion of sales; increased profits; new horizons, markets, and production; improved service; and/or successful relations both externally (with the public) and internally (with the employees).

Confidence in Campbell Soup's Potential Pays Off for Outstanding Executive

Campbell is a well-known, well-regarded company that has shown solid success in the recent past. Applicants spot this. One outstanding Campbell executive said, "When I was looking for a job a few years ago, one of the first firms I thought about was Campbell. This was partly because of its good reputation, but mostly because I liked what it had accomplished in the past. I realized, of course, that the company couldn't keep on growing as fast as it had. Things had moderated a bit. But I figured it would do nearly as well in the future. I was hired and then got a real shock! They assigned me to an old, beat-up wooden desk, all full of scratches and splinters, with a creaky old straight chair to match. I figured maybe they were trying to tell me something. Or testing my patience, or my humility. So I kept my cool—a decision that paid off well a few months later. It seems the company was not only expanding into a new product line and a new market but moving into a beautiful building with all new equipment and furniture, too. The future brightened pretty fast. Since then, I've been promoted twice! The potential that had attracted me to Campbell proved to be a reality. And incidentally, I'm glad I stayed cool about that old wooden desk."

DEMONSTRATE AN EXCITING PERSONAL FUTURE

Above-average people may be strongly "company-minded," but they are strongly "I-minded" at the same time. Famous consultant Peter Drucker once said, "Many managers make a major commitment to the old sailor's slogan, 'One hand for the ship and one hand for yourself.' " High-quality employees often have particular self-interest as it relates to the near future. Companies will attract top producers when candidates learn that they really can play a participative role in company growth, expansion, profits, and success. That they can operate and advance with some real freedom, authority, responsibility, and creativity. That your firm offers them movement, action, excitement, and progress, even if the company itself is calm, controlled, and moderate. A peaceful, solid company can provide dynamic personal growth.

3M Attracts Above-Average People With "You're Somebody" Ads

The Minnesota Mining and Manufacturing Company's TV commercials say, in effect, "You can play a role in our success. You will be free to create. You will be heard. And we will respond to you, because we regard you as a somebody, not a nobody." This promise and philosophy run through much of the 3M literature, speeches, and everyday activities. "I really wasn't sure they meant all that," said Ray W., an outstanding 3M design engineer. "But I decided to take a chance. My supervisor, Art, was pretty close to what the TV ads claimed, although I must say Art has a mind of his own and a personality to match. But the company gave Art sort of a reputation to live up to that has become a self-fulfilling prophesy." 3M attracts a great number of high producers and has done so for years.

OFFER A "LACK OF NEGATIVES"

Now offering a "lack of negatives" is a strange-sounding way to attract good people, isn't it? But just stop and think a moment. Aside from recent graduates, why are above-average applicants available? They have either left or are about to leave another company, voluntarily or by invitation. Something bombed. A "divorce" is occurring. Why? Clearly, because of some problem. If and when you survey your best people about why they like your company, you might also ask them what they *disliked* in other companies. Such surveys usually identify problems that you can convert into pluses or attractions for your company, such as: "We don't ignore people here. We don't put them down, stifle them, or abuse them. Supervisors don't have a petty, jealous, or "big me, little you" attitude. Instead, we give you more than full credit for your personal contribution."

United Airlines' Friendly Skies Attract Many High Achievers

United Airlines' applicants at all levels are convinced that the sort of negatives found elsewhere are less serious or don't happen at all with United. "I've worked for other companies in this industry and outside it," Ned J., a United executive, told me. "And frankly, there really are good firms out there. Of course, none of them is perfect, and that includes United. But top managers in some firms allow far too many negatives to creep into their human relations at all levels. I know one company where they have six departments, none of which will talk to any of the others. Can you believe that? It's damn near paralysis! When I was interviewed by United executives, I was amazed at the good feeling between groups. It was like a breath of fresh air. I'm lucky to be flying the friendly skies. Why? Mainly, mighty few negatives."

SHOW TOP QUALITY IN YOUR PRODUCTS OR SERVICES

True you may need to sell some, or even most, of your goods or services at low prices because of market strategy. This may win customers. But the above-average prospect is usually attracted by above-average products, value, performance, or public services. Even if your products are priced low, your service might be excellent. Bear in mind that top producers have a positive self-image and a good reputation to maintain with their friends and relatives. They like to stand tall among their peer group. They are attracted to firms that support and enhance such stature. Top-quality people look for companies that are known, accepted, respected, and even admired. They will say they want to work for a company that is "worthy," "respectable," "honorable," "significant," "meaningful," or even "important." Some, but not all, will say "aggressive." They really mean "a firm that's above-average—like me."

Kodak Quality Wins Respect

Kodak connotes quality, and that attracts a host of high producers. Most Kodak items are in the middle and upper range of excellence, and many are unsurpassed. The public knows this, and so do the higher-quality job applicants. "I look on myself as a far-above-average person, a top-caliber executive, but not necessarily a risk-taking, high-flying entrepreneur," says Tim R., a Kodak executive. "And I feel this company is the same way. I figure we match up pretty well. We fit each other's public and personal images. That's a key reason I applied to Kodak. Maybe Rodney Dangerfield likes to say, 'I don't get no respect!' but *I* sure wouldn't enjoy making such a statement. I'm always proud to tell where I work, and I notice people even seem to look up to me just a little more because of my affiliation."

PARTICIPATE EFFECTIVELY IN TRADE SHOWS

At trade shows, you are putting your best foot forward to your industry, usually through some sort of booth, display, poster, movie, or sign. You need not be big, fancy, or extravagant. The key is to emphasize the most attractive side of your firm, along with any basic promotional message. Sometimes your most important selling point may be your people—the way they look, dress, and relate with trade show visitors, who are rarely junior clerks. More often, they are leaders, achievers, and high producers representing their companies. Be sure they are greeted cordially, and you will enhance your firm's reputation. When possible, make it a point to visit competitive and related booths. Introduce yourself to some of these people, and in a stroke, you will have contacted a few above-average individuals, who now know you and your company. They are likely to remember their favorable impression of you if and when they need a job. Even big industries operate in a small world.

Firestone Tire Shows Wheels Within Wheels

At one of the better trade shows, Firestone made it a point to provide a particularly attractive display. The presentation emphasized the company's major product selling points, of course, but it also dramatized engineering features that not only were attractive to technicians but also nearly shouted "quality" (in a tasteful way). In addition, Firestone had a number of key executives present at times. They looked and acted like the high-quality top producers they really were. Unlike many other exhibitors, the Firestone staffers went out of their way to be accommodating and most gracious to visitors making inquiries. (I was one.) People noticed this and were favorably impressed. Later, a Firestone personnel specialist told me, "You know, we had an unusually large number of high-quality people applying to us shortly after that trade show."

GAIN RECOGNITION THROUGH PUBLICITY

Well-planned publicity, skillfully executed, can get all kinds of high-quality people knocking on your door. Bad public relations, on the other hand, can get people leaving in bunches. A solid, effective PR program starts with a good understanding of public opinion—the public's awareness of you and the image it holds of you. PR moves next to a realistic objective. (What kind of awareness and image do you want?) And then to ways and means of reaching that goal. The PR program should be a written business plan consisting of careful steps, well timed, and scheduled to make the best impression at the right moment. This should include officer appearances, talk shows, interviews, panels, and speeches. These might be before any worthwhile assembly that will listen, including the general public via radio and TV or civic, commercial, legislative, and educational groups. Consider print media releases of any interesting, newsworthy items—especially about people, personal successes, awards, promotions, business breakthroughs, discoveries, accomplishments, or new products and services. Include success stories from customers and suppliers. Don't overplay the company name or be greedy for attention. At times, you may want to give the company only minor mention, focusing the major story on other people. If the material is well prepared, with high reader-audience interest, sent to the right people on a reasonable schedule, you'll get plenty of recognition—sometimes more than you anticipate, if you don't push too hard. Firms can do very well in these areas, even if they are relatively calm, not highly motivated by entrepreneurial dynamics.

Royal Crown Bottler Builds Prestige with Publicity

Royal Crown Cola was an old, well-established firm in a quiet market. RC management noticed that not many above-average people were applying to the company. "W.D., our best approach would be to improve our image through better publicity," said Tim B., the plant manager, to his boss, the president. "Here's my plan: We feature you, W.D., Mrs. Brown, your secretary, and me as spokespersons. I have a set of short speeches for each of us, and the broadcast people say they can work us into various talk shows. I have a list of stories on company and personal awards and promotions we can do, as well as a series of success stories about our top ten customers." Tim's program was put to work, and the company won the state public recognition award. It also enjoyed improved sales, profits, and value of its stock along with a string of high-quality applicants—all at a very low out-of-pocket expense.

USE ADVERTISING-MARKETING TO ENHANCE YOUR STATURE

Tailor your company advertising and marketing programs not only to make sales but to build company stature and selectively invite applications. This does not mean you must have a high-quality, high-price image. You may be selling merchandise at the K-Mart level. If so, fine, but whatever you do, do it well. Look and sound like you're doing it with some authority, assurance, and expertise—as if you know what you're doing. K-Mart does. So do Ralston Purina, Campbell, Kodak, and Firestone. Your advertising should be the kind you would be glad to sign personally. It should reflect a proud, prosperous past and a promising future. High producers do not need to work for a fireball company that projects a Hollywood image. In fact, many top people are turned off by these as being unstable, flash-in-the-pan qualities. But above-average people rarely want to work for a company they must apologize for. Make employees proud of their company's advertising and you'll get lots of top achievers waiting in line to join you.

American Express Says, "Don't Leave Home Without it"

American Express's highly successful, award-winning TV commercials, with their realistic "slice of life" traveler's checks episodes ("Lost your wallet? Don't worry. There's an American Express office nearby"), are believable, sensible, and reflect a concern that middle- and upper-income people easily identify with. The credit card spokespersons are mostly above-average, high-quality, well-known people. "I felt that American Express was doing a good job in its market and has an excellent future," says Bob K., outstanding new executive with an American Express office. "But more than that, I believe the company's reputation—the look, dress, and face it uses to meet the public—is my face, too. Although I do think I'm better-looking than our spokesman Karl Malden!" American Express marketing clearly attracts above-average people. Even handsome ones.

BUILD GOOD EMPLOYEE MORALE

You will find that good morale is contagious, favorably infecting your whole team and the economic community—even suppliers and customers. This need not be a feeling of spirited entrepreneurship or high-risk venturism. It can simply be the quiet confidence of a team of people who believe in their company as a solid, successful, reliable operation and in themselves as people of quality doing something worthwhile with their lives. You might say, "Fine. A good objective, but that's really easier said than done." And you're right—but it's not impossible. Let's look at an example—the Japanese.

Inscrutable Orientals at Matsushita Are Quite "Scrutable" About Morale

Japanese firms use many morale-building techniques that are basically copied from approaches once employed by American companies but dropped years ago (although they are still used by some of our better firms). "Here at Matsushita (Panasonic), we have tried to make morale development into a fine art," Department Manager Hajame Mitoto told me during a recent visit to central Japan. "It's pretty simple, costs little, and uses methods once employed by you Westerners. We use these 27 points: respect, awards, communication, courtesy, discussion, negotiation, consensus, loyalty to employees, socializing, training, few direct orders, long-term thinking, hope for the future, innovative freedom, job permanence, stable conditions, clearly assigned responsibilities, special welcome to new people, lots of smiles, much please and thank you, thoughtfulness and consideration, receptiveness to criticism, generous help with retirement, dedication, determination, discipline, and industrious hard work." Morale at Matsushita Electric is very high, sales and profits are growing, and the company has thousands of top-quality people from whom to select its new employees.

DESIGN POLICIES THAT ATTRACT PEOPLE

Developing policies deliberately designed to build your reputation and attract applicants may seem difficult, but it can actually be quite simple, especially when you recognize that above-average people are seeking just a few basic conditions. They want opportunity, fair treatment (the assurance that promotion is inevitable, given a decent roll of the dice), reasonable freedom (no needless shackles), near-term-future orientation (good bucks now, but better bucks tomorrow), and good communication (both ways, up and down, below and above them. Peter Drucker says, "poor communication is modern management's major mistake." This costs so little to correct and pays off beautifully). You might strongly consider picking up on most of these points. Emphasize them in your dealings with employees, customers, suppliers, outside service firms, and the public. All these groups greatly influence the flow of better people toward your firm.

Sears Roebuck's Policies Spell Opportunity

Sears Roebuck attracts thousands of above-average people each year. "We talk to our applicants and ask them why they have come to Sears," said one of its top executives. "Do you know what most of them say? Well, boiled down into a few sentences: 'Sears's policies. We like the way Sears treats its employees and the public. Sears means opportunity to me. Opportunity not only to buy good stuff as a consumer but the chance to be fairly recognized as an employee, to prosper and grow in a healthy, steady, stable way.' These applicants know that Sears is not a hot-shot, dynamic outfit. But we're not asleep, either." This applicant-attracting image didn't materialize overnight. Sears has been working at it for years. But it would never have happened without a deliberate decision to design policies that attract people.

TEN COMMANDMENTS FOR ATTRACTING ABOVE-AVERAGE APPLICANTS

1. Have something to offer and to trade on.
2. Show the company's potential for a good future.
3. Demonstrate a promising personal future.
4. Offer a lack of serious negatives.
5. Show quality in company products or services.
6. Participate effectively in industry trade events.
7. Use well-planned publicity, skillfully executed.
8. Tailor your marketing to attract quality applicants.
9. Build good employee morale.
10. Develop policies that attract high producers.

The OBI. (one best idea) for attracting above-average people is to offer top-quality goods and services, high morale, effective marketing and publicity, positive policies, and solid future prospects.

CHAPTER 4
How Your Screening Can Find the One Best *Person*

A Mobil Oil division manager recently told me, "Oh, brother! Did we waste a lot of time flying purely by guess and by God. We used to pick people practically by tossing a dart at a list. Sort of by dumb luck. And it really was a pretty dumb way to go. We batted about 50–50. Half were good, half were costly losers. Low morale and low production are both very expensive. Finding and training new people also cost big bucks. We were really concerned. Then we talked with a consultant who suggested ten steps for better screening. We tried these for a year. Result: We are now much better ball players. Would you believe 95 percent success? Plus fewer of those distressing time-consuming, nasty people problems and much lower turnover! What do you suppose that's worth?"

Let's assume you have found some good candidates or have several who have found you. What should you do next? Make a stab in the dark? Not if you want to avoid a lot of trouble and expense. Now you are in an excellent position, even if you are just "half smart" in your next steps. You are in the driver's seat—in unusual control of your destiny.

Your objective is to select the best among your various options. Or even to decide that none is satisfactory. Some of the group are going to be below average. Lemons. Some will be fair. One or two will be a peach or a top banana. But out of your market basket, which is which? They all look pretty good, with their pressed suits, shined shoes, sparkling smiles, "yes sirs" and "no sirs."

Here's how you can efficiently screen these candidates to separate the good grain from the sour mash.

DON'T GET CONNED BY APPEARANCE

Don't fall in love with your candidate's baby blue eyes. This is one of the most common errors made by employers—being overimpressed with appearance. "My God, that fellow Joe Smith looks and acts just like our dynamic young executive vice-president! He'll sure impress everybody! Joe can't miss!" Oh can't he? Any chance he was in trouble with the law or drugs or John Barleycorn? Perhaps he got let out for incompetence or because he couldn't get along with four bosses in a row. *Now* how does he look? The key point is that you can't tell a horse by its harness.

So don't get conned by appearance. It happens all the time. Even with very sophisticated executives on Madison Avenue. (Maybe especially on Madison Avenue.) Oh, sure, appearance can be important, but unless you are mainly looking for that quality—a doorman or a receptionist—count it only for what it is—just one good point. And then go on to the next item. The ideal-looking applicant may end up as your finest employee—or your worst. Your best approach is to keep a sharp eye, an open mind, and cool emotions. In fact, mild skepticism.

For example, you might ask yourself, if this person is so darn good-looking, what is he or she doing here? Why is this candidate looking for a job in the first place? What, if anything, is he or she hiding? Nobody's perfect. Everyone has flaws, Best to find them now, not later. Mark Twain suggested, "Keep your eyes wide open before marriage, half shut afterwards."

Appearances Are Deceptive at Leo Burnett Agency

I was a brand-new account executive at Leo Burnett's booming, thousand-employee Chicago ad agency and had not yet met the top man. One day, on my way back from a client meeting, I passed this dumpy little guy carrying a wastebasket near the reception desk. Short, with a pudgy body, thick facial features, and bulgy eyes, he was without a jacket, his sleeves rolled up, a cigarette spilling ashes down his unbuttoned vest. "Sort of early for the janitor," I remarked to the receptionist. "Mr. Rice, that wasn't the janitor. That was Mr. Burnett." (Fortunately for me, Leo was out of hearing distance.)

No, millionaire Leo Burnett wasn't famous for appearance, but he was pretty good on performance. Some small, struggling little brands had come to him in the 1930s and later—brands that Leo had helped quite a bit. They included Hoover, Maytag, Kellogg, Motorola, Pillsbury, Jiff, Secret, Camay, United Airlines, Green Giant, Pfizer, Parker Pen, Curad, and Marlboro, to name just a few.

HOW TO USE YOUR SPECIFICATIONS

We saw earlier that your specifications, or candidate requirements, can easily be pulled out of the job description. Your best bet is to list about six "essential" or "must-have" qualities. Then about six more "preferred," "not necessary but good to have," or "ideal" items. Be very fussy, dreamy, and demanding with this last group of specs. If the perfect candidate would look like a film star and have a brain like Einstein, list these characteristics (appearance and genius) but decide which are essential and which are just nice extras. Include category areas like education, experience, attitude, and proven skills. Also list such practical, nitty-gritty items as health, driving record, past attendance, living location, family obligations and freedom to travel, speaking style, performance under pressure, and ability to get along well with people.

The great advantage to listing your specs briefly, coldly, and honestly is that it is doubly fair—fair to your candidates, in that you are judging each by the same criteria, and fair to you, in that you have sidestepped emotion. You are just using plain, hard facts to evaluate each applicant—usually leading you closer to the one best selection. (As we will see, there is definitely a time and place for emotion—but later, *not* now.)

Close Call at Bristol-Myers

A Bristol-Myers department head told me, "I really had a narrow escape last year. We were looking at two candidates for an important job in our department. I interviewed both Mr. A and Mr. B. They each looked pretty good. Frankly, Mr. B made a much better appearance and had a good personality. He complimented me a lot, and I could see he was a smart cookie. But Mr. A looked good, too, and I really wasn't quite sure what to do.

"Then our personnel manager reminded me to be sure to list my specs for the job. In all the hurly-burly rush around here, darned if I hadn't forgot about that. Well, I made my list and judged each candidate by the same criteria. I got a big shock. Mr. B bombed out in all but personality. Mr. A had everything I needed. You know, the essentials plus most of the extra goodies I had sort of dreamed about. What a find! He has done a super job. Far better than I ever expected. I later found out that Mr. B took another job and lost it in a few months. And to think that I nearly hired the guy! That was a close call."

ANALYZE CANDIDATES WITH YOUR COLD FISH-EYE

Study each applicant carefully and coldly. Every minute you put in, every fact you discover now could save you tenfold time and trouble later. Your best mind set is: Find both the flaws and the strengths—right now, not later. Later is too late. Look under the rocks. Learn your man or woman.

Look at the application. Question every little detail. If even the smallest item looks strange or doesn't add up, check it out. Ask about it. Behind this little detail, a major problem could be lurking. Do the same with the résumé. Remember, the application is a standard set of data, while the résumé is a flexible, nonstandard "selling" piece. It is edited to tell you what the candidate wants you to know and to leave out what he or she does not want you to know. Pay particular attention to what is left out. It may be a warning of danger.

Learn where the person was born, raised, and went to grade school and high school. That might not seem important, but it is usually a good indication of the background, attitude, and viewpoint of the candidate—especially during his or her vital formative years.

Learn about his or her parents' occupations and relationship with the candidate. It clues you in to his or her view of authority. Check education, additional training, hobbies, outside activities, work experience, kinds of jobs, duties, and duration.

Pay special attention to why the candidate left each job. To encourage a cards-on-the-table response, you might ask, "If (or when) we check your references at the ABC Company, what reason will they give for your leaving?" You may be amazed at the horror stories you will hear. Just judge these carefully.

Standard Oil Finds Winner by "Fine-Tooth-Combing"

A Standard Oil manager was interviewing for a head computer clerk. "We had several candidates, and frankly, they were a mixed bag, but fairly good," said Mel J., the department head. "At first glance, no one seemed to stand out much above or below the others. But then we started to 'fine-tooth-comb' their résumés and applications. Wow, what a difference! One gal in particular showed great care and accuracy in providing data. Everything added up and checked out. We even found some special strengths in math training, which were just what we needed. And we saw a few flaws—she had flunked Latin—which really didn't matter. Everything she listed matched our job specs. The same was not true with the other candidates. On that basis, we made our selection. And we found a real winner!"

FOCUS ON YOUR INTERVIEW OBJECTIVES

Emphasize the interview's goals as you visit with your applicant. This will make the meeting smooth, efficient, and productive for both you and your candidate. It will be a good experience and a better investment of your time.

Your best three goals should be: first, to give information; second, to get information; and third, to make a friend. If you keep these easy points in mind, you will probably do a little thinking, plotting, and planning even before you meet with your prospect. For example, you might make a little list of key facts about the job you feel the candidate needs or will want to know. Perhaps some items about the company's past, present, and future. This is both a considerate and an efficient step. It will save each of you some time and avoid misunderstanding. You might outline key duties, summarizing the job description. A second list might cover points you need from the candidate, such as clarification of some résumé items.

As a third step, when the interview starts, immediately try to put the candidate at ease. Remember, he or she is probably pretty uptight. So relax, speak calmly. Take his or her coat. Offer a cup of coffee. Be sure the sun isn't in his or her eyes. Thank the person sincerely for visiting you. The interview will be far more pleasant and productive for you both. Why make a friend? Your applicant may end up as your customer's or your supplier's key person. Or your best employee—or even your boss!

Now surprise the candidate—have a little list of questions you wish to ask. (By actual count, not one interviewer in 50 does this. Most of them are terrified amateurs, almost as uneasy as the candidates.) It will impress the candidate, and you'll learn things other interviewers don't. Your questions might be about past experiences, present goals, and future plans. Such as: "What were your most interesting projects?" "What are your long-range objectives?" "What do you hope for or see for the future in our industry?" You may be amazed at some of the comments you'll get. They could make your selection a whole lot easier.

Union Carbide Manager No Longer Dreads Interviews

"As a Union Carbide manager during my first few years in this position, I frankly dreaded interviews," said Les R. "I didn't know what the hell to say. What do you talk about after you say, 'Hello. Sure is a nice (or nasty) day out there'?"

But Les discussed this problem with his management consultant, and they agreed on the give info- get info- make a friend formula. Les put the simple system to work. "I can't believe it! Not only am I ready for the applicant, but I feel relaxed, so the applicant feels relaxed. We cover a lot of ground in a hurry, because neither of us is uptight, standing on our tiptoes and sparring around." Les now has a reputation for being the best interviewer in the division—and for finding the best people. How does he do it? He keeps his three main interview objectives clearly in mind.

ENCOURAGE THE APPLICANT'S QUESTIONS

Inquiries from candidates, either during the interview or later by phone or letter, can be highly revealing. They tell you (1) the amount of study or homework your candidates did before the interview, (2) their level of thinking, (3) their ability to articulate ideas, (4) the kind of questions they are likely to ask during their first days on the job, and (5) their ability to handle themselves and deal with others under some stress.

Ask the candidate, "Do you have any more questions about any of this?" If he or she is slow to ask, you might help the person along by saying, "May I tell you anything more about the situation here? The job? Our goals? The activities of the department? Or the people?" (The candidate couldn't possibly know all those things.) Don't ask in a perfunctory way, rattling the questions off like machine-gun fire. Pause at each question. Give the candidate time to think. Ask in a nonthreatening way. Let the person know his or her inquiries are most welcome. Answer in an approving way with something like, "That's a good question," or "Oh, I'm glad you asked about that."

If the applicant still has no questions, this tells you that he or she is either very unresponsive to your obvious encouragement, very bashful, or terribly well informed. Your decision depends on how well one of these alternatives matches the other information you have. And you have just learned a lot about the candidate— even through his or her silence.

Top U.S. Steel Applicant Is Ready with Questions

A U.S. Steel interviewer asked an applicant if he had any questions about the business. "Yes," said the man. "It just so happens I do. In fact, I have a list of ten basic things I'd like to learn." The interviewer was a bit startled. "Well, I'll be damned! I've asked that question a lot of times but never had an answer like that. Let's go to lunch and talk it over." Their lunch lasted three hours, and the candidate was later offered an excellent position. With some regret, he declined it to become president of a closely related business grossing several hundred million dollars a year. The interviewer sure knew how to smoke out an above-average producer.

GET YOUR ASSOCIATES' OPINIONS

Have several trusted associates visit with the candidate. One of the best methods is to select interviewers who have the sort of judgment you can trust. Four eyes and four ears are better than your two of each, and they will notice things that got past you. Urge your colleagues to be particularly attuned to strengths and weaknesses. Then, later, compare their observations with yours. This step is especially useful if your associates can each see several candidates, rank them, and say why. If your own ranking differs widely from theirs, you may need to do some careful rechecking. Experience shows that seasoned and fair interviewers working from identical job specs tend to rank applicants in a very similar way.

The advantages of putting several minds to work on the problem are: (1) Second and third sets of opinions tend to reconfirm your decision. (2) They help to reassure any reviewing authority (like your boss) who must approve your selection. (3) The other interviewers almost always come up with some added strengths and/or weaknesses to help with your decision. (4) If and when the selection is made, these interviewers feel they played a role in the decision. Therefore, they are more likely to help the person become successful, as a sort of self-fulfilling expectation. (5) A final advantage is that this approach is a double precaution against your getting sold on a candidate simply because the person has one or two traits that you may be over- or underrating.

Associates Spot Nearly Overlooked Colgate-Palmolive Winner

A Colgate-Palmolive district sales manager was interviewing several candidates for a key territory. He tentatively favored Bob A. but also felt that Chuck D. was a good prospect. The manager wisely asked two of his closest associates to check both candidates. One of the alternate interviewers was a top sales representative in the manager's own division, while the other was sales manager in another department.

The results were surprising. Both interviewers agreed that Bob was a good candidate but felt that Chuck would be a far better choice, and they gave several reasons. The sales manager reviewed these, realized he had missed some key points, selected Chuck, and ended up with a sales award winner.

HOW TO CHECK REFERENCES

Checking references is one of the most useful yet underemployed devices in the whole screening tool kit. Why? Because by the time interviewers get to this point, they have often sold themselves on the candidate and don't want to hear any bad news or be confused by new facts. To avoid this, try to withhold your judgment. Promise yourself, "I'll wait until I check references." Why make such a check? Because these reference people often have years of experience with the candidate, compared with the few hours you have. They know him or her much better than you do. You may be horrified or delighted at what you learn.

Your best technique? Don't ask for references in writing. People are very reluctant to put much good or bad down on paper. Visit in person or by phone. Begin by asking about good traits. Then you get to the bad—normally a touchy subject, but very important. You and the applicant may be "married" a long time, so you should know what you're getting. You have paved the way with the reference person by reviewing favorable factors. So now he or she doesn't feel so bad about mentioning unfavorable ones. You can take the curse off the question by saying, "All of us have some less than good traits. What are some that we should protect John from, if we hire him?" This almost sounds as if you're helping the candidate and so is more likely to get a candid reply. And you really are helping him or her, if it ends up with a better match all around. Incidentally, be sure to check with other people besides just the references listed by the candidate.

Weigh remarks from references with care. If someone has a very positive or very negative point to make, try to get some extra information. Ask about this same point when you talk to other references. See if this is confirmed or refuted. Even a candidate's good friends or bad enemies can provide you with helpful pro and con data if you are careful what you ask and even more careful how you interpret the answers they give you.

Mars Candy Unexpectedly Discovers a High Producer

A Mars Candy executive was considering several candidates for a staff assistant job. Mr. A did not come off too well in the interview, since his verbal skills were not strong. However, a check of his references and past associates showed him to be greatly superior in the job specs needed. He was hired and proved to be a far-above-average producer. Thorough reference checks had avoided a serious mistake and identified an outstanding person.

USE THE CIRCLES AND Xs COMPARISON CHART

Remember back there a few pages ago we talked about your specifications? We said you should have about six required specs and six more good-to-have extra elements. Now you're ready to use the Circles and Xs system. It has three important advantages. First, it will save you time, trouble, and effort. Second, it will find you some high producers. And third, it has been well proved to get good, practical results, based on five years of field testing.

Here's how it works. On a sheet of paper, list your 12 specs down the left side and draw horizontal lines under each and across the page. Then put in several vertical columns off to the right and enter your candidates' names at the top of each. Now make an entry in each box formed, by marking a circle for every favorable attribute and x-ing through each unfavorable attribute as shown in the example here. Let's interpret what our Circles and Xs comparison chart is telling us. It says that Mr. A has little to recommend him, Ms. B is about 50-50, and Mr. C has a very good score.

If you wish to refine this system further to match your needs, you might give each spec a weighting in terms of its importance to

Job Specs	Mr. A	Ms. B	Mr. C	Highest Weight
Education	X	O	O	15
Experience	X	X	O	5
Job training	X	O	O	5
Key skill	X	X	O	15
Attitude	O	O	O	10
Speaking ability	X	X	X	2
Outside interests	X	O	O	5
Health	X	X	O	10
Attendance	X	O	O	10
Diplomacy	O	X	O	15
Travel	X	O	X	2
(etc.)				

you, as shown in the last column on the right. Education and skill may be very important, so you might give them a maximum of 15 points. Speaking ability or travel may be least needed, so you might give those 2 points. Other specs fall in between. Now going across on the education line, Mr. A gets zero points, Ms. B gets 15, and Mr. C gets 15. Do the same for all the other lines. The numerical scores can then be added up. Again, Mr. C comes out a winner. Your selection becomes much easier.

People who insist on hiring in direct contradiction to this system almost always end up with a far inferior staff when compared to those who use this plan. In addition, the system is objective, quantified, reduces or eliminates emotional bias, and is demonstrably fair to all concerned (in case of legal challenge).

Circles and Xs Pays Off for Federal Agency

A well-known federal government agency has about 60 branch offices across the country, one of which showed such dramatic improvement in output and public service in the last few years that it was cited as "the No. 1 office" in the United States out of all the branches. This occurred even in the face of severely adverse publicity, a fire, a tornado, and a break-in.

The secret? The branch office's administrators had been using the Circles and *X*s system for building an above-average staff. It also brought them two important extras. First, they trimmed their turnover level to under 5 percent a year (a fraction of the average for such offices). Second, they achieved exceptionally high spirit and positive attitude, as measured by semiannual morale inventory research studies. Double proof that the Circles and *X*s system pays off big.

GET A FEEL FOR THE PERSON

Up till now, you've been cool, calm, and calculating. You did your homework and made the measurements, holding your feelings carefully in check. Now is the time to release your emotions. Set them free. Enjoy them. But more important, use them to your advantage. Facts are fine, but there is also a time for feelings—hunch, emotion, intuition, and just plain gut reaction.

You have input to your mental calculator thousands of data bits, not only of facts but of spirit and emotional chemistry. Use that huge data base to make a further assessment. You might want to add to it by going out to lunch or dinner with the finalists. In the end, if you simply don't like Mr. A but find Ms. B to have a most pleasant personality, you would be foolish to ignore this. Other people may feel the same way about the candidates. It's a vital element in the equation—often the final most important factor, especially if other data were checked first.

Now that you have considered facts plus emotion, it's time to add it all up, set your teeth, and make that decision, secure in the realization that you have done about as much as anyone could do to assure success. You certainly did far more than most. "To succeed you must be willing to do those things known to cause success," goes an old management proverb—and you have done exactly that.

General Foods Uses Well-Rounded Screening Technique

"I had applied to General Foods as a brand manager," my friend Rod W. told me. "And I have got to say those GF people are impressive. They had their job specs well in mind, held an excellent interview series, gave me some tests, and checked my references. But then I noticed a big change—a sudden shift. They put away their charts and graphs, and we got a chance to know each other and become friends. We established a mutual rapport and liking for each other. They offered me a fine job, and I felt that their emotional judgment of me played a really good and fair role, along with all their statistics, in making that decision. They used a well-rounded screening approach." Rod subsequently proved to be an outstanding producer.

WRAPPING THINGS UP

Now you've come to a crucial moment—closing the deal, planning the next steps, and following through. You and the candidate have both looked each other over pretty carefully. You know a lot about each other, and it's rather obvious that you are at a decision point. At this moment, you have a golden opportunity that comes only rarely. Right now you can lock things up neat, clean, firm, and final for your mutual benefit by getting a commitment.

You might say, "Can you do the job?" and/or "Do you think you would like the job?" In responding, an applicant will usually make a pretty deep commitment. But you haven't. Listen to the reply. If the candidate is really sharp and savvy, he or she will say something like, "I sure believe I can do it well and would enjoy it. What do you think?" Go ahead and speak your mind. Saying "I agree with you" does not fully commit you, unless you make a further statement, a formal offer or acceptance of the candidate. Just be very sure you understand each other. You don't want any bad slips at this stage. You may want to discuss a few things (like when the candidate would be available) or suggest that he or she come back for a final visit to meet other people or the big boss.

At this point, if you want this person on your team, you had best show a very strong interest. Have clearance and be prepared to make a firm offer. After all, if the candidate is truly above average, as you now believe, he or she probably is being considered by other good companies. Set some firm dates and follow your schedule carefully.

Chevy People Close the Deal

The president of a large Chevy dealership had been screening for a chief clerk. The process had taken months, but his staff had finally found the ideal candidate. She fit all the specifications. Her interview was excellent, references were superb, and she obviously matched the personality and style of the group. She was being interviewed by the assistant treasurer, who wasn't familiar with good screening. He thanked her for coming in and said, "We'll let you know."

At this point, the president came by the office, heard the comment, sat down with them, offered the candidate the job, and she accepted. She turned out to be a leading employee. It was only some time later that the president learned that she had been just about to accept a similar position with the Ford dealership down the street. Clearly, you reach a point when you must act decisively or lose the ball game.

TEN COMMANDMENTS OF GOOD SCREENING

1. Don't fall in love with those baby blue eyes.
2. Start with your own well-thought-out specifications.
3. Use your cold fish-eye to study candidates.
4. Give information, get it, and make a friend.
5. Encourage questions. Listen carefully to the answers.
6. Have trusted associates visit with the candidate.
7. Check both references and the candidate's other associates.
8. Use the Circles and Xs chart to comparison-shop.
9. Get a feel for the person and make your decision.
10. Close the deal, plan next steps, and follow through.

The OBI (one best idea) for screening and finding outstanding people is to give and get information carefully, make friends, compare both cold facts and warm emotions, and then decide.

CHAPTER 5
How to Sell *Your Firm to a Quality Applicant in the Interview*

"Here at Sperry Rand," a department manager said recently, "we had a few fiascos in trying to find high-quality people. We made our share of mistakes. A major change, installed in recent years, was a better way of selling our firm on top candidates. We found that a simple program worked best. It really is bad news to hire a high producer who isn't sold on the company—not really convinced that he or she will be doing something worthwhile."

Remember your goal—quality. You are looking for an above-average employee. If you feel you have a pretty good insight into the person you seek, if you have found some possibilities and have screened and identified your one best selection, then the time has come to set the hook. Lock the candidate up. Sell the candidate.

To be sold, your prospect must first of all be persuaded mentally and emotionally that he or she is doing the right thing. Sure, money is important, but money alone is seldom enough. Not for top people. Don't forget, you're dealing with a high-quality person. Chances are, if this person is really as good as you think, he or she can get the same money somewhere else. Maybe more. In the end, top achievers usually go where they can get both financial and emotional fulfillment. No, very often, money alone won't do it. In fact, emotional conviction—plain old sales effort—can often substitute (at least in part) for cash. Many top people have joined a company that did not make them the largest salary offer. There is a saying among high-quality people: "Don't always go for the top dollar." They suspect that the high-roller company often must bid so high to offset a closetful of secret problems, troubles, and negatives.

Second, remember that, as a top-quality person, your candidate is looking you over about as carefully as you (also a high-quality person) are looking him or her over. You would be wise to put on a pretty good face and make your best presentation. Third, a job is a contract—a two-way street. It takes two parties who each feel they came out well to form a lasting commitment. Fourth, top people *are* available. But it's often a matter of finding them and selling them. Scores of fine companies got where they are largely by recognizing that high-quality people can be recruited, found, and sold. (Emphasis: *sold*.) The company executives made the selling effort—successfully.

Unfortunately, most employers do not know how to sell their own firms. Worse yet, they don't even try. They think it is unnecessary. Then they wonder why their competition boxes their ears off in the marketplace or with a better organization. Obviously, a good sales effort is very much in your own interest. A sold tiger is a better tiger and a happier one, who is likely to perform closer to his or her top potential.

When you make a sales effort, you really have everything to gain and nothing to lose. If you do hire the candidate, you get a better producer. If you don't hire the candidate, at least you part friends. That may (and often does) pay off handsomely in the months to come. Either way, you have gained. Let's look at ten tough, tried-and-true techniques to tie up the top tiger.

SELL WHILE SCREENING

Think "selling" right from the start. This doesn't mean you should come on like a sleazy, phony, high-pressure con artist. It does mean you should put your best foot forward. You have a good company and a good job opportunity, and you're a good person. At least you think so, or you wouldn't be looking for a good-quality candidate. But don't hide your shining light under the proverbial bushel basket. Turn it on. Display it. However sharp, your candidate is not a mind reader. He or she can't pick up facts and feelings purely via osmosis.

Resolve that you will make a good impression right from the

start. Especially from the start. First impressions really are lasting. You don't need to go overboard or kiss the candidate's feet. Just be polite, friendly, and cordial. Pretend he or she is a customer. Above all, use the AIDA formula: Get your prospect's *a*ttention, *i*nterest, *d*esire, *a*ction (commitment). A further advantage to you is that the more he or she is sold, the stronger your bargaining position, the more you can ask for, and the more you can demand and get.

When you first contact the candidate to invite him or her for an interview, be polite and friendly. Remember, no matter how blasé or sophisticated he or she is, you are still a strange name and a strange voice. And don't forget, you hold that mystical magic power of potential economic life or death. Maybe *you* don't think you do, but the candidate does. So he or she will be a little apprehensive.

Before your interview starts, have a simple plan. You might use the SOS formula: *s*ituation, *o*bjective, *s*trategy. The situation reminds you to get the facts. The objective says to look at your goals and at your applicant's targets. The strategy means to check the methods you plan to use.

At the start of your interview, as mentioned in the preceding chapter, go a bit out of your way to be pleasant, relaxed, cordial, and sincere. This actually has a double payoff. It will not only begin building an interest and desire within your candidate but will make him or her more likely to open up. The candidate will often say more than he or she had planned, and you will learn more than you had expected.

Sales Pitch Sparks Candidates' Enthusiasm at Gillette

A Gillette executive, Bud R., was looking for a product brand manager. After reviewing applications and résumés from many candidates, Bud selected six for interviewing. As he called each applicant to arrange an appointment, Bud introduced himself carefully. (Some hurried executives give their name and title so rapidly the candidates are not really sure who is talking to them.) Bud thanked the candidate for his or her résumé, saying that it was of real interest, and asked the candidate if he or she could come for a visit. A meeting date was then set up. During the interview, Bud went the extra mile to sell himself and Gillette. The result was that nearly every applicant became quite enthusiastic about Bud and his company. He weeded out a couple of strange characters he really did not want to hire and ended up with an exceptional employee, which isn't surprising. Bud had been selling right from the start.

STATE THE FACTS

As you visit with each applicant, give the facts, opportunities, and a few basic policies of your company. This has the double advantage of orienting and educating the candidate as well as permitting him or her to tailor responses and further questions to fit your interests. It also fills his or her information needs. (After all, the candidate is a fish in a strange pond and knows it.) Plus, this gives the applicant time to think and makes him or her feel more comfortable.

In this way, you are killing a lot of birds with one stone. You are also saving time for both of you and quickly covering the "situation" portion of your SOS formula. Remember, you know a lot about your prospect through his or her résumé. Now he or she knows something about you. A true exchange of information and feelings has begun.

Here's how to do it. Be fairly candid. Give both pros and cons. Remember, you're selling. This person did not drop by to hear you complain about the company. Any cons should be touched on partly to cover some obvious negative that is common knowledge and partly to build your own believability. Emphasize the pros. The candidate believes you have a good situation, or he or she wouldn't be there. Included in these positives, or advantages, should be basic facts about the company, a few major policies, and reference to at least a hopeful, if not shining, future.

Quaker Oats Levels with Candidates

An advertising executive at Quaker Oats, Ken D., recently told me, "We try to be extra careful to give each candidate more than a fair shake. By this I mean enough information about us and the realistic future possibilities for the prospective employee personally. This isn't so much because we are swell guys. It's just that in doing this, we also do ourselves a favor. Obviously, a good exchange of information benefits everyone in a great many ways. Of course, I'm also proud of our company, so it is easy for me to talk about it. I feel that giving good information in a positive way has helped us land some awfully good people who might otherwise have been lured away by other companies."

UNDERSTAND THE CANDIDATE

This may surprise you, but a good insight into your "customer" is one of the first laws of good salesmanship. Therefore, be extra sure you understand your prospect. It gives you four advantages: First, you put the candidate at ease and show him or her a courtesy. Second, you demonstrate that you care, thereby building the candidate's interest and enthusiasm. Third, with greater understanding of him or her, you now know what questions to ask and how to adjust your own statements. And fourth, you learn more, so you are better able to evaluate or assign this person later.

How do you do this? To understand a person better, ask questions. Most people like to talk about themselves, given a non-threatening listener. (Next time you hear two people talk, notice how often they say the word "I." It will appear in at least every other sentence and sometimes three or four times in the same sentence. It's the most heavily used word in the English language.)

Ask the candidate about his or her background and major interests, professional or personal. Then listen carefully—not just to what the candidate says but also to how he or she says it and what he or she chooses to talk about. One of your key objectives at this point is to learn where this person is coming from and what he or she is aiming for. But most of all, at this stage, you are selling. You want the applicant to like you, and he or she will tend to like you more if you show sincere, personal interest. (Real interest, not phony solicitude.) You can do this by truly listening and understanding.

Mennen Supervisor Draws Out Applicants

A supervisor at a Mennen toiletries plant, Vic G., used to like to say, "When I'm interviewing people, I let them talk. I pull a little trick on them. I just ask a simple question like, 'Where were you born and raised?' or 'Where did you go to school?' I don't say what level of education, just 'school.' Then I listen. When they stop, I say something like, 'That's interesting. Tell me more,' or 'What did you do next?' I just sort of keep nodding my head and smiling softly, nudging them along. It works almost every time. They relax, get friendly, and I learn lots about them. In half an hour we both feel like we've known each other for years. Strangely enough, they end up wanting to work for me real bad. And I hardly did a darn thing!" In reality, Vic did plenty—for himself, his company, and his candidates.

SHOW A STRONG POSITIVE ATTITUDE

Stay positive, but don't go overboard. Don't load your conversation with artificial enthusiasm. Your candidates will see through it instantly. Most of them can spot a phony a mile away.

How do you stay positive? Your secret here is simply your own belief in your company—your conviction that you have a good personal future and that whomever is selected for this job will likewise have good things in store for him or her. What if you don't have very great faith in your company or your personal future with it? Then you have a problem.

But you have a solution if you at least believe honestly that the job you are discussing right now would be good for the right candidate. This is where you can demonstrate your own sense of fairness, professionalism, and maturity. If the job would offer at least some important benefits to the proper candidate, then you owe it to him or her and to your company to reflect that belief in a strong and positive way.

How? The easiest way is to tell the truth. Explain that you feel the right person would have a challenging and rewarding assignment. Show him or her why. Point out the strengths, challenges, advantages, and positives. If you are strongly sold on your company, say so—and give your reasons. Illustrate your reasons with short examples of what has been happening. Perhaps what you, your department, or other groups have done to help promote the company. Also what is being planned for the future, in both the short and long run.

Phillip Morris Approach: Genuine Enthusiasm, Not Hype

A Phillip Morris quality control lab supervisor told me, "When I interview scientific-type people, they usually say, 'Just give me the facts. No hype. No sell.' So that's what I do. But, to be honest, when our screening system has found us a really top-quality person, I deliberately let some of my own personal faith in our company come through along with the facts. This influences what subjects we talk about and even my tone of voice. Scientists or not, the candidates are still human. And frankly, they want to be encouraged. Their decision is based on more than just cold facts. I find my enthusiasm is contagious. It lifts their spirits along with my own. Pretty soon, I start believing my own sales pitch. Well, almost. Anyway, it sure has helped me land some outstanding people."

LEVEL WITH THE APPLICANT

We said earlier that you should cover the pros and cons, but mostly the pros. Now that you have the candidate's enthusiasm raised a bit, though, you will have to know how to level effectively. If there is some key disadvantage associated with the job, such as moving to a less desirable city or lots of travel or overtime for a while, you had better cover it at this point.

This has four advantages. First, you've got to bite the bullet eventually, and now is as good a time as any—better, perhaps, since the candidate will be in a positive frame of mind. Problems won't look so big. Second, the candidate will respect you for bringing the matter up forthrightly and not surprising him or her with it later. (If your prospect is really outstanding, he or she may have found out already and may be waiting for you to level with him or her. By doing so, you will impress the candidate with your honesty.) Third, it will give you a chance to minimize the problem or present it in its least negative light. You will also be providing the candidate with a way to explain the drawback to his or her family. And fourth, all this gives the applicant a chance to ask you some questions and gives you a chance to provide some answers that will at least moderate, explain, or perhaps even resolve the problem. Good selling also means good answers to objections.

Your best approach is to come flat out and say something like, "There are a couple of matters that need consideration." (Don't call them problems.) Or you might say, "I'd like your opinion on a few things." Express these briefly and as mildly as you can while still staying factual. Don't debate. Listen to the candidate's objections. Resolve issues that are easily handled. Explain that some other issues are flexible and negotiable. A lot can change in just a few weeks. If a particular condition is very firm, admit this and say, "Let's get back to that a little later." Then go on to other matters.

Playing It Straight Snares Scott Paper Winner

An executive at Scott Paper Company said, "Frankly, we had a terrible problem. We had found an ideal candidate. She was so far superior in training, experience, skills, and spirit that no one else even came close. She had said right from the start, though, that there was only one condition—that she not be required to move out of New York City, where we had first located her, and that was fine with us.

But during the interviewing, things changed. The decision was made to move her prospective department to a distant state. We had no choice but to tell her that we felt she was one of the greatest candidates we had ever seen—but that things had changed. She listened closely. We discussed it and finally came to the conclusion that we might actually create a job for her in New York. Before that could happen, however, she told us that she and her husband were so impressed with both our integrity and our enthusiasm that they had decided to make the move after all. It turned out to be an excellent decision—for all of us. We played it very straight-arrow and honest injun—and it paid off big."

MAKE YOUR PITCH

Now is the time to make a simple desk-top sales presentation about the company and what's going on. The main advantage is that this reinforces your AIDA program (*a*ttention, *i*nterest, *d*esire, *a*ction). You will certainly grab the candidate's attention, since only two interviewers in fifty do this. And if you do it in a way aimed at where he or she is coming from, you will surely generate interest in and desire for the job.

How do you make a presentation? There are dozens of things you can do. Here are some that work especially well: (1) Show the candidate an organization chart illustrating where your department and "his or her job" fit into the big picture. (Your prospect is already starting to feel like one of the team.) (2) Show the candidate some exhibits or examples of the resources or tools that he or she will have available. (Now the candidate feels even closer—almost imagining himself or herself at work and using these.) (3) Show examples of earlier, finished projects, especially some good ones—and maybe some poor ones that he or she could easily surpass. (You are whetting the candidate's appetite still further.) (4) Present other charts, pictures, and graphs. Visuals usually have twice the impact of unadorned printed matter. (5) Briefly review any short, descriptive booklet about the company, such as an annual report. (6) Give the applicant a little kit, file, or folder of some sample exhibits to take home. He or she will be favorably impressed and may show this to his or her family. In doing so, the candidate sells and resells himself or herself, to a certain extent. (7) Take him or her on a tour of the plant or office and explain what goes on at some major areas. Introduce the candidate to a few key people and openly praise their strengths, so he or she will be proud to work with them. (By now, your prospect should feel as if he or she is almost doing just that! The candidate is nearly one of the group.)

Manager Sells GE with "Simple Routine"

A General Electric manager gave a little talk about how he personally likes to present GE to visitors. "I have a confession. Frankly, I'm all ready for visitors. We get a lot in my area. Some are from other parts of the company; others are suppliers, friends, and job applicants. I have a simple routine that I can easily expand for people who show a greater interest. I give them a couple of charts, some work examples, a walk through the shop to meet a few people, and a little visitor's kit. It's just a colored folder with an annual report and some booklets about our products. I watch my 'audience' pretty closely, and I notice they are nearly always turned on by this stuff. It's pretty easy; you might call it the lazy man's pitch. I do about the same thing each time but adapt it to the individuals who are visiting. With above-average people, I allow a little longer, discuss a little more, and give out more statistical data. I encourage their questions, then pick up on that subject and explain it in a lot more detail."

ARRANGE A SHORT VISIT WITH YOUR TOP EMPLOYEES

The advantage of having the candidate meet your above-average people is fourfold. First, like attracts like. Your better company people will usually quickly recognize a superior candidate and will frequently make an effort to sell him or her. Second, the candidate will likewise recognize the better employee and be favorably impressed. You will have some two-way chemistry going, really fast. Third, these visits will give you one more source of insight into the candidate. And fourth, after visiting with a few top employees, the above-average candidate is likely to feel all toasty warm toward your group. After meeting "his or her kind" of people, the candidate's enthusiasm for you and your company is growing. Your prospect is nearly sold.

How do you arrange such visits? A simple way is to line up two or three people before the candidate arrives. Many more than that gets a bit pointless and confusing. Give these people a little information about the applicant. Suggest that they tell him or her a bit about their jobs, encourage questions, and—most important of all—make a friend. Explain that you will have told the candidate that the employee is one of the top-caliber people in the company. Give him or her a reputation to live up to. Explain that it is important that they know, like, and respect each other: They may very well be working together. You have now put out the cheese and set the mousetrap. If you really do have high-quality employees, they will probably do a superior "selling job" for you, even though you never used that phrase.

Then, before you take your candidate to meet the employees, tell him or her a little about each one—the person's name, title, duties, and how he or she would relate to the candidate on the job. And, most important, indicate that you feel the employee is one of the top-quality people in the company. Your candidate will probably jot down a few notes. Again, you are selling by showing the good quality of your people, by showing respect and consideration for the applicant, and by orienting the applicant so his or her visits with the employees will have greater personal impact. When you introduce the two, use their names loud and clear. Review both employee's and applicant's backgrounds and duties in a sentence or two. Now give them an assignment and a time limit. Otherwise, the visit may be much too brief or run on far too long. "The objective of asking you both to meet is for you to discuss each other's backgrounds a little, over the next 30 minutes." Then tell them what to do next. "Charlie, when you two have finished visiting, please bring Dave back to my office, OK?"

Chrysler Engineer Introduces Above- and Below-Average Workers

During a talk to a small luncheon group in Detroit last August, a Chrysler engineer said, "Now some authors tell you to introduce your top candidates to your top employees. Frankly, I don't always agree with that. Sometimes it's a good thing to let applicants talk with your below-average workers. Then they can see what they're up against. Why deceive them? But along with that, when you really want to nail down good candidates, you're smart to get them with one of their own kind. Good fish swim in schools. To be honest, I use both methods: I introduce candidates to the above-average and below-average people. Whenever I do this, I talk to each of the employees first. Yes, I tell them a few things I'd like them to say. I'll admit it. I put a few words in their mouths. But so what? They are honest words—and they get the job done. Our department out-produced every one of our competitors last year. Very few other groups in our company can say that."

SHOW THAT THE CANDIDATE'S ROLE
WILL BE VITAL

What could appeal more strongly to you than to have someone say, "I realize what outstanding skills you have. You're terribly important to us. We want and need you. And if we don't have your help, we're in big trouble. But if you will work with us, we will all succeed as a team. We will win and you will win, because we will know you were the reason for our success. And you will be rewarded." Pretty strong stuff, isn't it? This is the sort of idea you should get across to your candidate.

How do you prove it? Four easy steps. First, start out by saying something like, "You have a right to know why your job is vital." (You just told the candidate what you want him or her to know and accept, and you picked a concept the candidate already at least partly believes.) Second, say, "Let's look at your job again, in closer detail. Then you'll see why it is essential"—or words to that effect. Third, don't forget to emphasize the particular goal of the job. And then, fourth, by all means, show that the job's goal is critical to the success of the whole department—even the enterprise. Or more.

Without much imagination, you can even convince a cab driver that his or her performance is the cornerstone, the focal point for the company. That without his or her success, the company could fail in this big city of New York, and New York itself would feel it and suffer. Ridiculous? Of course it's ridiculous. But it is not totally wrong, either, for this reason: If every cab driver failed, New York certainly would feel it and suffer. So there really is a lot riding on every single job.

Plus (and here you've got something big going for you) the applicant wants to believe you. Research shows that nearly every person feels that he or she is doing an important job, whether or not the boss admits this. A large portion of these people even believe they are doing a key job. Try it yourself. Ask a few people in a nice, nonthreatening way: "Don't you think you are doing an important, even vital, job?"

As a clincher with your candidate, go back to his or her potential on-the-job resources. You can say, "As evidence of how vital this position is, just look at the facilities top management has made available. They are certainly putting their money where their mouth is." (Resource measurement is a matter of definition and can be as broad or as narrow as you define. There is some overlap, but you can still make your point.)

Supervisor Shows How Shell Supports Key Position

A Shell Oil word processor supervisor told me, "I try to hire only the very best people. When I find an ideal candidate, I show him or her how vital the assignment is in relation to our company. I dramatize what would happen if we fail. And what happens if we succeed. Then I say something like, 'If you doubt that for a moment, think about this: Our company backs up your job with $50,000 worth of equipment! That's putting real commitment on the line. Think about that. It tells you something, doesn't it?' That kind of talk impresses almost anyone. Especially above-average people, who know the value of a thousand dollars."

TURN QUESTIONS INTO SELLING POINTS

Earlier, we looked at the advantages of encouraging your candidates to ask questions, but that was to learn more about them as a means of screening, or judging their value. You can also use those very same questions to help sell yourself and your company. Here are eight simple ways to do so:

1. Listen carefully to each question. Your candidate will appreciate that. You may be the first interviewer who really paid that much attention.

2. Show you care by the way you listen. By your concentration. By taking careful notes. By nodding and smiling.

3. Repeat, paraphrase, and play back the question in a pleasant manner. It shows you heard correctly and are thinking.

4. Compliment the candidate if you can. "That's a very perceptive question," or, "I'm glad you brought that up," or, "Not many people think to ask that," or, "Thank you for giving me the chance to talk about that." Or some thought along those lines, phrased in your own words.

5. Provide a careful, considerate, factual answer, using the same manner you would with a good friend or close relative. Not short or brusque and not too long. Use a pleasant tone.

6. Try to turn the answer into a selling point. "When you ask about our products (or sales or research or staff), you are getting into what's responsible for our excellent reputation. That's where we take real pride." Elaborate a little. Explain why.

7. End by asking, "Did I answer your question adequately? Is there anything more you'd like to know about this? If so, I'll try to answer it."

8. If you don't know the answer to a particular question, say so promptly. Don't hedge. It gives you an excellent opportunity to show your honesty—and your willingness to be accommodating. "I'm sorry, but I must confess that I just don't know the answer to that. But if you'd like, I'll be glad to make a note of your question and get you an answer. I know people who should have that data readily available."

There's no special need for you to memorize all eight of these steps. The key is simply to show real interest, understanding, empathy, and approval. And use each question to make a friend by the way you respond. It can be pretty simple.

Uniroyal Executive Uses Questions as a Springboard

A Uniroyal executive and I got to talking during lunch. "I agree that you can sell people with their own questions," he said. "In fact, you should add in your book that I've done you one better. Even before the interview, when I'm talking to the candidate on the phone, I ask him or her to bring a few questions along. This system works quite well. Candidates often give this a lot of thought. Frankly, I have put them to work—at no cost to the company—and given them their first project assignment. Their questions are generally quite good. Fortunately for me, they are both predictable and repetitive. Rarely unique. I praise their insight and pretend to give their inquiries deep thought, but I have actually answered those same questions several times before. Then I use the question as an entrée to make a few key selling points about the company and to give the candidates a couple of little booklets on the subject that I just happen to have on hand. I'm plenty aware that the candidates aren't always all that serious about the questions. They're selling me, just like I'm selling them. It's partly a game, and we both know it. But of course we never say so. That would ruin it."

FINISH ON AN UPBEAT NOTE

Always leave 'em laughing—or at least smiling and with a good taste in their mouths. All's well that ends well, and final impressions, like first ones, are often lasting. Many professional entertainers or sales representatives like to appear last on the program. Done right, the finale is an excellent opportunity to look good, lock things up, cement relations, and start off your new association on an upbeat, happy note. This can also favorably impress your candidate, your associates, and your boss. Here are a few suggestions for how to end in style and, even more important, start your next stage off beautifully.

First, be sure you did all you reasonably could to establish good, friendly relations. Remember, *how* you say things, your tone of voice, is much more important than *what* you say. Second, agree between you as to what is to happen next. Don't leave things "dangling." (You may never see your candidate again!) If another interview is needed, set a mutually convenient date. Third, if you made a job offer and it has been accepted, then you have an agreement. Set a starting date or agree to be back in touch with each other about this by phone or letter at a certain time. Fourth, if you had agreed to pay any travel expenses, reconfirm these arrangements and explain how the candidate should handle this. Fifth, follow up the visit with a letter or phone call within a few days. Thank the candidate for visiting and again recap what happens next.

In short, tidy things up. Don't leave any uncertainties as to where you both stand. A buttoned-up understanding is a buttoned-down sale.

Interviews at Sony End with "Sincere Selling"

A Japanese executive at Sony told some middle management people recently: "Friendly relations are essential. We are selling people all the time—certainly all the way through a job interview. But the end crowns all. It attones for a multitude of errors. Be extra polite, extra gracious, extra friendly. In Japan, we have a word for this that, freely translated, means 'make your visitors glad they came to see you and anxious to come back again.' This is one of the best and most sincere sorts of selling."

TEN COMMANDMENTS FOR SELLING TO AN APPLICANT

1. Start selling immediately, while you are screening.
2. Present facts, future, and a few policies.
3. Be extra sure you understand the candidate.
4. Keep a strong positive attitude throughout.
5. Level on some problems.
6. Make a simple desk-top selling presentation.
7. Introduce other outstanding employees.
8. Show that the candidate's role will be vital.
9. Sell with the candidate's own questions, properly answered.
10. End on an upbeat note.

The OBI (one best idea) for selling a top-quality candidate is to begin immediately with understanding; a factual, relevant presentation; and a positive, open attitude. Then keep everlastingly at it—from start to finish.

CHAPTER 6
How to Get Big Results from Good Orientation

"At General Tire," said a sales executive, "I made a serious error with a person who much later turned out to be my best employee. The mistake was that I never did bother to tell her enough about our company. This caused all sorts of trouble. She misunderstood a couple of key instructions and assignments. This created conflict, some bitterness, and even embarrassment for me and my boss. Personally, I have a cardinal rule: Never make the boss look bad. But I had broken my own rule that time. I may be a slow learner, but I'm a good one. Since that unfortunate episode, we set up a strong basic introductory program. It not only saved us a lot of trouble, but I saw the difference in people's performance. Especially in our better folks. And incidentally, we made the boss look good, too."

Some executives feel that an orientation program is unnecessary, especially for top people, who are supposed to know everything. Surprisingly, the opposite is true. Top-quality people are particularly interested in the company—partly because of their native intelligence and inborn curiosity, partly because they often see things in broad scope rather than through tunnel vision, and partly because they want to know more and make faster progress. They are well aware that information, education, and knowledge will be a big help to them.

This is a great opportunity for the company. Never again will the high producer be quite so receptive, coachable, and malleable as he or she is right at the start. Unfortunately, most companies either have no orientation program at all, or they have some sort of half-hearted, hit-or-miss patchwork affair. "Give him pitch No. 31, Charlie—if you ever have time!" And of course Charlie almost never finds time, so the new employee picks it up helter-skelter as he or she goes along. With your better workers, this can lead to a very bad impression, to poor producers, and to embarrassing errors for you and your boss.

Here's how to plan and execute a low-cost, quick and easy orientation program. It can get you big results from your better people. With your help, they will usually find ways to deliver, not just half, but their full potential, toward your mutual goals.

KNOW YOUR COMPANY

You can't explain something you don't fully understand. You would be surprised at how many executives get so engrossed in their own departments that they can't describe the overall operation. A good test is to see if you can draw a simple organization chart. Eight or ten boxes or circles will do nicely. Know who's on top, who's next, and roughly what each group does and how it relates to the others. If you can draw that on a plain sheet of paper, you will be able to inform and impress your top-caliber employees. Only about one manager in ten can do this.

The organization chart is basic to your business and to your orientation effort. Why? Because it permits you to picture the whole operation—who's where and who can do what—in an orientation program, so you can begin a plan, and it also provides an easy, pertinent, and helpful tool for you or your "students."

Eastern Airlines Shows Newcomers the Big Picture

An Eastern Airlines executive addressing a small chamber of commerce group said, "My assistant, Tod, would hire top people into his department and then find that they spent too much time going around asking about how their unit fit in with the others. I discovered that Tod had never told them. So he and I worked out a basic organization chart. In fact, we drew it up with a bunch of those colored felt pens. We used it from then on to help orient new people, and it worked beautifully."

PLAN A SIMPLE PROGRAM

Orientation can take place in a week or a day or perhaps an hour a day for a few days. Companies make three major errors in orientation programs: They are too long, too short, or nonexistent. A fourth error is that when such programs are held, they are disorganized or done poorly and so become a gross waste of time. A few suggestions:

1. Have an orientation objective. A good one is simply to give new employees their bearings—an understanding as to where they are personally and where they fit within the whole. The objective should be to offer a quick insight into the work environment, not to present detailed job procedures or solutions to specific problems.

2. Have a plan. A program. Know what subject is first, second, and so on. Start with basics, like the overall industry—what it does in our world. Then show where your company fits. A good procedure is to cover the processes of goods or services chronologically, from start to finish. A few sentences on each phase is usually enough. Don't bog down in details. Get to the employee's department role and personal job as quickly as possible.

3. Have some visuals or examples of work done. Take a tour, particularly if it helps this step.

4. Arrange for enough time, especially for above-average people. Some topics can easily be covered very rapidly. On others, employees will have an unusually large number of questions. Tailor the program to the time available. Don't try to jam a two-day course into half an hour. If that unfortunate need arises (and it probably will), just summarize and hit the high points.

5. Be sure your boss gives full approval of and support for your orientation plan early on, in the idea and proposal stage. Then, when your boss discovers that you and your new employee are spending time on this, he or she will endorse, not criticize, your action.

Wrigley Gum's Flexible Program Offers Excellent Insight

A manager from the Wrigley Gum operation long ago worked out a simple orientation program. It's just a set of twenty 3″ × 5″ cards, each with a subject and three or four sentences. It is highly flexible.

Using the cards, he can orient a new employee within an hour—or he and the employee can spend a day of discussions. When they are finished, the new person has an excellent insight into the industry, company, department, and job. On several occasions, the very same high-quality people the manager oriented subsequently borrowed the cards and copied a set to use for indoctrinating their own new people. It's a simple, low-cost, well-liked plan—and it works.

HAVE A COORDINATOR

The guide or coach for your orientation program might even be you. (In fact, it probably should be you at first, just so you know the routine and can teach it to others.) Whoever the coordinator is, this person's job should be to implement, coordinate, and execute the plan—arrange the times, places, and attendees and see that the goal (good, quick insight and understanding) is reached.

Your approach to orienting above-average people had best be light on the reins and briskly paced. Your coordinator, who should also be an above-average person, should be tuned to that approach. Try to make this a permanent, part-time assignment for someone who likes doing it and can do it well. Do not slough it off on someone incapable of handling it. Better to scrub the mission than to do it like that. Require your coordinator to attend one or two of your orientation sessions to get the feel of the process. Then you should let the coordinator do it, while you note how well he or she manages things.

Orientation Handled by Specialists at R. J. Reynolds

An executive from R. J. Reynolds said, "We are proud of our company, so naturally we have no trouble telling new people about our operation. Yes, we certainly do require above-average people to go through a little orientation program. There is no doubt in my mind that it is a good investment of time. Education never hurts and usually helps. Top people seem especially good at using extra knowledge. We find it best to have a few specialists give the overall company orientation and then let individual department heads see that the final details are added."

PREPARE OTHER SUPERVISORS

Let the supervisors within your department as well as the heads of other groups know what's going on, and that you are in the orientation phase with a new, high-quality employee. This has several advantages. First, supervisors like to avoid surprises. Once alerted, they can mesh their own plans with yours. Second, sometimes they can help you. Occasionally, they will have ideas or urge your new person to tour their operation. Or they may want to be directly involved. They may have a key message or a point that they want to make. As a third advantage, they will get to know the new person a little, and working relations tend to get off to a good start.

How can you do this? Begin by showing your simple plan to supervisors, so they can see what you have in mind. Second, ask their opinion and really listen to their ideas. Nothing says you must agree, just keep an open mind. Third, ask them if they wish to play some role or if they would like you to cover any particular point.

Fourth, be a little careful that, in bringing supervisors into the orientation process, this does *not* become an invitation to someone who has a particularly strong personal, selfish, or vested interest— or an opportunity to spread dissent. While it is good for the new person to know about problem areas, it is sometimes best that you or another objective party touch on this briefly during orientation rather than getting the new employee all embroiled in what may be confusing, possibly conflicting, and even erroneous data. This could do more harm than good.

Miles Laboratories Improves Orientation, Saves Snafus

Said a department head from Miles Laboratories, "I used to get pretty damn ticked off! They would bring good new people into other departments and never even tell them about our operation. Some cats were here a year before they even knew we existed! Can you believe that? I often felt, if ony I had ten minutes to talk to them right at the start, it would save me and them a whole lot of trouble. Then the boss urged us to cooperate on these orientation sessions. At first, I would talk directly with the new employees. But later, the coordinator covered my material, so I didn't need to attend personally. What an improvement! That simple change saved a lot of people a ton of costly mistakes!"

REVIEW YOUR PLAN WITH NEW EMPLOYEES

Now that you have worked out a program, have a coordinator, and have gotten input from other executives, it's time to bring the new employees into the process. To do this, first touch on the problems that can develop when new people do not understand the company. One or two horror stories about new-employee mistakes will surely make the point to your newcomers. You are "selling," and you want their attention and interest. With your better people, this should be no problem. Second, state the orientation program goal—yours and theirs. It's simple—a quick insight into the organization and the 5 Ws, with particular emphasis on who does what and why. Generally, the above-average person quickly realizes that this will help him or her "hit the track running," with a minimum of stumble, fumble, and fall.

Third, in reviewing the plan, show the employees the logic of it, why it was set up this way, and how it flows naturally from the start of a company process to its finish. Fourth, emphasize that a strong positive attitude on your part and theirs is vital. It will help you both to reach your goal—a fast, useful insight into the company structure and mechanics. Fifth, emphasize that this is a great and rare opportunity for you both, for two reasons: (1) most companies don't even bother with such a program, and (2) this will happen just *once* while they are with the company. They never get a second chance.

Coordinator Seeks Input from Top Standard Brands Employees

A supervisor at Standard Brands told his assistant, "Ira, I want you to handle the orientation program from now on. You've seen enough of these sessions so you know we have a pretty smooth system, and it gets us good results." The supervisor underrated Ira. Ira not only took over the program but he asked the new employees to help by outlining what they wanted to know. Together, Ira and the new employees made a list of subjects and then used that to modify their past program.

"That Ira!" the supervisor chuckled. "He's something else! I never could trust that guy! Now we have the best orientation program there is. And to think he even got our new hot shot to help him. Wait until I tell the boss. Maybe I'll get a raise. Maybe Ira will get one, too."

ARRANGE A FLEXIBLE TIME SCHEDULE

One of the problems with above-average people is that, by the time they've gone through all that screening and interviewing and testing and selection, company people want some action—not more meetings. And you can't really blame them. Said one Mr. Big, "I don't understand why that new man of ours doesn't seem to be doing much. He's been around here for weeks." His assistant answered, "But Mr. Big, he doesn't go on our payroll until next month!"

Try asking Mr. or Ms. Big at this point for approval to run an orientation program. He or she may think that too much time has already been invested without any results. That's all the more reason for you to have obtained the boss's endorsement for the program long ago—right from the start. If you had done so, you would have fewer problems in proceeding now.

But even with the boss's approval, time is running out. You have already invested a lot in the recruiting procedure, and everyone is getting anxious for the new person to start producing. This tells you that your two-day orientation session may need to be cut to a half day. Or less. That's why you should have a very flexible program. Long enough and informative enough to fill two days (or whatever) with good results for every hour spent, but flexible enough to be boiled down and highlighted in two or three hours, if necessary.

Plans for your group size should also be flexible. There may be a large number attending one session, whereas another session may have only one person. In your preparation, you should specialize primarily in the one-person orientation. That's the size "group" you may have most often, especially when you are dealing with the above-average new employee.

Here are some more ways to assure flexibility:

1. Talk about the orientation program midway in the screening process. Perhaps after you have selected some finalists, but before the agreement is made. This brings the matter up and fixes it in everyone's mind as a pending item on the agenda.

2. Soon after the agreement is made, set an orientation date that is mutually convenient for all concerned. Agree as to who's running the program and who's attending. If it's just an informal series of meetings between you and the new employee, say so.

3. Circulate a note outlining the program, objective, time schedule, agenda, and key people involved. Then everyone is singing from the same song sheet.

4. Hang loose. Be ready to change at a moment's notice. Some managers have not yet fully realized the profitability of a good orientation and thus give it low priority. It can very easily be bumped by other urgent projects, sometimes out of pure necessity. When a company hires a person, particularly a high achiever, that usually means there is a project that needs immediate attention.

Flexible Orientation Program Keeps Westinghouse Turnover Low

An executive from Westinghouse recently said, "I leave very little to chance. Early in the ball game, we have all talked about the need for orientation of our new people. We schedule it automatically for their second day on the job. Everyone understands this. The new employees know the plan and the time and place. They have the names of the people they will visit, the subjects they will cover, and how much time they have at each point.

"Our particular program is a sort of do-it-yourself plan. The new employees go from place to place—with a little help from their friends. It goes like clockwork. It is also plenty flexible. If a new employee gets interrupted with one person, he or she just goes back later and picks up at the point where the meeting left off. In our division, we usually orient just one person at a time, since we don't have much turnover.

"Then I have a 'phase two' program, consisting of my personally spending one hour a day for five days with each new employee. Again, we follow a list of subjects. When we're finished, by God those new people know as much about the basic overall operation as do most employees who have been here for years. And it sure turns on those above-average people we've been finding recently. Maybe that's one reason we have such low turnover."

KEEP IT FAST-PACED

The program had best move fast and be challenging if you want to hold the attention of quality people. This will also assure that you'll get a good return on the time you both invest and that you'll spend less time overall. Here are some effective methods for doing this:

1. Leave only enough time to cover each subject properly. Don't load in extra time. It makes things drag. High producers are usually allergic to wasting time.

2. Move right along. If you cover one topic adequately in less time than you allowed, go right on to the next. If you finish early, you can always pick up some optional subjects. And then, there's usually no law that says you must use all the time allotted. Break off when you've done the job and go back to other duties.

3. Keep the tempo brisk. Again, this will appeal to high producers, who also usually think at a fast pace. You will hold their attention.

4. Let the new employees set the pace, to a certain degree. Remember that you are dealing with above-average people. Don't talk down to them. Pour it to them as fast as they can handle it. You may be surprised. Most people can listen three times faster than they can talk. If you see their attention lagging, you may want to speed up. Then, if and when you see them falling behind, slow down. Watch them and let them give you the cue on speed.

National Distilling Top Achievers Rapidly Grasp Orientation Package

A National Distilling executive, whose company has interests in many fields besides gin, said recently, "My department is small, so we don't bring in many new people each year. When we do, we have a loose-leaf notebook that covers various industry facts—size, trends, competition, markets, customer opinions, and the like. It combines statistics, pictures, graphs, and short text material. Then we have an annual operations plan, with goals and steps to reach those goals. Plus we have a bunch of other stuff—exhibits, booklets, photos, documents. Things like that. I find that by going through the industry notebook and the operations plan, we pretty well cover the waterfront. I let the new employees—often junior executives—turn the pages at their own speed. They usually move pretty darn fast—at least faster than I would go with most people. Yet I can tell by their comments that they understand things about as well as I could expect. Of course they don't memorize the stuff, but that's not the objective. They dig it pretty well."

ENCOURAGE SOME QUESTIONS

The advantage of encouraging questions is that your new employee will get a lot more out of the orientation meeting if there is an exchange, if it is a two-way street. People, especially high producers, don't like to be "talked at" for an hour or two. Top achievers may tolerate it better than others, but they also like it a whole lot less than most. Here's how you encourage the right kind of questions:

1. Explain right from the start that this is an orientation project—the goal is to give the new employee plenty of usable, even helpful, information. The company has already learned a lot about the employee. Now it's the employee's turn to learn more about the company. So the data flow will be mostly one-way.

2. The operative word in the last sentence is "mostly." That means there can and should be some flow from the employee to the coordinator. In other words, questions. Even comments.

3. These are welcome and encouraged.

4. However, there's a "but": the questions and comments should be aimed strictly at the goal—a quick, useful insight. Meaning they should be brief, basic, sincere, interested, fact-oriented, and to the point.

5. Employees should be discouraged from asking challenging

questions. This is not an inquisition or a debate. Also, the coach is not all-knowing. He or she is there to give good, solid, basic, useful data and to do it quickly. More than that can and should wait until another time and place.

S.C. Johnson Exec Turns Tables on New Employees

Said an executive from S. C. Johnson, "I pull a little switcheroo on new employees, especially the better ones. Oh, yes, of course I tell them to go ahead and ask a few questions as we move through our orientation. Some of them seem a little more interested in the modernistic glass tubing of our beautiful Frank Lloyd Wright building than they are in the formulas of our products. But maybe that's not all bad. The switch I make is that I ask *them* the questions. I warn them ahead of time that I'll be handing out a little self-graded quiz at the end of the orientation!

"I have two little lists of true/false questions—one for the average people, the other for the top-quality people I'm sometimes able to find. Of course I made that quiz pretty tough. You'd be surprised at how it grabs their attention. It's their first on-the-job assignment, so naturally they give it their best effort. Talk about first impressions being lasting ones! The other day, I had a guy tell me that he still remembers some of the questions I asked him on my little orientation quiz—ten years ago! In the meantime, that same fellow has won three top company awards."

MAXIMIZE SUBJECT SCOPE AND PEOPLE CONTACTS

Orientation will be the first and last chance most new employees will ever have to personally see and review the company as a whole and to meet a lot of its key people, all at once, in place, and at work. This is especially important for the above-average employee, who will be a much more valuable worker if he or she really understands the big picture.

To do this, first talk in broad-brush, general terms. Don't get bogged down in too many details. Yes, give a few specifics here and there, to sharpen the focus, but mostly speak in terms of the overall perspective. Second, contact and introduce as many key people as possible. Eight or ten are not too many. Talk a little about what they do and let them tell the new employee a few things. This is a great way for the employee to pick up the feel and the flavor of what's going on and how things are done.

Third, point out to new employees that this is a rare opportunity for them personally. They will not only learn more in the next few hours than they could in several years of work, but they have a great chance to establish contacts they will need with people who will help them get things done. A company runs not just on facts but also on feelings. People progress partly that way, too.

Challenging Volkswagen Orientation
Broadens Employees' Horizons

A food service manager from Volkswagen said, "Good orientation doubles the value of top people in some areas, because they look on the world as their oyster, their arena to work in. So we show 'em the world, or at least our world. Even if the new employee is only going to be involved in a small part of that world, we particularly want the top-quality people to know what all of it is about. Maybe we throw too much at them too fast, but we didn't pick them for spoonfeeding. We challenge them to stretch their minds. We introduce them to lots of people, not just to chiefs, but to Indians, too. This works really well. The high producer gets into the swing of things much faster. And do you know something? It seems to have a good effect on the rest of the people as well."

SUMMARIZE AND EVALUATE THE ORIENTATION

As you wrap up the orientation, review and discuss it. Give it that little extra lick to make the hair stay down. In a sense, this is your quality control—to see if the program "took" and was understood. After all, you don't need to go through all this just for the exercise. You want and must get useful results. A good finish helps assure this. Here are a few practical suggestions for doing it:

1. Recap and summarize the whole program—whether the orientation lasted an hour or a week. Boil it down, perhaps into 10 or 20 key points. Especially things that you know to be most useful, things the employees should remember that will help them in the long run. Your editing of these and your selection of data can build in lots of value here.

2. Give the new employees one last chance to ask about anything that they may not have understood.

3. While the employees are directing verbal traffic your way, try to get them to give you their overall impression of the orientation plan. You might also ask, "If *you* were doing this program, how would you change it?" You may pick up some good tips. And it sets the employees to thinking, since in fact they may very well be conducting the program at some point in the future. This step also increases the efficiency of the procedure and raises the return on the time you have both invested.

4. Make sure, as a final point, that the overall program was handled well. It sets an example for your new employees and says, in effect, "This is the way we expect to see things done in our operation."

Summary Smooths Transition to Jobs at National Biscuit

A purchasing manager from National Biscuit Company said, "Orientation is highly important to the procurement function. I suppose this is true for any aspect of production. It helps people to see how all the parts fit together, even though an employee may be only one little cog in the big machine. When we finish our orientation, naturally we recap or summarize as best we can. It's really pretty informal in my department. Sure, we ask if the new employees have any final questions, but in reality, they've been asking their questions all along. Anyway, we do the average program one better: We hand out a little summary of the orientation—plus giving the new employee any standard company manual he or she may need. This is especially appropriate with above-average people, who are likely to be in one level of supervision or another. That way, the orientation leads smoothly and directly into their own personal jobs."

TEN COMMANDMENTS FOR GETTING BIG RESULTS THROUGH PROPER ORIENTATION

1. Know your company's basic structure.
2. Plan a clear, simple goal and program.
3. Put a qualified person in charge.
4. Prepare other supervisors by getting their ideas and involvement.
5. Review situation, goal, and plan with the employee.
6. Arrange a flexible time schedule.
7. Keep it fast-moving and challenging.
8. Encourage factual questions, not debates.
9. Maximize subject scope and people contacts.
10. Summarize the orientation and collect feedback.

The OBI (one best idea) for using a good orientation to stimulate and help high producers is to have a basic plan, capable coordinator, general involvement, flexible schedule, fast pace, broad scope, and constructive wrap-up.

CHAPTER 7
Supervising High Producers
So You Get Their Full Contribution

"We had a whole bunch of dynamic people in one department here at Campbell Soup a while back," said a plant manager. "But it was a disaster! For some reason or other, most of them quit. We had to fire the rest, because they just got too darn big for their britches. Then we began to wonder if perhaps we were at least partly to blame. Maybe we had even missed an opportunity to really harness up those wild horses. We held a long skull session and talked it all over pretty frankly. We figured out a few things about what we were doing right and wrong. Then we came up with a new set of supervision methods aimed at high producers. These systems proved to be really effective. Our turnover rate dropped like a rock."

Most companies seriously shortchange themselves when it comes to supervising high producers. Managers could eliminate most of their trouble if they would just avoid two major errors—involving quantity and quality of supervision. "Quantity" means giving top producers somewhat less supervision; "quality" means giving them a somewhat different kind of supervision.

The old-fashioned kick-'em-in-the-butt methods of autocratic leadership are not always very effective today, even with average or below-average employees. These methods are even less productive with high-quality persons. They can usually find employment elsewhere and may have an offer or two in their pockets. Managers who use brutalizing tyranny are generally only cheating themselves, their organization, their stockholders, and their other employees, who would gain from company progress. The high-quality person, too, is penalized, but mainly as a temporary inconvenience.

Earlier we used the analogy of horses—some needing stern words, others performing at the slightest sound. This might be extended to compare a racehorse with a trail horse. They clearly have two different missions, and mixing these two types of horses up will greatly reduce your results. This is not to say that racehorses don't work as hard. Quite the contrary. They may train twice as long and twice as hard and put in twice the work hours and effort. They may also cover two or three times as much ground. But you ride them very differently.

How do you superviser high-quality people to personally enjoy their full potential, full value, and full contribution? Here are ten tested techniques that will get you good results.

KNOW THYSELF

When you set down your specs for your high-quality person, you were, of course, considering an imaginary, hoped-for individual. But you were also, consciously or unconsciously, looking at yourself in relation to that individual—your wants and needs, your expectations, your goals, and even your *modus operandi*. You were saying, "This is the kind of person I really want around, the kind I want on our team." In short, you have an image of both your candidate and yourself. You can see yourself working with this person.

It is wise for you to recognize that you have this mental picture. Why? Because there is an old saying among managers to the effect that "people tend to hire in their own image." Therefore, if you hired, sold, and oriented your ideal person, you probably found someone either very much like yourself or at least like your image of yourself. Only very high-level, self-confident managers hire above themselves. And you may have done just that—another reason to know where you are and what you like.

Now that you have taken a fresh look at yourself, you can ask yourself how you personally prefer to be supervised. This will give you an excellent starting point for deciding how to supervise your new high-quality employee.

Goodyear Exec Hires—and Supervises—in Own Image

An executive from Goodyear Tire and Rubber said, "It took me years of fooling around with recruiting before I got wise to the fact that I was often trying to recruit in my own image. Yes, to hire myself. When I saw that, it was a whole lot easier for me to know how to supervise. I simply used the methods that worked best on me. I'd be lying, of course, to say this was always a big success. But it sure was always a good place to start. Then I fine-tuned things from there."

KNOW THY TIGER

You certainly should know that high producer by now. You did a lot of screening, orienting, and selling. During each of those steps, you were giving information, but you were also getting lots of data, too. Here are several ways to make that final check, as it relates to your supervision of the newcomer:

1. Be sure you are being objective, not looking only for the good features and ignoring the bad, or vice versa. Be sure you have removed your colored glasses, whether tinted rose or black. Try, in short, not to see things—good or bad—that simply aren't there.

2. Don't be influenced by past high-producer patterns. Recognize that no two high producers are identical. The person you are about to supervise is totally different from those who may have gone before.

3. Look for his or her peculiarities, strengths, and weaknesses. These are things to utilize and appeal to or to avoid when you supervise.

4. Put on your supervisor's cap and remove your orienter's or sales representative's hat. Look now at your new employee in terms of what supervision style will be best for you, for him or her, and for your company. What style will encourage the employee to be most responsible, controllable, and coachable? Notice especially, where he or she is coming from, literally. Is it from an environment that was either highly disciplined or extremely permissive? How did that work for your employee?

Tigers Checked Inside and Out at Mattel

"Here at Mattel, we faced reality," said one manager, "and we do it in a very practical way. By the time we bring a tiger on board, we know him or her pretty well—almost inside and out. We know about what the person can and cannot do, judging from past experience with other people. Sure, we realize that no two employees are alike, but we know our man or woman because we hold a couple of meetings with the people who found and screened him or her. This means we know what kind of supervision we should use. Of course we can't tailor-make a different approach for every individual. Tigers had better be flexible and adaptable enough to fit in around here. And that's no problem. We already know they'll blend in with us, because we checked it out. If they wouldn't fit, they wouldn't be here."

USE THE TIGER'S "ON" BUTTON

Since you know your tiger so well by now, you should have a pretty good idea of what turns him or her on. Consider it and use it in your supervision procedures. It will pay off. That's really why you have this high producer on the staff—to pay off in progress for the company and in gains for you. If not, what's he or she doing here?

How do you find and use your tiger's "on" button?

1. Keep your eyes and ears open during your screening and orientation, so you know his or her strengths.

2. Realize that your tiger's strengths are also the very things he or she probably most likes to do. They are the things that turn this employee on. In short: Strengths *are* his or her "on" button. Bull's-eye! You've located the key to the tiger's power—and yours.

3. Now use these strengths and preferences. Aim your supervision in that direction. For example, if your tiger likes numbers and not people, then give him or her plenty of number problems and few people problems. If his or her preferences run the other way, reverse things.

4. Guide moderately. Now that you have found and used your top producer's "on" button, keep his or her attention on this hot

project. Keep the project flowing toward your tiger. As these two forces meet, stand back. You should be getting good—even out-standing—results. Your supervision step at this point should basically be one of focusing and uniting the person with the project, plus some fine tuning.

American Airlines Puts Employee Strengths to Work

American Airlines made an advertising slogan out of the company's strengths: "American Airlines—doing what we do best!" One of American's top supervisors of ticket and travel check-in counters personnel recently said, "We have lots of jobs to do, as any agent will tell you. But believe it or not, our success at the service desk and ticket counter has largely been traceable to a combination of high producers plus smart supervision. The supervisors know their people, find employee strengths, and put these to good use. If the employees are good with people, that's what they spend most of their time on—working with people. No wonder every year surveys show that air travelers rank us as the No. 1 airline! It's not magic; it's just that our supervisors know how to use employee abilities."

BEWARE OF PUT-DOWNS

Don't rain on your tiger's parade. Your above-average employee reached his or her level of excellence by seeing what is needed before others do—often even before anyone else thinks to ask. The tiger spots it ahead of time. He or she is unusually percep-tive and is generally sensitive to conditions and responsive to re-quests. These are great skills—assets that can and should be put to use for your company and your department. A put-down can kill it all.

A good racehorse will respond to a few words and a touch. A stubborn mule may need a two-by-four clout between the eyes merely to get its attention. The manager who mixes these up and uses a two-by-four on his or her racehorse may quickly lose a good performer, who knows that there are other riders and other race-tracks. How do you avoid the put-down?

1. Evaluate your racehorse. Look specifically for his or her level of perception and sensitivity. Does he or she respond quickly? Slowly? Not at all? This will tell you something about the need for you to avoid or not avoid the put-down.

2. Try other corrective measures first. If you see something you feel is being done wrong (unless it's something that can lead to immediate disaster), don't invest too much time condemning that action. Spend much more time and effort seeing that another procedure is used in the future. After all, your main goal is not usually to cut something down, as much as it is to see that something is done differently and properly.

3. If that initial try doesn't work, then test a mild put-down, perhaps criticizing indirectly, like, "People in other companies use that procedure, and it causes all sorts of trouble." Let your employee keep his or her self-respect and save face as much as possible.

4. Expand the put-down as needed. Some racehorses don't respond to a gentle word or a touch. They might require a two-by-four clout between the eyes. But use it only as a last resort.

5. There is even much merit to the sharp and firm rebuke, given early in the game. It establishes you as the supervisor, reminds everyone and reconfirms it. It clarifies the ground rules and illustrates just who's on first base. Above-average people, being a bit pushy and aggressive, are often doing a little testing and want to discover their limits. Teach them. But such a step should be used sparingly and followed by expressions of confidence, no hard feelings, praise, and appreciation, where possible.

Polaroid Supervision Accents the Positive

"Polaroid makes a fine effort to locate and hire many above-average people," said a Chicago management consultant. "And this effort is usually successful. But it would all fall apart if it were not for effective supervision. There's no sense in having good people, good equipment, good financing, or good products if you don't know what to do with them after you've got them. The most effective supervision of high-quality employees, it seems to me, accents the positive and minimizes the negative, destructive, or insulting comments."

AGREE ON GOALS

Reaching mutual agreement on the results that should be achieved will usually make a tremendous difference in the total utilization or the total waste of a high producer. Such an employee who has a clear understanding of the target, of what is to be accomplished, and is in full agreement with this becomes highly productive. You know yourself, that when you understand your objective and believe in it and agree with your supervisor that this is important, you generally move in a very constructive direction. So it is with your quality employee.

A high achiever (says Maslow) is rarely motivated only by the desire to amass dollars for life support or for security against future problems. He or she is much more stimulated by status within the group and by self-esteem. He or she gains much of this by knowing, striving for, and reaching worthwhile goals. Here's how to agree on goals and results to be obtained:

1. As supervisor, you are in an excellent position to describe the work situation. This may involve a problem or opportunity or more likely a combination of these factors.

2. Make sure your high producer understands these factors, too. Since you've gone through much orientation on a general and specific level, you probably have conveyed the message pretty well by now.

3. Relate back to the company goals and to his or her role. You have already showed your tiger how important his or her job is to the company.

4. At this point (if not long before), the employee has already been considering goals. Permit and encourage this. Ask his or her opinion. Planners find that people who set their own goals ordinarily tend to establish higher targets than the planner would. But top producers tend to set still higher goals. Such people have a greater tendency to aim for targets that are too ambitious rather than ones that are too easily reached.

5. Now make some kind of decision. Bring the top producer's goals back into line with reality, resources, and company or department objectives.

Schlitz Aims High Achievers at Best Targets

"The Schlitz Beer people do a fine job at supervising high-quality people," said a beer industry analyst, "largely because they get the guy or gal aimed in the right direction. Heading for the best target is, to me, the name of the game. Sure, I believe in letting the high producer pick his or her goal, but I also think the supervisor should have a strong input on this. Especially in the beginning, when the employee is new. This sets up an important pattern that continues year after year."

SET PRIORITIES

Now that you have your top-quality employee hired and oriented and have agreed on the goal, there are usually lots of roads that will get you there. You and your new employee have many options regarding possible steps you can take. All may be good, but not all should be taken at once or you'll have a total log jam. You'll get paralysis, chaos, and poor results.

Tigers like a load—a heavy load. But they do not usually deliver well if they don't know which projects or steps come first, second, and third. Your supervisory effectiveness will therefore be greatly improved if priorities are set. Decide to do first things first. An orderly tiger is usually a more efficient and productive one. Here's how to set priorities with above-average people:

1. Look at the situation, the problem, and discuss it with the tiger. He or she may have some clear ideas and reasons for planning certain actions as first steps.

2. Review some of your most likely, and even some unlikely, options. You and your new employee may see some surprising opportunities.

3. Some projects may nearly cry out for attention. Perhaps these are emergencies, big threats, or very large opportunities. These might be given an *A* priority.

4. Certain projects are not important, not threatening, or offer little chance of much gain. Give those a *C* priority.

5. The remainder might be given a *B* priority, but some should be assigned a *B+* or *B−* if possible.

6. Your most important mission in setting priorities is rarely to line up all the options in a neat little row from *A* to *C*. For one thing, you won't think of all the possible alternatives. For another, new options will come on the scene, while others will fade. Further, priorities have a nasty habit of sliding around and shifting from day to day. Your main objective should be to decide on your very next two or three most important steps in a proper order.

Setting Priorities Multiplies General Mills' Effectiveness

"General Mills is great for putting priorities on projects," said one of their suppliers, "and that multiplies the effectiveness of their better people. I remember one time they realized that sales of a certain package size were going so well that the container would be in short supply just a few months down the road. It was one of their most complex packages, requiring lots of lead time. The problem got high priority. A first-rate young executive expedited the project, and the matter was solved long before crisis day arrived. Heads-up supervision used priorities to get great results from a high-quality employee."

PLAN RESOURCE USE

If you really want to supervise a high producer in a manner that will utilize his or her full talent, you should be sure that the employee and his or her resources are properly engaged. Mesh those gears. Here's how: First of all, be sure you know what resources you have, how many, and how good. This might include things such as machines, outside services, staff, space, time, money, or material.

Second, make certain that your quality employee also has a good understanding of his or her resources and, most important, knows how to put these to work effectively so that progress is made toward your objectives. It is a sad commentary on many American businesses that we have so many resources that we occasionally ignore, misuse, or underuse them. Don't let this happen to you. It can waste another valuable resource—your high producer.

Third, be sure your employee understands the important concept of assigning part of the workload to his or her resources. Otherwise, the employee becomes overburdened, while the work-saving resource is underutilized. Case in point: A man down in a ditch is shoveling vigorously, yet he ignores several workers who are standing around watching and complaining that they have nothing to do. Who has made the error? The supervisor, who has one tiger and several sleepy pussycats. A comparable situation occurs in at least one out of five work groups.

Smart Resource Use Frees Up Revlon High Producer

"The Revlon Company does a great job of using its resources," said an assistant production manager, "because the company makes sure its best people know and take advantage of what they have available. One guy had been spending many hours doing statistical tabulations when his boss discovered this and showed him how their computer staff could do the whole project in a few minutes."

AVOID CONTRADICTORY ASSIGNMENTS

Very few things turn off a high producer like a second project that conflicts, or even seems to conflict, with the first one. "Get out there and visit 20 percent more clients and, incidentally, cut down your travel expenditures by 20 percent!" A conflict? Sure sounds like one. The supervisor may have meant to say, "Visit 20 percent more clients but do this locally, cutting out the long-distance visits, so your total travel costs drop by 20 percent."

Along the same line, avoid assigning two or more projects as an $A +$ priority—"Do this first." This is a frequent request. The supervisor is really saying that both are important. If the supervisor doesn't differentiate between the two projects, then he or she may mean that the employee should use his or her own judgment—or take action according to immediate opportunities that may change periodically. Here's how you can help avoid contradictions:

1. Realize that avoiding contradictions won't always be easy for you. Almost anything you ask your employees to do may seem to conflict with something assigned earlier, if only because few people can do two or three things at once. So proceed and make requests with considerable care.

2. Put yourself in the employee's place. Ask yourself, "Would this seem like a conflicting assignment if I were running that guy's work station?"

3. Give full and clear instructions. Not so much that your quality person bogs down in details, but enough so that any apparent conflict is resolved, as we saw in the travel expenditures example above.

4. Give your employee and yourself a break by indicating clear priorities whenever possible. Avoid saying that everything is $A+$. Clearly *something* has got to go first. And usually one project truly is more important or more urgent than the others, and as supervisor, you are probably in the best position to make that judgment. It's fine to delegate, but don't abdicate the privilege, the right, the authority, and the power to set your own priorities on options.

5. When in doubt, talk it out. Discuss the projects with particular emphasis on how they relate to one another. In this way, apparent or real conflicts can be solved and hard decisions made about the true priorities. A good high achiever can often help you in resolving seeming contradictions and deciding which actions really are the most urgent.

Clear Priorities Maximize Merck Executive's Performance

"As an executive for Merck Pharmaceuticals, I was considered a high achiever," said one market analyst. "I was always pleased with the way my supervisors kept an eagle eye out to avoid assignments that might seem contradictory. They realized that each new project impacted on previous tasks and programs. They not only realized it, but they acknowledged it and told me what was needed first. This sharp supervision helped me to maximize my own performance and my contribution to the company—and my supervisor's personal progress as well. We both gained."

DON'T CRY "WOLF"

Sure, circumstances change and so do priorities and their urgency levels. New targets appear and must be met. But good executives try to avoid routinely crying "wolf" (assigning an "emergency" project), then promptly forgetting about it and pointing to a new wolf. Tigers hate wolves—especially in packs. This becomes "management by crisis." It turns off your high achiever—especially if it happens several times in a row, as is the case in many companies. Soon the achievers' response drops to a shrug or a chuckle. The spark grows dim. No wise person can or will stay at a fever pitch all the time. The cry of "wolf" has been heard too often. When the real wolf appears, the reaction may be inadequate, and the manager may exclaim: "Those so-called high producers are worse than the others!" The manager has sadly deprived himself or herself and the entire unit of much unused talent.

Here are six steps for avoiding the "Fire! Fire!" syndrome:

1. Recognize that above-average people will usually put out great effort on an important assignment. Such employees concentrate their thought and action on the problem. They will often even wake up in the middle of the night thinking or worrying about it. They take it very seriously. Thus, the assignment should never be given lightly, casually, or capriciously.

2. Once you've made the assignment, be sure to at least consider and mention some sort of time frame, even if this is just tentative. That way, your high achiever knows his or her deadlines. Realizing how much time he or she has to work with, your tiger can budget or spread that time most effectively. High achievers tend to be better than others at time management.

3. Be slow to interrupt work in progress—for your own sake. You have something going for you. If you switch in midstream to something else and then switch again, the weeks and months can go by, and you can become furious at the failure of your so-called quality employee to ever finish anything.

4. Weigh the true advantages to you and to your unit should a project be dropped midway through in favor of another. Sometimes the switch is very wise. It may get you much greater progress or

avoid major losses. Just be sure you are not trading down to a project that seems exciting but is ultimately of lesser value.

5. Talk with your high achiever and discuss the changeover. He or she may be able to complete the original project rapidly, finish a key part, farm out a portion of it for a while, or otherwise put the thing on the back burner. Then the new urgent matter can be handled, and later, attention can return to the original project without losing very much. Maybe you will get a net gain. But you might not get this without first discussing your "midcourse correction."

6. Sometimes, simply load it on. Most high achievers like to be busy, even overloaded. That way they can juggle schedules, fit things in, delegate things out, stall some things, push certain projects, cogitate or worry about others. Don't forget, you hired this tiger because he or she is supposed to be able to produce a lot. Sock it to the tiger. Challenge him or her. Demand a lot. You may be surprised at how much tigers can handle. But, as with feeding material into a powerful buzz saw, don't misjudge the speed or get your fingers caught. And do be ready to hold back a little, for your own sake as well as the employee's, should you see him or her start to choke on the volume.

Schering-Plough Avoids Crisis Management

"The better executives at a Schering-Plough Drug Company division use what to me is an excellent system for avoiding crisis management," said a business consultant. "The plan is the very essence of simplicity: Before a supervisor interrupts key people who are on a priority project, he or she is urged to talk it over first. Not with the high achiever. There's no sense in bugging him or her until absolutely necessary. No, the supervisor is supposed to talk it over with his or her boss, whenever practical, since the boss is usually the person who has the new emergency. The top person is often in a better position to see the big picture and to revise priorities. He or she, as well as the supervisor, stand to gain or lose, depending on the wisdom of the switchover decision. So it makes sense that the boss be a part of it."

USE PARTICIPATIVE MANAGEMENT METHODS

Participative management can enable you to get the most good out of your high-quality people. They may or may not have management skills, but they usually do have above-average insight, perception, intellect, and a sense of participation or involvement with the group.

Here's the approach to use:

1. Level with your high producers about problems. Challenge them to show initiative and to participate in finding solutions and in setting goals.

2. Show reasonable respect for their abilities and expect the same from them toward all other members of the team.

3. Permit, encourage, and even insist on at least some planning meetings. Anyone associated with the project, especially high producers, should participate and provide suggestions for steps to be taken.

4. Don't be afraid to delegate work to top achievers. Just be sure it's meaningful—that is, aimed at reaching mutual goals.

5. Butt out and let your high achievers be their own bosses and run their own show, at least as much as is practical.

6. Provide awards and recognition to top producers, if and when they earn it. Very few work only for money. Most put out extra effort at least partly for boss, peer-group, and subordinate approval and respect.

Nestle Levels with Top Producers

Said one Nestle plant executive, "We always felt that we could get a lot more out of our high achievers if we got them involved in a project at the earliest practical time. Sometimes that means as soon as we see a problem. Our best method is to level with them. A system we tried last year was to put them in a conference room with other members of the team and let them work out a solution. We would ask them to make a recommendation within three hours. If we took away their chairs, we discovered they could do it a lot quicker!"

TEN COMMANDMENTS FOR SUPERVISING HIGH PRODUCERS TO GET THEIR MAXIMUM CONTRIBUTION

1. Know thyself.
2. Know thy tiger.
3. Use the tiger's "on" button.
4. Beware the put-down.
5. Agree on goals and results.
6. First things first, but get agreement on priorities.
7. Plan the best use of your resources.
8. Avoid the contradictory assignment.
9. Don't cry "wolf." Tigers hate wolves.
10. Use participative management methods.

Your OBI (one best idea) for supervising high achievers is to know yourself, know your employee, push his or her "on" button, utilize available resources, establish mutual goals and priorities, invite participation, and avoid put-downs.

CHAPTER 8
How to Motivate Above-Average People

An executive from Procter & Gamble said recently, "Motivation of average people makes for major progress, but motivation of high producers makes for miracles!" It seems that some time ago, the company's top management decided to introduce a new hand soap. It was designed specifically for the dirty, greasy, hands of people doing manual labor. Several talented executives were assembled and told of the need and the goal. Each was given an important role. More planning meetings were held, and these faced up to a number of emotional and intellectual challenges, such as package design. Much aggressive action was taken as the brand moved forward in a fiercely competitive market. The product, which was named Lava soap, eventually became a major brand, representing many millions of dollars in sales. Motivating a talented team produced dramatic progress—and substantial profit.

Most high-quality people are, almost by definition, self-motivated. But not all of them and certainly not all the time. They are only human. Like everyone else, they have their ups and downs. And generally, they are only partly turned on—sometimes much less. Having capabilities available but unused is a waste for the company, depriving you of the progress these able people can bring you. And in a sense, it is a waste to the quality people themselves, because they are neither living up to their potential nor achieving what they could.

Clearly, one of your major objectives should be to get the full value from your top-caliber people, for your sake and theirs. After all, you're paying for it, and you have a right to it. But as we recognized earlier, money alone will rarely suffice to reach that objective. Taken by itself, it's simply not good enough. Nearly all quality people can earn money—good money. Many other motivators can also produce dynamic, constructive action. At times, these will work in place of some money or even much better than money.

Money wages reach a point of diminishing returns once people are earning enough to cover their basic needs—food, clothing, shelter, transportation, recreation, and some savings. This is especially true where the high-quality people are living with partners like themselves, with both earning a substantial wage. At this point, an added $1,000 a year is nice, but after taxes, this may come to only an extra $15 a week, which does not exactly represent superexcitement.

Many research studies, as well as astute observation and ordinary common sense, tell us that high producers and high achievers seek career fulfillment and job satisfaction—generally above all else. Consider the fact that high-quality people who feel they are truly accomplishing something they consider worthwhile will usually stay at it, even when they can get somewhat more money elsewhere. But high producers who earn top wages but feel they are doing useless work will eventually leave. Apparently, in many cases, job fulfillment, not money, makes the big difference.

Here is how you can provide this fulfillment fairly easily and at low cost. In fact, most of these techniques cost nothing. They're a matter of working smarter, not harder.

USE THE SOS PLANNING SYSTEM

Most top-quality people respond well to planning. They understand it and do it a lot in their own lives. They have usually worked out some sort of system for themselves. But you have a better one with the SOS (situation, objective, strategy) technique. Where we are. Where we want to go. How we are going to get there. It's simple. Easy to remember. Easy to use. And well proven in both the military (Navy, World War II) and in the finest corporations the world over. It's useful and highly effective with large problems and small, both in business and outside. In fact, we all use the system unconsciously, almost every day. The words just make it a little more structured. Here's how to put it to work:

1. Explain the system. A simple statement will do. You may want a few items under each heading, like: *situation*—facts, problems, opportunities; *objectives*—short-run, long-run, quantity, quality; *strategy*—how we will reach our goals with product, package, price, promotion, advertising, service, schedule (who does what, when, and where).

2. Demonstrate how the system can be put together. Set up a simple test problem, not your big, tough one. You are selling and educating at this point, not tackling the major issue.

3. Let your high producer try it. Better still, let him or her work with it and present it to others, leading the others in this simple planning procedure.

SOS Spells Results for McDonalds Manager

"As a manager," said one McDonalds top achiever, "i realized that I needed some kind of simple system, not only to solve problems but to reach goals. I met with some other employees who felt the same way. One of them said he was using the SOS planning program, and he explained it to us. Now I have a reputation as a high producer, and I'm proud of it. But I confess I felt a little stupid for not having thought of that SOS thing myself. Naturally, I could see how handy it is. To make a long story short, I picked up on this and have used it for years. I've not only had good results, but of all the little sayings, slogans, tricks, and systems I learned as a manager, the U.S. Navy's SOS program has proved to be about the most useful device ever to come down the pike, at least for me personally."

SET OBJECTIVES

Your tiger probably likes to be goal-oriented, to be aimed at something. If you don't have a target, he or she is likely to make one up. Beat him or her to the punch and suggest one or several objectives for the group and for the high producer. Most achievers find this challenging, stimulating, and highly motivating. Picking an objective might seem simple, and sometimes it is. But it is also a powerful tool. Used right, it can accomplish great things. Goal setting has become an art and a science in modern management. Here's how you might do it:

1. Pick a goal that is worthwhile and important both to the company group and to the achiever—a priority objective. Ask yourself, if I could reach any goal I wanted, what would it be?

2. Don't hesitate to have several goals. Two or three are fine. Ten are probably too many. This spreads your resources of time, money, and effort too thin. Multiple, but not excessive goals increase the challenge and interest levels for high achievers.

3. Set priorities for your goals. Decide what is most important, next most important, and so on. Label these. This is an almost surefire way to increase achiever interest.

4. Let nearly everyone concerned participate in selecting these goals. This develops what are sometimes very high levels of personal commitment.

5. Set goals that require stretch and effort but still are feasible, reasonable, and reachable. If you do so, your high producer will find this quite motivating.

6. Set some sort of time frame and standards. You may want a short- and long-run goal plus quantitative and qualitative ones. Even with the qualitative targets, have some kind of general criteria for success.

7. Establish what happens next, when the goal is reached. Have some kind of worthwhile and significant follow-up. This will be highly motivating to an achiever. If you simply lean over, pat his or her head and say, in effect, "Good doggy," your achiever isn't likely to chase *that* bone again.

Goals Are Powerful Motivators at General Motors

"At General Motors," explained one analyst, "some of us always tried to look on our goals as a sort of personal contract between each individual, his or her boss, and the company. Maybe it really is just a contract that the individual makes with himself or herself, I don't know. But I do know that setting goals and doing it wisely is one of the greatest motivators of high-quality people you'll ever find. It works like a charm and, in my judgment, is a major reason why the company continues to be one of the most powerful in the world. Goal-generated motivation is a giant step toward personal and corporate success."

ENCOURAGE MUTUAL RESPECT

Show respect and expect it in return. Even demand it. In other words—mutual respect. You are not being a snob or a stuffed shirt. You are being very wise and practical and operating in the best interests of your company, yourself, and your quality employee. He or she wants, needs, and craves respect and in turn needs to respect his or her supervisor and others. How can people do their best working for or with someone they don't respect? Or who doesn't respect them?

The Japanese economic system is, to a large degree, built upon and thrives on respect—up, down, and sideways. It's a great factor in making both big and small wheels mesh well, work together, achieve higher goals, maintain greater harmony, and motivate major effort from high achievers. Some would almost die from humiliation if they failed to deserve the respect and live up to the expectations held for them by others.

Here's how to show respect and get it in return:

1. Recognize your employees' abilities and their strengths and let them know this. You can do it directly by saying so or indirectly by showing it. Defer to their expertise, whether they are cab drivers, economists, or executives.

2. Show appreciation. Surprising as it may seem, the applause of even one person can be highly motivating. Look at what people will do to impress mom or dad, or one sister, brother, spouse, or neighbor. Or the boss.

3. Use the LLAD formula (look, listen, ask, and discuss) when working on problems with a high achiever. This very procedure signifies substantial recognition and regard for a person.

4. Demonstrate your respect partly by the very kinds of assignments you make to a quality person. Simple, childish tasks handed out on any regular basis can be just a bit demeaning and

insulting. Tough jobs are a challenge, but they are also a compliment.

5. Express your confidence freely, openly, publicly, and sincerely. When you say, "I am proud of you, and I believe in you," this becomes highly motivating to most quality achievers.

Scott Paper Motivates Through Respect

Said a Scott Paper Company senior consultant: "Scott management realized long ago that respect for people has a strange way of motivating them strongly in a highly positive direction. When I first joined the company, my new boss told me they had selected me out of a whole bunch of other applicants. He explained why he made his choice and let me understand that he knew my abilities very well. He showed that he respected me and that he expected the same in return. And he got it. I never forgot that. I worked my heart out for him and for the company. It was worth it. They are a great operation, great people, and they always treated me very well."

HOLD PRODUCTIVE MEETINGS

Accomplishment-oriented meetings will turn on your high achievers. Among other things, these achievers usually have a keen sense of good time management as well as effective and efficient planning procedures. If your meetings are productive, you are also likely to have similarly efficient people. Here's how to do this:

1. Know your reason for holding a meeting, your objective, and state it clearly beforehand in your oral or written invitation.

2. Plan your meeting carefully, so it is aimed at accomplishing your stated objective. Work out the 5Ws, of who, what, when, where, why—and how. Be sure the mechanics are checked out, such as room size, table, chairs, lighting, and screens or other equipment.

3. Send an agenda to prospective attendees as part of your invitation. List subjects to be covered and a general, overall time frame. Perhaps provide some background detail on the subjects. This stimulates achievers.

4. Also cover, or at least mention, the problem to be solved. Ask attendees to give it some thought *before* the meeting and be ready to comment on it as it affects their area of operation.

5. As the meeting starts, restate its purpose. Then get a brief input from each attendee. Encourage constructive give-and-take discussion but avoid pointless arguments—particularly those that become irrelevant. Keep the discussion on track. High producers are turned off by time-wasting harangues.

6. Maintain control. Keep each and every effort aimed at reaching the meeting's goal. Don't spend too much time on any one subject.

7. End with a recap, especially mentioning what was decided, who does what, when, and "where we go from here." High achievers will usually be motivated to move forward aggressively from this point of departure.

Meetings Impressively Well Planned at Bristol-Myers

A woman from Bristol-Myers said, "As an executive for some years with a division of this company, I can't help being impressed with their meetings. Talk about organized! People around here know the value of time, of human resources, and of getting it all together. They don't hold meetings just because one of the execs is lonely and wants to shoot the bull. They always have a reason, a plan, and an agenda. When people get there, they've done their homework. They are ready. And they get right to the point, make a decision, and plan where to go next. In my group, a summary was prepared the next day and sent out to everyone concerned, including the big boss. He didn't attend very often. I guess he felt we did OK without him. But he sure was impressed."

USE INFORMAL "SKULL" SESSIONS

Casual "group-think" meetings can be helpful for planning details, checking progress, and getting going on next steps. These might be held every day or two, perhaps for just a few minutes, between some of the people playing direct roles in the program.

Such gatherings stimulate better people simply because the group is in the actual act of achieving the very thing high producers relish: getting things done. Here's how to hold good "skull" sessions:

1. Keep it informal, unstructured, and spontaneous. "Hey, Bill, do you have a minute? Let's get Charlie and look at this servicing problem."

2. Have not only a purpose for the session—a goal—but also collect a few facts. Exchange these and try to put the pieces together, so they point to a solution, or at least one step toward this. Don't just meet to commiserate. Instead, use your able people, and they will produce.

3. End with some sort of conclusion as to what happens next. "Well, it seems we all agree that the servicing delay happened because we didn't send the request to all the right people. We learned something! We'll cover that base on the next request. In fact, I have one right here that needs the full treatment, Charlie." And you just motivated Charlie.

Working Lunches Prove Productive at Pan Am

A Pan American Airlines executive recently said, "You know, we sometimes get more troubleshooting done over the lunch table than we do all morning. I'm talking about actually exchanging information and ideas for resolving problems. We don't call them 'groupthink' or 'skull' sessions, but that's what they are. These working lunches are relaxed, yet productive. We all become more enthusiastic—including me."

STIMULATE BOTH HEART AND MIND

One of the world's greatest motivators, Leo Burnett, often said, "For maximum impact, use ideas that are emotional—but seem logical." Even brilliant people are still ruled by their feelings, so fire up both their hearts and their minds. And don't forget, a motivated achiever often accomplishes double or triple what others can.

How do you stimulate both emotion and logic? First, attack problems and assign projects that are an intellectual and emotional challenge, where a solution is logically needed and emotionally wanted. For example, better communication to your employees. Second, avoid projects that are routine, boring, or so childishly simple as to be almost insulting. Third, stimulate your high achievers by encouraging brainstorming. This is where all ideas are welcome, anything goes, and no idea is ever criticized, because even bad ideas can lead to innovations.

Best Coca-Cola Managers Tap Both Logic and Emotion

An executive with one of Coca-Cola's key advertising suppliers remarked, "Some people say Coca-Cola is stimulating. Well, I don't know about that, but I do know that they have a stimulating operation in some divisions. I have attended hundreds of formal and informal get-togethers with their people. Their best managers have always displayed a very wise awareness of both heart and mind. I remember one top officer who got his best people together and said, 'We have a tough problem that will take some sharp thinking. Some people say you can't solve it, but I think you can. I believe in you!' And he was right. Heart and mind are mighty motivators."

PROVIDE MEANINGFUL WORK

Yes, work itself is a strong motivator! Especially of high producers and achievers. After all, they could hardly earn those personal labels without any tasks to do. They love work! But here's the secret, your secret: It must be the right *kind* of work. It must be an assignment or project aimed at your mutual goals—yours and your top producer's.

Here's how you can make work motivate: First, when you think of work, immediately think of your secret word "goals." Second, be sure your high producers actually have some goals that you know about. Goals you can both share. Without this, work won't produce much motivation. Third, now dress up that work with some excitement. Make it challenging and meaningful. Show how it solves a real and present problem—or wins a big reward—from their perspective, not yours. Speak, act, and assign in terms of their own personal interests. They may like you, but they like themselves even more.

Union Carbide Sparks High Achievers

Union Carbide is a company I have always admired for its ability to motivate high-quality people through work," said a major consultant. "It seems that some of its managers use a particularly effective method. They not only explain but dramatize and emphasize the problem and the personal rewards to be achieved by solving it. Those top producers get worried, and then they become driven to high levels of activity. If that's not constructive motivation, tell me what is!"

DELEGATE EFFECTIVELY

Your high achievers represent a splendid opportunity for you to shift some of your tasks to their shoulders. They are hungry and anxious for, and even demand, delegation. It stimulates them. And face it, they can often do a better, easier, and faster job than you, if only because they have some special training, or simply because they have the time. Further, delegation is flattering and ego-inflating to high achievers. They want to be somebody (a goal), and you are helping them through assigning an important task.

Here's how to use delegation as a motivator:

1. Select tasks that someone else can and will do properly. An ideal starting point for delegation is to split up a large task into smaller, manageable chunks.

2. Use the formula "pride plus responsibility equals action." This means that people who have self-confidence and self-respect and who are given an appropriate task to do usually take strong, constructive action.

3. Avoid dictating much detail about the method to be used. There are lots of routes to reach a goal. Let the achievers use the system that serves them best, and they will also serve you best.

4. Once the delegated task is well understood, with resources and time frame reviewed, then step out of the way and let it proceed.

Recheck progress occasionally and interfere only if the goal is not reached sufficiently.

General Mills Executive Wins with "Hands-Off" Style

"An executive friend at General Mills had a simple system for using delegation to motivate achievers," explained a consultant. "He actually let them pick which part of the task they wanted to do. An approach I particularly liked was that he realized that each person—and especially the high achievers—has his or her own management style. So he used a policy of never butting in on a method unless the person wasn't making good progress. Sometimes it nearly killed him to have to hold his tongue and keep his muddy fingers out of the clockwork, but in the end, he got great results."

COACH USING THE "EX-DEM-PRA" FORMULA

"Ex-dem-pra" means "*ex*planation, *dem*onstration, and *pra*ctical work." It is a simple system, easy to remember and easy to use, that has produced excellent results in officer and leader training of high achievers the world over, particularly at the major advanced U.S. and German military units. Here's how to implement this approach in an executive environment:

1. Play the role of a coach with your high achiever. Here you are acting as his or her senior adviser. Together, you check the problems, opportunities, and objectives. Together you try things, discard what doesn't work well, keep what does, correct, improve, and polish it and go on from there.

2. Explain your view of the problem and your best recommendation for solving it—but get your employee's suggestions, too. Consider these fairly, impartially, and objectively. Admit when his or her concept is superior. In the end, this will pay off best for your company and for you.

3. Demonstrate briefly just what you want done. You might do this only partially or with a few words, sketches, or graphs.

4. In the practical work phase, let your high achiever do it. Even allow him or her to make small mistakes. It won't kill you—or

the employee. And he or she will catch on more rapidly and perform with greater enthusiasm.

"Ex-dem-pra" Spurs Top Kellogg Achievers

"At Kellogg," said one executive, "I found the 'ex-dem-pra' formula worked pretty well as a motivator for quality people. We added one extra element to it—a noncritical, nonthreatening environment. No put-downs. This was effective with most people but worked especially well with high achievers. Those people already have a pretty good opinion of themselves. It worked so well for me that I was offered a much better position in the airframe industry last year, where I'm using the same techniques—and still getting good results."

COMMUNICATE OPENLY

Free and effective communication will motivate high producers. They cannot and will not operate well in a vacuum. They must hear from you and exchange ideas. Ideas are the beginning of action. They have consequences. Three criteria must usually be met if a true exchange of ideas is to occur: The message must be transmitted through some medium to the individual involved. It must be received by that person. And finally, to be certain that communication has actually occurred, the message should be confirmed. When the message has been sent, received, and confirmed, then you have achieved communication.

Here's how you might improve your communication techniques:

1. Beware of extremes. Don't deluge your recipient with information, nor starve him or her for it, either. Adjust the flow to fit the need.

2. Consider using the advertising formula for high-impact and highly motivating communication—FOWD/PA (meaning, *fre*-quently, *o*ral, *w*ritten, *d*one carefully, *p*layed back, and *a*djusted). Then follow these directions: Communicate often enough, both orally and in writing. Get playback of reaction and results. And

change or fix as needed. As a package, this approach will substantially increase the motivation of most high achievers.

3. (This is a tough one!) Find and present one central idea in your message. For example, there is a basic concept to this chapter: "ways to motivate your quality employee."

Ralston Purina Speaker Displays Top Motivational Techniques

"Most Ralston Purina executives seem to be particularly skillful at using communication," said a young market analyst. "They are really good at stimulating leaders. I once attended a United Fund drive where a Purina executive made a presentation. He had one pervading theme woven into his message and knew just how much to present and how fast. It was very interesting to see him watch his audience, check with them, and adjust to their interest. It was a living, breathing demonstration of using communication to motivate high achievers. I wrote down some of his methods, and I've used them with darn good results."

DON'T OVERSUPERVISE

Butt out! Oversupervising can actually demotivate people, especially high producers. They can start to feel smothered, inhibited, and even insulted. Result: You don't get the value of their full potential. Here's how to win the supervision game:

1. You can be tough, definite, and firm in your directions—*if* you do this in three ways: briefly, impersonally, and early on in the game.

2. Then shift to an easier, more permissive stance. But don't go too far this way, or you will have a total loss of control, which hurts everyone.

3. Avoid either extreme—too tough or too easy. Seek a midpoint but stay flexible. That means move somewhat away from the midpoint in either direction, depending on the needs of the situation, and then return.

4. Stand back. Let your tigers have their own turf and let the

action happen. Allow small mistakes. But watch out for and protect them and yourself from major disasters.

Textron Tigers Select Their Own Supervision Level

"Some Textron executives have always impressed me as being especially skillful at motivating their best people by using the 'butt-out' technique," said a manager with a competing company. "But they use an interesting twist. After they lay down the law on what needs to be done, then they actually ask their top performers just how much supervision they want! They themselves set the permissiveness level. Surprisingly, their high achievers almost never say that they want a zero level of supervision. What they really want is to stay wired to their boss, not chained. And they do become a superbly motivated and highly effective team. I have the scars to prove it!"

OFFER AWARDS

Your high achievers may be tough, driving, and bright, but they aren't made of stone. They are flesh and blood and feelings and pride—just like everyone else. Awards reinforce their self-image and give them a higher reputation to live up to. However, there are several steps you should be careful to take in making awards to high producers if you want maximum impact and results.

First, be sure that any citation is truly earned. Wait. Watch. Have patience. Then, when exceptional effort, performance, and especially accomplishments are made, that is the time to give an award. Second, the most effective method is usually to present the award in front of the high producers' peers. The award should be strong, simple, straightforward, and sincere. Recognize a specific achievement, not a general one. Third, avoid the temptation to give out honors casually, excessively, or just because "It's award time again." Too many citations debase the currency. However, it is better to give out a few too many honors than for accomplishments to go unrecognized.

Awards Have Ideal Impact at Parker Pen

"I'll never forget one Parker Pen award presentation," said a former manager, now an executive with another firm. "There were only a few top citations, and these were for truly outstanding accomplishments. These were presented before a major gathering of employees. Each award was accompanied by a short, unhurried story, told with dignity and heartfelt appreciation, reaching a crescendo as the first prize was presented. By that time, there was hardly a dry eye in the house!"

DON'T PUSH TOO HARD

Beware of overstimulating the self-motivated person. This is the same as beating a racehorse that is already running at top speed. It can lead to an overload that destroys far more than it builds.

Here's how to guard against this: First, keep an eagle eye out for the level of performance you are getting from your high achiever. Judge this in relation to his or her potential. He or she should not operate much below that level. But no one can perform at a flat-out, high-speed sprint all the time. Second, when performance has been well below potential for some time, load on the assignments and employ some stimulating motivation methods. Third, when performance is close to top capability, back off on assignments and stimulation, or you'll strip a gear. Eat the eggs, but not the duck.

Managers at American Home Products Know Their Tigers' Limits

"It seems to me that American Home Products managers are especially sharp at knowing when to motivate their high producers and when to exercise constructive restraint," said one consultant. "I remember one time a high producer had been putting in a lot of overtime, when suddenly a priority project came along. One of the top managers wanted the hard-working guy to take this on in addition to his current task. But his supervisor switched the project to another achiever, and it was done beautifully. Later it came out that the hard worker subsequently helped out on the project voluntarily, but he had not been pushed into it, and that made a big difference.

DON'T FRUSTRATE YOUR HIGH ACHIEVER

You brought your tiger into your operation because you recognized his or her high delivery capability. Naturally, you want to benefit from that potential and convert it into flowing productivity. You don't want to turn off the tap by second-guessing or chaining up that achiever. How can you prevent this?

1. Recognize that frustration means your achiever headed for a goal and was then totally blocked. He or she is not just hitting an obstacle. Impediments are expected by high producers. No, here he or she is completely thwarted. Be sure you or other elements under your control do not deliberately or accidentally cause this. It will totally deprive you of the value from this resource.

2. Try not to restrict the achiever's goals or methods to the point where his or her alternatives become narrowed down to just one. Again, it cuts your tiger's value to you.

3. Wise managers not only delegate to high producers. They also accept the result, rather than rejecting, revising, substituting their judgment for their tiger's, and generally second-guessing him or her. Don't go out and buy a dog and then do all the barking yourself.

Talented Tiger Surprises Green Giant Supervisor

"The Green Giant Company has a reputation among my group for fully utilizing the skills of its high achievers," said a manager from one of Green Giant's suppliers. "On one occasion, a Green Giant supervisor had delegated a package design project to one of his most talented people. When the employee came back with the design, the supervisor, who was not an artist, thought it was simply awful. But he didn't block, frustrate, or second-guess his designer. He went along with the design, and it won not one, but three, important awards."

TEN COMMANDMENTS FOR MOTIVATING
HIGH ACHIEVERS

1. Use the SOS (*s*ituation, *o*bjective, *s*trategy) system.
2. Agree on the problem, goal, and procedures.
3. Show respect and demand it in return.
4. Hold productive meetings and group "skull" sessions.
5. Appeal to both emotion and logic.
6. Provide meaningful work toward personally relevant goals.
7. Delegate, then coach by explaining, demonstrating, and practicing.
8. Communicate clearly, then butt out and let the work proceed.
9. Use emotional rewards but avoid overstimulation.
10. Don't buy a dog and then do the barking yourself.

Your OBI (one best idea) for motivating above-average people is to recognize that while they may be very sharp, they are still human and will respond well to a whole spectrum of motivators, including planning, goals, respect, meetings, emotion, logic, work, delegation, coaching, communication, and awards.

CHAPTER 9
How to Train Tigers for Top Results

"Here in Japan, we place great emphasis on training, even for our best people," said Mr. Suzuki, owner of a large musical instrument firm, during an elaborate penthouse dinner in Tokyo last year. (His cousin, Mr. Kenzo Suzuki, is Japan's prime minister.) "This is partly because we are very competitive with many other good Japanese companies. They train their people, so we train ours. Also, we want to stay current with advanced technology and up-to-date management thinking. As a final objective, we want to hone the fine cutting edge of our top people so their skills will be as sharp as our famous samurai swords. And it works. We cut down lots of competition."

Even top tigers need training. Skills learned long ago can get rusty without a refresher. New methods are constantly coming along, and competitors are learning them. Training is most effective when the "student" is receptive. You would be wise to give it some selling effort. Convince and persuade, don't demand and force. As one executive says, "Seduce, don't rape."

Don't try telling high achievers that, in effect, they are dummies and need this training. That approach is not calculated to raise anyone's enthusiasm a whole lot. Instead, put it in terms of their own interests. "Here's a great opportunity for you! You can pick up fresh knowledge and new tools. You'll be able to use these to help you reach your goals a lot quicker, with less effort. Why not work smarter rather than harder?" If convenient, remind your tigers that even the nation's finest scientists—including nuclear physicists and neurosurgeons—spend some time almost every year updating their training.

Another approach is to recognize that the high achiever has

probably already had considerable training and may, in fact, have actually taught this subject at some time. In which case, bill it as a refresher course. Also, welcome his or her constructive critique of the training. If appropriate, you might also say, "Please take a few notes and come back prepared to give us an oral or written summary of the course. This will help all of us and bring the knowledge to many who might need it much more than you, but who could not attend—and who would never be able to re-present it as well as you can."

Training offered properly to your high achievers will be accepted. In fact, it is usually welcomed. They expect it and even occasionally request it. The real keys are values, appropriateness, and practicality. If the training is neither useful nor helpful to the employee, then it is unnecessary, and you should scrub the mission. This is especially true if the training can be taken as degrading or insulting, such as teaching first grade math or language skills to college graduates. Ridiculous? Of course it is—but it happens.

Another common problem is that you can't always have a training program just for above-average people. They must often attend and mix in with everyone else—good, fair, and poor. Your best solution in this case is simply to take your achiever aside and explain the facts of life ("Charlie, it's just required, that's all."). But also emphasize again that this is a fine opportunity for him or her personally. And repeat the request for a later recap presentation.

Here's how you can give tiger training maximum effectiveness.

PLAN USING THE FIVE Ws

Who is a particularly important factor, because it is double-barreled—who should attend and who should give the training. Make sure the achiever you send can really benefit from the course. And be certain that the person giving the course is well qualified in two ways—that he or she both knows the subject and knows how to present it effectively, with some sparkle, excitement, and impact.

Sending a person to an inappropriate training unit, given by an unqualified, unskilled individual who is also a poor presenter, is not just a waste of money. It demotivates the achiever and reflects badly on management. Yet this is done all too frequently. In some areas, 25 percent of the training involves some or most of these errors.

What refers to the subject. Make sure it is both (1) appropriate for the trainee's job and (2) needed by the employee.

When and *where* should be a matter of common sense. If there is not going to be any extra free time for recreation, it can be both a financial waste and a tantalizing unkindness to hold the meeting at a resort area—especially if it's difficult to reach. A better alternative might be some centralized business location, such as a hotel close to a major transportation hub.

As to the time schedule, consider when trainees will travel. Will this be on their own time, such as traveling the night before, attending a full day of instruction, and returning home that evening? Or will travel be on business time, such as coming in one morning, meeting from noon until noon the next day, and traveling home the second day in the afternoon? A compromise might be to travel one way on personal time, one way on business time. Also, are attendees allowed or encouraged to bring their spouses before or after the meeting to enjoy the recreation, shopping, touring, and other facilities?

How refers to the hundreds of details that should be checked out to insure effective training. One bad mistake in this list can cause disaster. These details really boil down to two major categories—creature comforts and effective presentation mechanics. For comforts, be sure the facilities are a proper size, with adequate chairs, tables, heat, light, soundproofing, carpets, drapes, air circulation, lightproofing, rest rooms, phones, and food and beverage service. Are facilities "barrier free" for wheelchairs? For the presentation, make certain that you have available any necessary movie or slide projectors, screens, flip charts, chalk boards, pens, paper, booklets, tape players, PA systems, and allied equipment. You will demonstrate real professionalism if you double-check all of these. Then check again. Failures here are a common cause of numerous costly errors.

HAVE A CLEAR, AMBITIOUS GOAL

Have a good, strong purpose for your training session. "Oh my gosh, it's training time again!" is a pretty poor reason to hold a training session. Don't train just for the sake of training. Millions make this mistake. Also, don't hold a training session merely to explain a simple new program, product, procedure, or system that can just as easily be covered with a few letters and phone calls in much less time. Training sessions are expensive—when you add up the cost of travel, attendee time, facilities, and presenters' fees. Make sure the purpose is strong enough to justify this cost. If not, don't have the training at all.

Here's how to set some economical and effective training goals:

1. An excellent purpose for a training program is to constructively modify attendees' behavior—to bring them something new. This might be a different product, system or machine, new information, or a new way of thinking or treating others.

2. The objective might occasionally be purely to motivate or, even more rarely, just to criticize. However, your high achievers are usually already motivated with "self-hype," and a long session devoted entirely to criticism will go over very poorly. It can seriously deflate people to the point where the cure becomes worse than the illness.

3. One of the best objectives you can have for training quality people is the bottom line—the end results: to have people leave saying, "I learned three things I can use right now. I'm glad I attended." With these results, you've won both hearts and minds and probably guaranteed some pretty constructive action.

A typical situation you might face could be where some of your key people clearly lack knowledge regarding some detailed and important steps that they should take, perhaps involving some area such as order processing or retail marketing. If you set as your goal simply to provide this information and to have it well understood, you then have a clear target. You can present the data, check with your people, and soon know how well you hit your objective.

REQUIRE STUDY IN ADVANCE

Assign homework. Does that sound mean and laborious? It's neither—not to high achievers. Again, remember that, by definition, a high achiever gets a lot done in a given time period. Therefore, time is a major variable in his or her equation of professional life. That means your tiger is very conscious of time and wants to make every minute count. Prestudy and homework mean that he or she will usually get more out of each hour of training than without such prior preparation. Most achievers like that. Here are three steps you might take:

1. Some preparatory work might simply be reading informational or background material. That's fine, as long as you resist the temptation to assign too much or get too far afield. Give a small amount, say 10 to 50 pages. A hundred is usually far too many. (But it happens.) And be sure the material has some direct, practical bearing on the program—and moves you toward your training objective.

2. Case problems are also very useful preparation. Here again, don't assign cases that are more numerous, longer, or more involved than is truly necessary. Again, achievers are highly time-conscious. Be especially careful to tie in the cases directly to the instruction. Never ask your attendees to prepare a solution and then say, "Oh, I guess we won't have time for the XYZ case." Either make time or don't assign it—or you will lose credibility.

3. A good preparation exercise is a series of brief self-tests based on several short readings. This permits the attendee to play back, demonstrate, and use his or her own newly acquired knowledge. Again, be sure this is really an integral part of the course.

PROVIDE A DETAILED AGENDA

Your agenda should cover things like a list of speakers, their titles, subjects, projects, times, dates, room numbers, and any other key "housekeeping" mechanics like where to park, hotel check-out time, and perhaps even a list of nearby drugstores, restaurants, bars, and theaters. Doing all this has many advantages for you and the attendees. High achievers are favorably motivated by sound planning. A thorough agenda reflects such a plan. They feel confident the whole thing is well organized, a good investment of their time.

High producers also do not like surprises, particularly sudden problems. A good agenda suggests that there is an orderly track to run on, fixed starting and stopping times with a specific person responsible for that time frame. Even if things get off the track, behind in timing, or speakers get switched around, if you have a detailed agenda, everyone still knows what is going on. That is reassuring, orderly, and comforting to many people—especially to well-organized ones.

Here are some suggestions for preparing effective agendas:

1. Give enough facts. Better a bit too many than too few. One page printed on both sides can provide hundreds of details—easily enough for a meeting lasting many days. Give a background sentence for each speaker. Maybe a postage stamp-sized picture, too, just to show that the speaker doesn't have two heads. State the meeting's main theme and its objective. Be sure to allow enough time for coffee and lunch breaks. End the agenda by asking if the meeting's goal was met and requesting that attendees indicate this by filling in the evaluation questionnaire in their handout packet and dropping it by the door as they leave. This both pleases the achievers and especially challenges the presenters.

2. If any particular demonstrations, exercises, or audience participation activities are planned, give these a special mark such as using asterisks before and after those items on the agenda. Then achievers are forewarned and are more likely to prepare for this if they can.

3. Hold the program closely to the scheduled timed slots. A meeting that gets out of hand timewise is not only wastefully expensive chaos but demoralizing to speakers and attendees alike. Also allow enough time to get in and out of the meeting place as well as time for some questions at the end. Really wise agenda planners deliberately allow a secret 10- or 15-minute time cushion both morning and afternoon. Studies show that 95 percent of all agenda troubles come from running short of time. Major cause: trying to cover too much per hour. Only 5 percent come from getting ahead of schedule. A time cushion can usually solve over half the trouble.

Pfizer Agendas Contribute to Trouble-Free Training

"Pfizer runs its training like clockwork," says one financial analyst. "One reason it's so smooth is that they usually have an excellent and complete agenda. One division also uses a little twist that I think shows sharp organization. They send the agenda to attendees about a week ahead of time, and it's dated. Then, when the meeting starts, they hand out another copy for people who forgot to bring their own. That's at least 10 percent. And if there has been any program change, a final agenda is given to everyone, marked 'revised' in big letters, dated, and printed on a different color paper."

ESTABLISH RAPPORT

Open the meeting by welcoming, introducing, selling, and establishing rapport with attendees. Done properly, this really gets things off on the right foot—and that simple act can be much more important than it appears. A bad start can take hours to correct, if it ever *is* corrected. Introducing key people (or everyone, if possible) makes attendees feel a part of the program as well as helps them become aware of who's present. They sometimes discover that old friends are there.

And keep selling. Even at this point, there may be lingering doubts in achievers' minds. They may have gone to a great many of these sessions—perhaps dozens—and suspect they have already attended too many. They fear a waste of their time—time they could be using to make more significant personal progress. Convince them that this meeting is truly a good investment of their time and effort. How do you do this?

1. Remember that some of your attendees have traveled many hours and miles to get there. Set a relaxed, friendly, nonthreatening tone. You can achieve a warm and effective welcome by strongly expressing your appreciation for and pleasure in their attending.

2. To introduce key people, simply state their names, ask them to stand, and give a sentence or so about them. If there are as many as 50 to 100 people attending, go quickly around the room and ask each to stand and give his or her name and title.

3. To convince the attendees that this is a good investment of their time and effort, recap the agenda. Reconfirm the authority of the speakers and then briefly relate the various subjects directly with the attendees' jobs. Show how the material is designed to help them personally to perform better and to improve their careers.

A typical problem you may have is where you are the emcee or the person giving the welcome. You might be wise to make a few light-hearted remarks to break the ice and put people at ease. Introduce yourself and others and express your personal pleasure at seeing the group. Then make a serious statement about how important the meeting will be for everyone. You might end by saying something like, "So let's get to work," or introducing the first person on the program.

RECOGNIZE THE ATTENDEES' SKILLS

Calling attention briefly to the attendees' status and accomplishments has the strong advantage of building self-respect among high achievers. They may have felt just a bit uncertain about attending a training session, suspecting that this implied some sort of failing on their part. Your simple acknowledgment of their position can often largely eliminate any vestiges of antagonism or humiliation. Here are some approaches you can use:

1. If possible, briefly recognize eight or ten key people in the audience. This might be a statement something like, "We are especially pleased to have the following department supervisors here."

2. Sometimes there are too many such people. Then you might use a blanket recognition statement covering them all as groups, without giving individual names.

3. You may have special guests from outside—from the public, press, government, or other groups. If you acknowledge these people, you further warm up the atmosphere.

4. A good simple device, when you have members from only a few specific groups, is to ask members of each of these groups to stand up together as their group name is called. This gives individuals an opportunity to gain a little additional unity, distinction, and identity.

Du Pont Greets Achievers Graciously

"Many people feel that Du Pont managers have a particularly gracious way of recognizing their high achievers at some of their training sessions," said one analyst. "Sometimes they simply give each person's name. On other occasions, one or two are told ahead of time that they will be asked to say a few words—half a minute or so. One time they started a meeting by giving out a series of awards to several large groups. You wouldn't believe how fast that warmed things up. The team spirit was right up there on cloud nine for many hours after that."

SET FORTH THE GROUND RULES

Give highlights, rules, and format of the meeting as a brief final step just before the presentation starts. This lets high achievers know what to expect and what they should do and not do. Again, this has the effect of unifying the group and making attendees feel they are part of the program. You help eliminate any sense of strangeness or disorientation.

Here's how: First, recap the objective and promise that it will be met. (Make sure you can and do deliver on this.) Even assign each person the task of helping to reach the goal. Achievers like to know they have something to sink their teeth into. Second, if there are any special rules of the game, this is the time to state them. This might include any added housekeeping announcements like elevators to be used, lunch locations, or check-out methods. Finally, attendees might be told of the procedures for asking questions or for doing group projects. Remind them of any request to do further preparation required after the first session.

Good Recaps Get Standard Brands' Training off to Smooth Start

"Standard Brands training sessions," said one executive, "always seemed to represent just the opposite from a fiasco I experienced a few years ago in which the sessions started out in total confusion and then disintegrated steadily downward. I never did quite figure out why we were there or what we were supposed to do, and no one else seemed to know either. I even went out and paid for a lunch, only to find out later that we had a special group luncheon—provided free! Some Standard Brands people must have seen similar disasters, because they always started meetings off with a quick, clear, and helpful recap of highlights and rules of the game."

PRESENT, ILLUSTRATE, AND DISCUSS

Presentation, illustration, and discussion represent a system that will build a substantial positive impression among your high-producing employees. And that impact and effectiveness is the whole object of the exercise. A "dead" training session is one that should never have been held. Here's how you can get a "live" one:

1. Present and explain the material in a brisk, clear, job-related manner. Outline the problem and the steps attendees can take toward a solution. Have a central idea to each area or subject on the agenda. Something they can hold on to, remember, and use. Watch their eyes. Make sure they are saying, "Yes, I dig it. I understand," not, "Ho hum. What a bore!"

2. Illustrate this key point with real-life examples showing how the information is used. Present visuals if at all possible—charts, graphs, pictures, or diagrams. These are often remembered and applied. Of all we learn, 80 percent is acquired through our eyes.

3. Discuss it a little. Let people ask questions for a while. Encourage questioning as long as it is held to sensible inquiry in a reasonable time period, say five or ten minutes. The purpose of the discussion isn't always so much to provide information as to generate an atmosphere of understanding and familiarity with the ideas and a sense of the attendees' own personal involvement.

4. Don't employ overkill. Don't dump the whole load of hay on your audience in each presentation. It is better to cover ten strong points thoroughly, in a way that the attendees can grasp and use, than to cover fifty points in a confused or superficial manner.

Bell Telephone Training Sparks Involvement

Bell Telephone people often seem to be experts in personal communication and their training courses show it," said one top electronics specialist. "As a technician, I'm not all that interested in dollar revenues or human resource management. But when these subjects are covered, it is done in such a clear, practical way that I can't help feeling interested, involved, and just plain turned on. And I notice that Bell's really good people seem to feel the same way. I guess it ain't what you do, it's the way you do it, if I may echo an old phrase."

STRETCH THEIR MINDS

Talk "up." Reach and make the attendees stretch their minds a little. The advantage here is that high achievers like to try for new ideas. They enjoy it, and they tend to latch on to these fresh concepts and seek good uses for them.

How can you do it? First, never talk down or be overly simplistic. Some achievers will tend to lose interest and let their minds wander, because they are not being fully used. Others will be irritated at what seems to be a waste of their time. Either way, training stops. If you happen to have a mixed group, so that you must cover some simple elements, say something like, "Let's stop here for just three minutes and look at a few basics." Cover them and then get right back on track.

Second, stay as challenging as possible. Present new ideas and concepts at a fairly fast pace. Even ask, "Think about this point! What can you do with a great new approach like this?" Set your audience to thinking, stretching, and reaching. Third, stay realistic and practical. Relate the new ideas as closely as you can to the achievers' everyday problems and goals.

END WITH SELF-QUIZ AND SUMMARY

A self-test and a summary are for all practical purposes a double recap that can thoroughly nail down your training and guarantee that you reach its objectives. Further, a quiz has the advantage of very real and close personal involvement. Psychiatrists say that this sort of action is one of the strongest possible methods of reinforcing the common, everyday garden variety of learning. So, again, you did it! And you did it in spades! Here's how you can be sure the spade digs in:

1. As you come to the close of the session, consider ending off with a short series of questions. You might simply ask everyone to number a sheet of paper from one to ten and give them ten true/false questions. Be sure these are well prepared, clear-cut, and directly tied in with the basic material and important points of the training, not insignificant details. Then read the answers. You'll get their

attention, all right—especially with your high achievers. Explain that the summary to follow will elaborate a little on these points, and that will avoid most of their immediate questions and challenges.

2. Then keep your promise and cover the highlights in a summary statement lasting five or ten minutes. Be sure to expand a bit on all the true/false answers. The quiz and recap can stand separately or go hand-in-hand, as you wish.

3. Give out any appropriate certificates of training completion, if this is in keeping with company practice. Whatever you do, don't make light of this. Do it with seriousness, if not ceremony. This means a lot to some people, even to some achievers (it's one more feather in their war bonnets). Others just like to add it to their award file.

4. Remind the attendees to leave their completed training evaluation forms on the table as they leave. You have taken strong steps toward assuring a favorable "report card." This may impress your own supervisor, but perhaps more important, when attendees give a high rating to training, they tend to believe it themselves and so gain more from it. Which brings us back to the beginning—to our specific objective right from the start.

5. Part friends. Thank the attendees for coming, for being such good listeners, and for helping everyone to share and gain from the learning process. You are orally sort of "putting your arms around" the members of your group, cementing their team spirit, and giving them a final emotional lift.

At Suzuki Instruments, Training Ends on a Ceremonious Note

Japanese training methods are quite similar to those used in America. The Japanese, too, recognize the value of a good ending. Their approach differs in several respects, however. Both the quiz and the certificate presentation are often given somewhat greater importance. In one Suzuki training course held in Kyoto, the quiz was extensive. It was handed in to be graded electronically and become part of the employees' records. And the certificates were presented with considerably more ceremony, even involving a representative from the local governmental authority as a presenter. But in the end, there were many good words of praise for the trainees, much good fellowship, and later, sake wine toasts from their instructors. Japanese training usually proves to be quite effective, especially for high achievers, who take it most seriously.

TEN COMMANDMENTS FOR TRULY EFFECTIVE TRAINING OF HIGH ACHIEVERS

1. Double your training impact by planning with the 5Ws.
2. Have a clear goal: "I learned something useful."
3. Require prestudy and advance homework.
4. Provide a detailed program agenda.
5. Welcome, introduce, sell, and build rapport.
6. Recognize the attendees' skills and status.
7. Give highlights, rules, and format.
8. Present information; illustrate it; discuss and try it.
9. Talk "up," reach, and stretch minds with new ideas.
10. End with a quiz, a recap, and a feeling of friendship.

Your OBI (one best idea) for training talented people is to have a good purpose, clear plan, thorough preparation, detailed agenda, warm welcome, and constructive and challenging material, closing with a pleasant and practical summation of key points.

CHAPTER 10
How to Control the Aggressive Achiever

A high achiever is a challenge—to everybody, at home and outside. A challenge in about every sense of the word. A high producer is a lot like a high-powered car engine—a great opportunity to make speedy, dramatic progress but also a problem to keep the darn thing under reasonable control. In a very real sense, you have a tiger by the tail. Even the roar can get a bit scary or threatening.

Having recognized your situation, with its problems and opportunities, your objective is clear: Use the good. Avoid the bad. Gain from the cutting edge's thrust. Duck the other edge. The key is control. If you have this, then you can use the good edge and the beneficial power—and avoid the rest.

With an engine, you must know how to start it, aim it, and be sure it is moving toward the target, not toward the ditch. So it is with your tiger. The danger is that the high achiever can take on his or her own direction, which can be disruptive to the team effort. Or he or she can take the wrong direction, which can be damaging to everyone. Your tiger can even take over control of resources and of other key people's job assignments—including yours. Out-of-control tigers can destroy an organization and a business, and have done exactly this. And then they simply get up, brush themselves off, and stroll calmly away from the smoking ruins.

One way to look at the high achiever is as a package of objective capabilities and subjective emotions. High achievers, by definition, have high capabilities, but they may have widely different subjective emotions. One may be tough as nails, another, tender as a tulip. Most will be somewhere in between these two extremes.

The purpose of this chapter is to outline some effective methods for solving the problem of handling aggressive achievers. How to control them when they are getting pretty assertive, on up to the point where they have become far too aggressive—even downright out of control.

BEGIN WITH ANALYSIS

The advantage of starting with insight and analysis is the same as that which the race car or racehorse owner has by knowing his or her machine or beast—thoroughly. The owner can often get and keep control by knowing not only what buttons to press but the limits on how hard they can be pushed and which ones had best not be mashed down on at all. Knowledge is power, and knowing these things often permits you to gain good control with a minimum of your own time and effort. Your high achiever usually has great power but equally great complexity. It is simply part of the package. You have a potent tool but a complicated one.

Another relevant comparison is between an automobile and a bicycle. The car can do a whole lot more for you in terms of comfort, speed, and style—but it usually takes considerably more knowledge, attention, and servicing to keep it in the proper condition so it will produce well for you. And control is even more important than servicing. An out-of-control auto can be far more dangerous and have more damaging consequences than falling from a bike and skinning one's knee. So it is with the out-of-control tiger.

To establish and maintain control, first be sure you know your company's needs and wants as well as your own and those of your high achiever. That way you won't misdirect, misuse, or overuse your resource. To reach a mailbox a block away, you might use the bike, not the race car. Second, understand the engine and its peculiarities—so you will know when you have control or when something is going wrong. Best to discover this before it's too late. Third, test your controls regularly. Make sure you can get things started, speeded up, slowed down, turned left and right, and shut off. Run these tests routinely, on small, not urgent matters, so if something does go wrong, little is lost.

Supervisor Tames Leo Burnett Agency Tigers

The Leo Burnett company is one of the largest and most successful advertising agencies in the world. As such, many of the nation's top marketing specialists apply there, and its team is made up almost totally of high achievers. "They are used to controlling tigers," said a top advertising executive. "I remember one day when two highly dedicated and talented guys each wanted a completely different photo treatment in an important ad. Tempers flared, and it looked for a while as if things might get out of hand. But matters were solved very quickly by one simple step: An equally talented supervisor with higher authority simply looked and listened carefully to both sides of the matter, and then he made a decision. Period. End of conflict. The tigers were each back in their cages."

USE GOALS TO MAINTAIN CONTROL

Match the personal targets of an aggressive achiever with those of the company, and your control over him or her increases. And here we come back to our old friends, goals and objectives, and we use these to help channel and direct achiever activity. The advantage to you is that using mutual goals is a lot simpler and easier than some other mechanisms. It also accomplishes the things you need done, gains you control, and avoids the disaster that can result from nondirected action. Here's how you can do it:

1. Constantly check both your tiger's and your own past, present, and future goal descriptions to find common ones. Circumstances are never totally static. They are always changing, at least a little. When they change a lot, this can mean that old goals are no longer mutual targets, but there may be new ones that are.

2. Add multiple goals wherever reasonable. Look for and aim at wider horizons and new worlds to conquer. This makes the whole program more interesting to a high achiever and so channels his or her efforts constructively. In other words, it builds your control. Tigers like lots of red meat to chew on.

3. Raise quality standards where you can. Again, you are controlling the achiever to the mutual benefit of all concerned. As your

tiger shows increased aggression, you can show him or her increased quality standards as a challenge.

A typical situation you may sometimes encounter is where
your high achiever is making such excellent progress that it almost
seems like a bit *too much* progress. Things get far ahead of schedule,
and your achiever starts wanting to branch out into a project or two
that might conflict or overlap with those of other people. As a supervisor, you have several pretty good options. One is to encourage
your tiger to keep right on doing more of what he or she has been
doing, perhaps expanding the service or activity to more people.
Another sensible approach you might consider is simply to execute
"operation quality upgrade"—having your tiger do the job a little
better in every step of the process. Emphasize performance results,
not just numbers. Encourage innovation. As an additional option,
you could check into the possibility of discussing any prospective
overlap. The other party might be delighted to switch those activities away from his or her job description and over to your
energetic achiever.

GIVE YOUR TIGER SOME ROOM

Agree with the high achiever a lot. Don't fence him or her in.
Now that may sound contradictory. Here we are, working out ways
to control high achievers, and then we turn around and seem to say,
"Let them go. Let them roam. Give them less control." There is a
saying among architects that "Less is more." Meaning, in their case,
that less fuss, feathers, features, and gingerbread actually has more
impact.

The same can be true with control of an achiever. Too much
attempted control can lead to resistance and hence to decreased
ability to manage his or her actions. Exercising less control, particularly on minor matters, can mean you customarily let your tiger
work on his or her own initiative, so that there is less resentment and
a greater feeling of freedom. Therefore, on the rare occasions when
you must have control, you have a better chance of getting it easily.
Here's how:

1. Give him or her the benefit of the doubt. Remember, you

have a high achiever. That's why you selected him or her. Surely that means your tiger has higher-than-average ability—a good reason to agree with him or her a lot and to give greater-than-average lead.

2. Emphasize freedom to your tiger, especially in the areas of his or her expertise. This will result in a feeling of flexibility, which becomes well recognized by the achiever and is thus not easily denied when the issue arises where you need, request, and even demand control.

3. Give in on the many small issues, again so that the feeling and the reality of freedom are generated. Know what the major issues are where you will request control and restrict yourself to asserting mainly on those points.

CHALLENGE OFTEN AND CHECK CONSTANTLY

High achievers usually work best when they have a load of important assignments that are varied, challenging, and fairly numerous. The advantage to you in such circumstances is that you get a lot of things done toward your goals, while you simultaneously soak up a lot of the achievers' excess energy that could otherwise get out of hand and cause problems. Here's how to do this:

1. Apply some pressure. This is not to say you should create a superheated pressure cooker, but most achievers like to feel the pace and the urgency of time. They respect it and use it themselves. And urgency is often a function of the number of jobs to be done in relation to the time available in which to do them. Therefore, assign a few more than normal rather than a few less. It can increase your control.

2. Make assignments that are not only numerous but varied, that use the achievers' talents, require some initiative, some innovation, and are challenging. In short, generate some quality pressure as well as numbers and time urgency.

3. Watch and listen. "Read" your tiger. Just as a race car driver listens carefully to an engine, so you should be alert to feedback coming from your achiever. It clues you as to when things are cool and controlled—or when the engine is overheating. Then adjust

accordingly. If it's laboring, back off on the pressure. If it's idling, add the motivators. If it's losing control, you may need to apply still more quantity and quality pressure.

Mobil Oil Keeps Its Tigers out of Trouble

"Mobil Oil company seems to have plenty of challenges for its high achievers," said a petroleum economist. "I like that, because, in my experience it helps keep high-powered people busy and constructive. I recall one case recently where a small team of tigers had completed a key job and won an award. Instead of inviting everyone to rest on their laurels, the supervisor immediately added a whole string of new projects to the team's schedule. They got so busy, only one member could find time to attend the award ceremony. The others were deeply involved in jobs with tight deadlines. And strange as it may seem, they were happy as pigs in mud! But without that new batch of projects, the supervisor would have lost a lot of important control and progress."

IN A QUIET COMPANY, KEEP YOUR TIGER'S ENERGY SAFELY CHANNELED

When you have a less-than-dynamic organization, the high achiever is perhaps a bit unusual or even a little out of phase with the group. A nondynamic company is not really a rarity. After all, most companies move into quiet times occasionally, possibly on a seasonal basis or as the organization matures or takes on less liberal, less aggressive, and more conservative policies. Under such circumstances, the achiever may appear to be a misfit and may seem less than well controlled. For your part, you may feel as if you have a tiger by the tail. Here's how you can keep from being mauled:

1. Know the procedures. Know what is permissible and what is not. This also means having an understanding of the company goals. Not just the stated ones, which may be partly for window dressing and public show. You want to grasp the real, deep-down, quiet, honest, basic objectives. These may very well be unstated. You may need to infer them from hints, clues, comments, and cir-

cumstances. But they are always there, one way or another. These point to opportunities for using tiger talents and hence for building your control.

2. Channel the high achiever's energy into these company goals, stated or unstated. This is a safe and harmless yet practical use of a high producer's energy. Now your tiger may say, "That's ridiculous! That isn't a very progressive goal." Then you can show him or her that not all goals are necessarily superdramatic ones. Some are vitally important holding actions, some are preventive, and some corrective. But these can still be highly strategic. No ship is ready for a race if it is leaking badly, or the time and weather are all wrong for setting out. What you are doing is reappraising, re-evaluating, and rebuilding the importance of the seemingly unexciting objectives—and strengthening your control.

3. A suggestion you must use selectively: Consider the reason why the company has become so quiet. Perhaps it's because it has hit a long-term, permanent brick wall or just a tough problem that no one can solve, or because it has become ensnared in some sort of circular self-entrapping difficulty or just simply suffers from insufficiently dynamic thought. Sometimes the high achiever can solve some or all of this. However, just *be sure that the top people really want it solved* and have some plan for the next steps in case the logjam is broken. If not, you may create far more problems than you solved. There is also something to be said for a nice, safe, comfortable, and profitable rut. Progress isn't always big cigars and motor cars.

IN A NORMAL COMPANY, ALLOW INDEPENDENCE

In a normal company, you have a situation where there is a mixture of high achievers, low achievers, and people in between. The tiger is not really that much of a rarity, but you still need control along with high performance. Here's how you can get both:

1. Be sure everyone knows the regulations—particularly your high producers and most especially anyone who might get out of control.

2. Do a little tailoring of the job assignment to fully utilize the

skills of the high achiever. For example, if the tiger is also a good public speaker, you might add that as part of his or her assignment.

3. Even bend the rules or adjust them a little, if that will help you get greater benefit from your high achiever without causing other problems. Using your tiger's skills to the maximum gets you double service—top performance and good control, because both of you want the high achiever to do exactly what he or she is doing.

4. Encourage his or her own initiative, innovation, and independence, within broad guidelines. Again you get greater output, but it is under reasonable control.

5. Since there is a mixture of low and high producers present, keep an eye out for how other supervisors control their tigers. Whatever they do might be accepted by achievers as standard procedure. If their approach fits your problem, works, and makes sense, use it.

A typical situation you might face in a normal company is a sales force of mixed performers, some excellent, some only fair at best. Naturally, you want the most you can get from each type, including your star players, who may do two or three times as much as your other people. Your best bet is to be sure they all know the regulations. But if one rule is that travel should not be by puddle-jumper airlines and a high producer still uses these to get big results, then the regulations might be amended to say, "except in Texas," or "unless by special approval."

IN A DYNAMIC COMPANY, SET TOUGH RULES

In a high-powered organization, you probably have many top producers. You may have a gathering of officers, leaders, managers, professors, or even business authors. This could be a roomful of prima donnas. Here your superachiever is just one of the crowd— one tiger among many. The following are some approaches that can help you manage many tigers at once:

1. Treat each tiger as what he or she is—just another member of the group, without any special privileges, a person who obeys the rules, is controlled, and controls himself or herself, just like everyone else.

2. Be sure he or she knows the standard operating procedures.

And recognize that, just as rules for college students differ from those for grade school students, tiger procedures differ from those for average and below-average achievers. They should be more in terms of broad policies, general guidelines, and overall philosophies than of minutely detailed nuts and bolts. Guidelines should be expressed mainly in terms of objectives and basic strategy.

3. Expect results. Pay more attention to what is accomplished than to how it was done (as long as it was legal and in reasonably good taste).

4. Let 'em roar. Roll. Perform. Accomplish. Just as long as your tiger is reaching objectives and not using any totally unacceptable methods.

5. If goals are being reached but methods are objectionable or borderline, speak up. Ask that these approaches be dropped and other more acceptable ones be used. Ask firmly. Follow up. Insist. Out of control, the greatest engine in the world is useless, damaging, and dangerous.

As a supervisor of at least one high achiever and possibly many, you have a unique situation. Typically, it is both a problem and an opportunity—the problem being to control the horsepower you have, the opportunity being to enjoy the benefits of such controlled power.

One excellent solution combines these goals along with a method for accomplishing them, and this actually works well in some of our nation's best companies. Here's the secret: Make a major effort to develop a constructive, positive attitude among your high producers. Try to get them feeling convinced that: "We all know not only the rules of our industry but the policies of our company. And the primary criterion for my group is accomplishment, pure and simple. Other than that, we have very wide latitude within the bounds of decency and efficiency. If we start crowding those boundaries, we hear about it really quick. I feel quite free, and yet I know that, within reason, I am controlled, both by my own common sense and by the good judgment of my supervisor." If you can develop that sort of attitude, you have gained a great deal of control over your high achievers—even in a very dynamic company. This is never easy and is rarely accomplished overnight—but it can be done.

DEMAND COMPLIANCE

When control is slipping, demand compliance but boost spirit (seduce, don't rape). Here is a situation where your high achiever is nearly out of control. He or she is no longer completely responsive to your requests to start or stop, to go east or west. He or she may even be going beyond the wide and liberal boundaries you have set. As we mentioned earlier in another context, your tiger may be testing you.

Also, being an achiever, he or she has never been overly impressed with obstacles—be they set up by competitors, circumstances, or the plain, old rules of the game. They all take on a similar hue as challenges—things to be overcome, one way or another.

Achievers are generally assertive. So it's not too surprising to see them rise to these challenges and bump against the barriers to measure their strength. This is an important moment. You are being tested as well. Constructive steps are urgently required before any major damage is done. You need to nip this thing in the bud and not let it get out of hand. And you want to come out of this well in control, yet without destroying too much of your tiger's enthusiasm. Here's how you might do it:

1. Be sure you are right. Get the facts and double-check them. They are your ammunition, and you don't want to go into battle with blanks. You'd just look foolish.

2. Review these facts with your achiever in a cool, calm, collected, and orderly manner. Remember, an achiever may be perceptive, well tuned, and sensitive as a tulip, but underneath he or she is rarely a shrinking violet. Most are made of pretty tough stuff, or they would not have accomplished what they have.

3. Restate the regulations. Lay it on the line. This is permitted, that is not. This is in bounds, that is out.

4. Let him or her save face if necessary, but not a whole lot of face. After all, it is your tiger, not you, who has gone overboard. You might ask him or her if some minor revision in systems and procedures would help. But you may need to mention the fact that if you were to make a major exception for him or her, you would also have to make it for many other high achievers, and that would damage the organization. In short, no special privileges.

5. Get some kind of reasonable understanding, acceptance, and agreement. Make sure he or she *says this*—voluntarily, if possible, or upon request, if necessary. But get it. Maybe it need not be shouted from the housetops, but somewhere in your conversation, *get an agreement to comply*. Get the next level of supervision involved, if only on a supportive basis.

6. Make it known that you are taking your tiger's word for this—and that you trust him or her and expect that the promise made to you and to himself or herself will be kept.

7. Also let your tiger know that along with your trust goes your confidence and faith in him or her and your enthusiasm for his or her ability and performance. You might say something like, "I am proud of you and lucky to be working with you. I know you want us all to keep on feeling that way."

8. End not only with an upbeat statement of enthusiasm but with a look ahead at next goals, new challenges, exciting objectives. Have a few listed and tucked in your pocket before your talk even begins.

ULTIMATUM: "COMPLY OR LEAVE"

When your tiger is totally out of control, things have reached the extreme. Control is not just slipping, it's nonexistent—gone. Your achiever makes little or no response to your requests or directions.

Your goals here must primarily be to avoid serious damage to yourself, your company, your employees, and the achiever himself or herself. You have reached the moment of truth: Things have either got to improve very much, very rapidly or you had best part company. Here's how to face up to this situation and move to a resolution, one way or the other:

1. Thoroughly inform your supervisor of the problem you face, particularly with respect to the damage and embarrassment this situation can cause him or her and the company. Outline the steps that you plan to take. Ask for any suggestions your supervisor may have and make him or her a part of the program. Be sure you have his or her full support.

2. We can assume at this point that you asked for your achiever's promise of compliance with your request, as we outlined above. Either your tiger gave this, essentially, or he or she did not. If he or she did not, then you have already moved directly into an uncontrolled situation, perhaps without realizing it. If you did receive assurance of compliance with your requests and direction but then did not get it, you are facing a broken promise. Your best step here is a blunt but calm presentation of the facts to the achiever and a request for some sort of clarification. There may be a reason—but it had better be a very good one.

(Warning: Your tiger probably saw this whole thing coming some time ago. He or she may even have planned it and could very well have some strong complaint, criticism, or demand in mind. He or she may also have some other plans or have taken other steps to circumvent or undercut you—or simply to move on to other things. Don't presume for a moment that you have taken your tiger totally by surprise.)

3. Assuming your tiger does not offer a good reason, or that you never got some sort of promise to comply with your wishes in the first place, you now have a hard decision but a clear one. You should come flat out and state factually and unemotionally that you have both reached a critical point. "Sam, we seem to have a very serious problem. It's simply lack of control. You're a fine person and a fine employee, but you are not responding to my direction." Let your tiger answer but do not change your own position unless new—and highly persuasive—information is presented.

4. Let him or her know that the situation is totally out of control and therefore totally unsatisfactory to you and to the company—including your boss. And ask what he or she plans to do about it and what he or she wants you to do.

5. At this point, you are poised at the fork in the road. Things almost have to go one way or the other. Let your tiger know this. You must have proof of his or her intention and plan to move in some major, positive new direction, or your relationship will have to undergo a substantial change. Say this in your own words, but put the monkey completely on your tiger's back. You have done what you could and can only hope for the best. The other party, after all, has a strong say as to his or her own future actions.

For example, a typical situation may be where you have screened, recruited, hired, oriented, and motivated a very fine assistant. But he or she has now gotten totally out of hand, doing things that you and the company had expressly prohibited and refusing to do things that you and the company had urgently requested. You warned him or her when you saw your control start to slip. And as is often the case, you got a promise of compliance—a promise that was not kept. Your supervisor is aware of the problem and strongly agrees that it is now a matter of complete correction or total separation. You tell your achiever this, and now he or she must clearly decide.

PARTING COMPANY

You were left hanging in the last paragraph. It was hoped that you would achieve your goal of saving the situation and pointing it in a new, positive, happy, progressive direction. It can and has happened. But it also—and at this point usually does—go the other way. It is not likely to go in the direction of a flat-out resignation, although that, too, is possible, of course, and you were surely aware of that. The reason that this is probably not the moment of resignation is that you are the one who initiated this discussion—and it was you, not your tiger, who selected the time and place. A high achiever, particularly a good strategic planner, is not too likely to convert this time and place into the moment for his or her "triumphal" resignation. More likely, your tiger will be the one to pick that time.

Again, you now want to act for the greatest good of yourself, your company, and your overachiever. Here's how:

1. At this point, you are obviously moving down the less-than-happy branch of the fork in the road. (Although by now, it may be rapidly becoming the more pleasant direction for you personally.) Unless you see a very convincing, documented, and proven turnaround by the employee, resign yourself to being past the point of no return and determine to move decisively on a new course.

2. Inform your supervisor and make sure he or she agrees.

3. Do not act hastily by saying something like, "OK. If you feel that way about it, you're fired." This can do you far more harm

than good in lots of ways. You can always play your ace—but once you've played it, it's gone and no longer has clout, power, or threat. Let the conversation simply end on the note that "Some decisions will need to be made by all of us." This leaves the door open for you both.

4. Sometimes your tiger can still be of great service to the company, but not in your unit. Check with others to see if they need or can use this type.

5. Check around with contacts outside your company. No person is really totally worthless. A high achiever who was carefully selected and trained has value. You will do him or her and the right new employer (and in the end, yourself) a favor by helping them get together. This can reduce the bad feelings that probably exist. It can even help build a good relationship. If you can't maximize your gains, you should at least minimize your losses.

6. Part friends, if at all possible. Since you are both of professional age, in the same industry, in the same country, on the same planet, it would not be at all surprising for your paths to cross again sometime. Possibly many times. As a high achiever, he or she may very well end up in a position that could do you a lot of good—or a lot of harm.

Armour Helps Problem Tiger Find Another Team

"At a division of Armour and Company," said a management consultant, "I had a high achiever working for me as one of my economic analysts. He was a truly talented executive—bright, willing, able, a high producer. The only trouble was, he kept doing some things I did not want done and doing other things I did want done much differently from the way, design, and format that I needed. He was causing me and the company some problems. I saw my control slipping and discussed it with him. He assured me there was no problem. But matters got worse. He began doing things behind my back—and then going around me to higher supervisors. People told me he was trying to get my job. I heard of an excellent opening in a fine company that I knew he admired and submitted his name myself. He was hired and has done a great job for them. We parted friends. Incidentally, I don't think he ever found out what I did."

TEN COMMANDMENTS FOR CONTROLLING THE AGGRESSIVE ACHIEVER

1. Begin with insight and analysis.
2. Match your tiger's personal targets with those of the company.
3. Agree a lot. Give him or her some room.
4. Make many challenging assignments and check constantly.
5. In a quiet company, channel your tiger's actions safely.
6. In a normal company, bend the rules a bit and allow some independence.
7. In a dynamic company, set tough rules, then let 'em roar.
8. When control is slipping, demand compliance but boost spirits.
9. When your tiger is totally out of control, it's "comply or leave" time.
10. If you must separate, try to do so as friends.

Your OBI (one best idea) for controlling an aggressive achiever is to understand him or her and adjust challenging targets, maintain company safety and flexibility, demand compliance, and part if necessary, but on friendly terms.

CHAPTER 11
How and When to Promote the High Achiever

Moving up is a touchy subject, and yet you definitely should consider and use the promotion in relation to your high achiever. This is for his or her good, your good, and for the benefit of your company. You almost have to get involved in promotion, either as a real consideration, a promise, or an action. Promoting people is a fact of life; it has been with us for ages and is here to stay.

But using promotion too little and too slowly is dangerous, while too much, too fast is disastrous. Clearly, you walk a narrow path between two pits of snarling crocodiles. A misstep either way spells big trouble.

You, as a supervisor, face a challenging little mix of emotional and economic elements. On the one hand, you want to give out a promotion. You are helping your company. You are presenting an award. You are pleasing someone. You are being a nice person. You are also building a partner and a colleague—one who owes you a debt of gratitude. And it is a display of your power. To say that supervisors never want to give pay increases and promotions is a comic-strip myth that people like to believe—but it just isn't true.

On the other hand, as a supervisor, it simply isn't all that easy to hand out these nice benefits. For one thing, there may be no opening, no place to which to promote the deserving person. For another, you may be plagued by three very reasonable fears: First, you fear that the promotion will fail—and that means you made a major mistake. Second, you may fear complaint and criticism from others—and that means conflict. And finally, you face the reality that you have now lost an important reward tool. Your ability to promote that person is gone and can't usually be employed again anytime soon—and that means you have lost power. Promotion is clearly a mixed blessing for the supervisor.

Now add to the equation the fact that most high achievers are very conscious of promotions. They know they are above average, and they have high hopes—and high confidence. They rarely have any real fear of failure. Some of these achievers get a little bit unrealistic in their assessment of themselves and their opportunities for advancement. At least a few expect to be president of the company by the time they are in their mid-30s—or by 40 at the latest.

This misjudgment is not too surprising. They see other people getting promoted. Some even do become president around age 40. They also compare their abilities to those of average or below-average people, and the comparison is sometimes rather dramatic. The achievers know they aren't perfect geniuses, but they are so far ahead of most others that they feel they should lead. They think of the old saying, "In the land of the blind, the one-eyed man is king."

They think about that and a whole lot more. Promotions are a subject of great debate at their homes or with their close friends. They ponder it, plan for it, and frankly, they expect it. If it doesn't happen or at least get considered somewhere close to their time frame, they become discontented, worried, and perhaps a bit angry.

Promotion or the possibility of promotion is one of the most effective programs you have for generating top action through happy, satisfied high achievers. But it must be done right to get best results. Done improperly, it can lead to more problems than it solves. Here's how to do it right, using techniques that have worked well.

STUDY YOUR TEAM

Take a good look at your achiever and at others who might be right under your nose. Don't just target one person as the crown prince or heir apparent. Yes, of course, you are already aimed at developing one or two, but just take the following reasonable steps to insure that you don't miss any other good opportunities:

1. Keep an open mind. Your well-known high achiever may be

your most promotable person or at least seems that way, but recognize that there may be others even better qualified. High achievement is not necessarily the only, or even the best, criterion for promotion.

2. Avoid being caught by the Peter Principle. You don't want to promote a person beyond his or her ability. Producing a premier performance, even a brilliant job, at level five doesn't mean the person would do well at level six. The higher level may call for a totally different set of skills, training, and abilities. A star sales representative may or may not be a good sales manager. These are two very different jobs.

3. Decide on criteria for promotion. List just what is needed to qualify for moving up. For example, "I'll consider promoting a person at level five when I see him or her doing certain things (like exceeding quotas), not doing others (like avoiding mistakes), and showing certain interests and abilities (like the capacity to supervise, plan, and do grade-six work)."

4. If you have trouble recognizing a promotable person, study each one and compare him or her to the qualifying list you just made in the previous paragraph. Sure clues to potentially promotable people are initiative, drive, creativity, action, and unusually outstanding results.

5. Try people out. Give prospective candidates like your high achiever the opportunity to demonstrate their ability and readiness to move onward and upward. You can do this by giving them advanced assignments or temporary appointments to duties in the next higher grade. Be careful how you judge their performance. Don't expect it to be like that of a seasoned pro in the position. Do expect it to be equal to or better than the performance of others who were given similar opportunities and who later went on to succeed at that higher level.

SET A REASONABLE PROMOTION GOAL

Think ahead regarding promotion, just as your achiever is doing. The great advantage to this step is that it helps you focus in on the future and build a logical, reasonable framework for getting there. If you have no promotion goals, you handicap yourself in two ways. First, you find yourself in a "crisis panic" every time the promotion matter reaches an intense stage of consideration. Whereas with a goal, all discussion becomes calm. You know where your achiever is heading, and there's little need for panic. Second, without a goal, you can end up with some pretty weird and bizarre arrangements that might leave both you and your boss wondering how it all happened—such as ending up with a person of doubtful competence placed in a position of high responsibility, perhaps far beyond his or her capacity.

In a real sense, lack of goals and objectives is a definite cause of the chaos described by the Peter Principle. And it is completely avoidable. Here's how:

1. Conduct a practical and realistic review of the organization structure. Know what it looks like. Who really reports to whom? Now ask yourself, Where can my tiger climb to next? What's the most reasonable step up? Chances are, there are several higher positions, and there are people already in those slots. What are the possibilities that any of them might vacate those spots? Probably slim at the moment but not out of the question. There is such a thing as turnover, even at upper levels. Sometimes especially at upper levels.

2. What about your own slot? If your high achiever reports directly to you, what are the chances that you may be going elsewhere? The thought may shake you up a bit, but this is a time for realistic thinking. If you have various other options and believe there is even a remote chance you might take one of them in the next one to three years, then you should consider your own slot as one possible goal for your achiever.

3. Be reasonable in goal selection. We can't all be president or board chairman or even a vice-president. And while we should of course all gaze far down the road to the dim and misty yet glowing and hopeful rewards of the future, we must also look to our footing right now, this year and next. Take this promotion thing a step at a time. And at this moment, the very next step is the important one.

4. Promotion or progress doesn't necessarily mean upward movement into a job having a higher position on the organization chart. Sometimes that only results in more burdens at little increase in pay. Other objectives may well be simply greater authority, recognition, power, prestige, pay, career fulfillment, and job enjoy-

ment, yet at essentially the same vertical level on the organization chart. In other words, horizontal movement. People on the first rung of the organizational ladder may laugh at such a notion and perhaps rightly so. But they don't usually laugh nearly so much once they go up a few steps.

5. If there are no obvious openings now and none likely, this calls for a little ingenuity in goal development. It is just possible that one of the higher-level people has an expanding part of the business. He or she may require an assistant. Possibly a new department will open that will need a manager. Perhaps the achiever himself or herself will develop a new product, service, or function that calls for a new, small, special unit (and leader). Consider these possibilities and list them.

6. Talk it over with your achiever. If you deceive yourself into believing that he or she is not thinking of a promotion, you are doing both of you a disservice. He or she may even have the next few steps planned. And your tiger could be right. More likely, he or she has some big flaws in the plan that could cause both of you serious problems. These need correcting. At any rate, he or she undoubtedly has ideas, and so do you. It is to your mutual advantage to exchange those views.

7. Tell your achiever you will help. Be supportive, especially if his or her goal setting is reasonable, productive, and not damaging to you or the company. This step has a lot of advantages, not the least being that you gain great respect and confidence from your achiever. And it lets you do some constructive counseling. You can help find openings and give him or her a leg up. Some supervisors have done this with a number of qualified people and soon found they had many good friends in high places.

PLAN A PROGRAM

Planning a program means identifying the steps that might be taken to reach the next career goal you and your achiever have selected. You are then continuing to manage by objectives—to use your time, effort, and other resources to progress toward a target. The advantages to you are that you gain increased control of your high achiever and increased motivation. He or she looks to you to help select actions best suited for moving toward the goal. This is the control element, because you are the one who can and should indicate activities and projects to perform. The program is also a highly motivating experience for most achievers, because it is meaningful work and represents something they can grasp hold of and sink their teeth into. Here's how you might approach this:

1. Work it out with your tiger. Talk about steps you and he or she can take together to move closer to the goal. You might look at some challenging projects. His or her job description is a good source. Explain which of these projects or tasks would be of greatest help to you and to him or her in moving up and getting promoted. You might assure your achiever that if this is accomplished, you will see that it gets on his or her record and that the next boss up the line becomes well aware of it. Then be sure to keep your promise.

2. Stay very flexible and encourage your achiever to keep an open mind on programs and projects. You don't want to get so locked into one set of tasks as being the "royal road to riches" that you can't switch to meet new needs as they arise. These new opportunities may have even greater potential for promotion.

3. Do not ever overpromise. Say something like, "Those projects should surely assist in building your skills and reputation—and that should help move you toward your promotion." Avoid statements like, "Do this, and your promotion is guaranteed." You can rarely be that certain of an appropriate slot up above. Requirements for it may change, the position may be eliminated, a better qualified candidate may appear, or important deficiencies in the achiever's performance may be found. Go to the firm promise only when you are pretty sure of your achiever, your slot opening, your circumstances, and your ability to take such action. Failure to keep your promise after the achiever has fully complied would greatly reduce your credibility, your control, and the achiever's motivation.

MAKE A REALISTIC TIMETABLE

List the dates when different steps might be taken. The advantage to this is that it organizes things into an orderly procedure and further aligns activities into a reasonable perspective from a time standpoint. It also performs the highly valuable service of emphasizing that full results are not likely to occur overnight. It gives you some breathing room and also prevents you from being pressured for faster progress by your achiever. You are in a position to say, "You are moving along nicely, right on schedule and maybe even a bit ahead," without finding yourself in a time bind in which you must provide some sort of instant promotion, accommodation, or a darned good excuse.

Effective scheduling has another great advantage of laying out some pretty tough projects to be done, some hurdles to clear, and some due dates. Here's how you might do this: First, break down the requirements to reach the promotion goal into small, reachable steps. Second, allow enough time to accomplish each of these, plus a little extra time for contingencies and uncontrollable delays.

Third, don't set up phony hurdles just to make your tiger jump through hoops. This is not a game. It may be tempting, but this will hurt you eventually. Set steps and dates reflecting real needs and real purposes that will accomplish things that are important for you, for your tiger, and for your company. Fourth, recheck actual performance and actual completion dates against steps assigned and dates due. This should be done almost continuously. It lets you keep your eye on the progress as it is accomplished bit by bit and make minor midcourse corrections. Due dates that are constantly missed tell you something. Dates constantly met or bettered tell you something else.

Royal Crown Supervisor Plans Well-Earned Promotion

An executive at a major Royal Crown Cola bottler said to his supervisor, "I have been on this job for two years, and you say I'm doing well. We have talked about promoting me to your assistant, and I'm really anxious to get this assignment. When will I be promoted?" (Ah, the perennial question, spoken or unspoken, but on the minds of millions! And not always easy to answer.) In this case, the supervisor agreed that the time was getting appropriate. He then listed six challenging key projects that he felt should definitely be done before he could grant the promotion.

Together they made a bar graph, listing the six projects down the side of the page with columns off to the right representing months. The first project was the toughest and would take the longest. A horizontal bar was drawn off to the right crossing the month columns, all the way over to the tenth-month line. The next item was another long project requiring a lot of lead time. That bar went right across the month columns, stopping at the ninth month. And so it went, with each succeeding project taking a little less time. The last, or sixth, project only went over to the fourth-month line. Each bar was made with a different colored felt pen. When completed, the graph looked impressive, exciting, doable, and important.

Then the supervisor checked each month with the achiever and reviewed the progress. Soon goals began to be reached, usually ahead of time. When they were all accomplished, the promotion was granted to an achiever who felt highly self-satisfied—and by a supervisor who could point to dramatic progress and a well-earned promotion that no one could very easily contest.

TRAIN YOUR TIGER INTO IT

You may have a situation where your achiever definitely has the potential. Together you have laid out some reasonable targets and even some steps to reach them. But you both realize that he or she is not quite ready. You recognize that some added training is needed. This has several advantages. For one thing, training is usually a scheduled activity with a known time frame, so you have at least part of a firm program. Also, you are channeling energies and inquiries away from you and toward constructive steps that will do some good. Here's how it might work:

1. If you elect to program some additional semiformal training, be careful in your selection. Pick courses that are really appropriate and constructive in building knowledge, skills, or a mind set that moves toward your achiever's goal. Many courses sound just great and may be fine for the specific grade for which they are given but deliver little useful or appropriate material that will help a person move up or be promoted to higher duties.

2. Be sure of real follow-through. This starts with a good, positive attitude on the part of the achiever-attendee. A course he or she is "ordered" to attend could have far less impact than one he or she is "allowed" to attend as a privilege, advantage, or opportunity to build toward the goal. Perhaps he or she should be permitted to "apply" and win permission or acceptance to attend the training. Follow-through also means getting the most out of the training. This might include taking careful notes and using the new-found information in his or her job, duties, and career. Both you and your achiever should double-check some months later to see if the course actually "took"—that is, made an impression and provided information that was applied to the job and to moving closer to the promotion goal.

3. Use on-the-job training if there is anything remotely resembling some kind of orderly learning procedure, moving from one point to another. This need not be elaborate. About all you really require is a list of subjects plus things to accomplish with each subject, due dates for each, and a method to check and see that all this has happened. On-the-job training might include some extra daily duties that both help you and help your achiever to prepare for or break in to the next job up.

4. Don't expect too much from training in terms of preparation for promotion. Formal plus on-the-job training is probably the best combination. But even this double blast rarely does the whole job. The key advantage to it is that it almost always helps at least somewhat, and thus is a legitimate element in the promotion development program.

CLEAR THE TRACKS UP AHEAD

Try to remove obstacles that are or might be out there to block the promotion. These could be requirements as to education, other qualifications, years with the company, or time on the job. Other roadblocks may be less formal or structured—for instance, "Nobody from the sales department is ever promoted to assistant plant manager. There's no special reason for it, but that's not how we operate around here. It simply isn't done!" Or, "Nobody gets any kind of management promotion in this division unless old Mr. X likes him or her. It's that simple. He likes you, you're in. He doesn't, you're out!"

Things like this can take years to resolve, which helps explain why people are rarely promoted "on demand" or nearly as fast as they usually would like. There is also the possibility that there are other well-qualified candidates who have been waiting many months, perhaps years, for an opening—an opportunity to roar down the runway and fly off into the wild blue. Here's how you can help clear the obstacles from that runway:

1. Make sure you really do have some obstacles. People may talk about so-called problems, but with a little careful research, you might find these are mainly imaginary.

2. Measure those problems that you really do have in terms of their difficulty. Some may be simple, others tough, a few impossible. Don't beat your head against a brick wall. Switch problems or people or goals. Solve what you can and leave the rest, but be sure you take the time to decide which is which.

3. Discuss these roadblocks with your achiever. This has lots of advantages for you. It shows him or her that you are working on the problem. This will be appreciated. Someone said that "The leader who is respected most is the one who helps people reach their goals, and they know it." By discussion, it also shows him or her that you are not the one who is holding back the promotion, but other people or other circumstances.

4. Enlist your achiever's aid in removing the roadblocks. After all, the tiger is the one who mainly wants the promotion and stands to gain, so he or she is the one who should put in the most effort to solve problems and make progress. If approval from Mr. X must be won, tell your achiever this and put the monkey on his or her back to get that little project accomplished. It's your tiger's promotion, not yours.

5. Let your achiever know that you view this as a team effort, and that you will do your part to remove obstacles. You'll help sell Mr. X. You plan to send him occasional examples of the achiever's best work or arrange to have others praise him or her to Mr. X. This is mighty fine service in anyone's book—service that only you can perform, and your achiever will know it. This will increase your control and motivation plus gain well-earned respect from him or

her. How can you not appreciate a boss who is making an outstanding effort to get you promoted?

6. Encourage other supervisors to welcome the promotion of your achiever. One of the best ways to do this is simply to show that such a development would be of benefit to them. This action builds a support base for your achiever and for the promotion recommendation you will be making.

Tiger Helps Clear the Track at Eskimo Pie

A major executive for an Eskimo Pie dairy, speaking at a recent luncheon in Chicago, said, "Promotion of our better people is one of the most important things we do. I'll confess it: We are selfish. We promote them because it's good for us. We make more profits. To be honest, the lunch we are all enjoying right now was paid for by increased profits from a new project launched last year by a high producer. We had trained him with some additional college courses and extra on-the-job duties. Then we cleared the track for him. One of the really tough problems was to convince another guy who also wanted a promotion that our achiever should go up first. Our tiger did the job by showing him that this program would help them both, and it did."

DON'T OVERLOAD

Don't dump the whole load of hay on your tiger at once. The promotion program obviously takes some doing, as we have seen from the preceding sections. You and your achiever are trying to arrange for progress, but at the same time, you must not only keep the present job functioning but also continue producing at an above-average level. A dud or a major error at this point can badly damage your promotion effort.

Here's how to run the promotion program smoothly: First, stick with your game plan and schedule. Don't accelerate or slow down too much. Promotion efforts have a bad history of either dying on the vine or of getting ahead of themselves, taking on a sort of life of their own, growing out of hand and interfering with regular duties. Second, take advantage of new opportunities to move more rapidly. This is not to say you should be overly pushy, but if a break appears—such as a new project, department, or opening—you might be wise to grab it.

Third, stay flexible not only regarding changing conditions like new opportunities but also regarding unexpected goals and methods. As you move along, you and your achiever may discover that the job objective has changed. It may be far less favorable, and a new goal may be indicated. The same goes for methods. A new training course may suddenly become available. Consider it, but don't get sidetracked. Use it only if it helps your achiever move toward the target.

BUILD INTO THE NEW JOB

Adding to your achiever's present assignments has several advantages. It increases the chances of success, which is important for you both. A major failure at this point would be very harmful to your achiever's career. Also, your reputation is very much at stake. Hitting the target will help you; a failure will hurt. Further, success is important to the well-being of your organization. Here's how to do it:

1. Ease into the new position, even before your achiever has captured the job. This can be done simply by assigning a few of the smaller duties and getting him or her familiar with handling them successfully.

2. Avoid moving too quickly into a full load. Overloading jams the mechanism, and your tiger will choke.

3. Have an orderly list of projects to add as circumstances permit. Be guided by his or her ability to absorb all this plus advice from others, such as your own supervisor.

4. Arrange the program so that when the promotion comes through, he or she is already doing many of the duties. This minimizes the shock to both the achiever and the organization. It smooths the transition.

5. The actual promotion recommendation should be made when you think the achiever is ready. This should be cleared with your supervisor and an effective date set. Then the achiever should be notified and congratulated. Be sure it is clear to your tiger that this occurred because of his or her own good performance plus your help and assistance. You might want to remind your newly promoted person that both your reputations now depend a lot on how well he or she handles the new duties, "so don't let either of us down."

6. Co-workers and the entire organization should be notified. People want and need to know where everyone stands. Also, it helps for people to recognize that a promotion occurred from within. That means each member of the group may also have a chance to move up.

STAY FLEXIBLE

Leave room for creativity and initiative. The great advantages here are that you will benefit from the achiever's full abilities. He or she becomes stimulated, fulfilled, and hence motivated to do more and better work—and to enjoy doing it. This further enhances your reputation and reflects well on your original decision to help with the promotion. That could come in handy for you next time you have a similar recommendation to make. Your own status has been strengthened.

How do you open the door for his or her initiative? First, even before the promotion, while your achiever was performing some of the smaller new duties, he or she probably had thoughts, ideas, and even outspoken suggestions. You wisely told him or her to keep those in mind "for later." Now is the time to bring these out and discuss them further. Second, encourage small tests—sort of a toe-in-the-water approach—on new methods. Try them on a small scale for a short time and check results. Third, be slow to shut off the creative juices or "initiative stream," even if results are not ideal at first. The flow may be hard to restart. Use what you can. Postpone the rest. Let success happen and tigers roar. The tiger's momentum helps build his or her success and yours.

Diet-Rite Phases in a Top Producer

A Diet-Rite Cola bottler executive said at a business meeting in Denver last August, "We needed an assistant advertising manager. Our merchandising coordinator had been taking evening courses in advertising at the university and showed outstanding ability and enthusiasm in the field. We moved him into the duties slowly, on a scheduled basis. At first, he didn't even realize what we were doing, but then we discussed it with him. He was delighted. Together we made a list of projects he should master, such as buying advertising broadcast time and print space. He rapidly learned this and even had some new ideas for improving our system. When we made the promotion, the transition was smooth, accepted by all, and has proved to be one of the smartest moves we ever made!"

FINE-TUNE THE NEW JOB

Adjust the new position a little to fit the freshly promoted achiever. The advantage here is that again you benefit from the full spectrum of skills that your colleague possesses. Each person brings a "package"—a collection of strengths plus some weaknesses. Sometimes the person has a whole range of special talents, such as speaking, writing, and graphics that are above and beyond those needed for the job. Naturally, both you and the achiever want to avail yourselves of these abilities and enjoy their use.

Here's how you might do it: First, identify and employ any special skills the newly promoted achiever brings. This means you may actually want to change the job description a bit. To a certain extent, "The person makes the job." We have all seen people in the fields of education, government, medicine, the fine arts, and management make major revisions to their careers because of their unusual abilities—and this benefits everyone.

Second, avoid his or her weaknesses. And again, a small modification in the duties and job description may be a wise step. This further helps you gain your objective of a successful promotion. Third, be on the alert to build an entirely new project, service, department, or business based on any new abilities delivered by your freshly promoted employee.

TEN COMMANDMENTS FOR EFFECTIVELY PROMOTING A HIGH ACHIEVER

1. Take a good look at both your achiever and others.
2. Set a reasonable promotion goal.
3. Plan a promotion program and manage it by your objective.
4. Make a realistic time schedule.
5. Train your achiever into the new job.
6. Clear the track ahead.
7. Don't dump the whole load of hay on your tiger at once.
8. Add to the present assignment, phasing him or her into the new job.
9. Leave some room for creativity and initiative.
10. Adjust the new job a little to fit the new skills.

Your OBI (one best idea) for effectively promoting a high achiever is to look carefully; establish a good goal, program, schedule, and training; and ease smoothly into the new assignment, so all skills will be fully and properly employed.

CHAPTER 12
How to Hold That Tiger

So now you have found your tiger. You invested a lot of time and effort landing him or her. You recruited, screened, sold, oriented, trained, supervised, motivated, and promoted him or her. Congratulations! That is a major project in anyone's book.

Yet after all your work and expense, you can suddenly lose your achiever's high productivity, just when the whole thing was about to pay off beautifully for everyone. How do you prevent such a revolting development? How do you hold that tiger? The objective of this chapter is to show you a few ways you can avoid this problem, retain your tiger, and enjoy the benefits of his or her high contribution to your program.

KNOW WHAT'S GOING ON

It is a serious mistake to go through all that training, processing, and promoting—and then just flat out forget about this fine person you have serving you. True, he or she does not and should not need a lot of spoon-feeding or frequent instruction. But it will pay off for you in greater staff stability and tiger retention if you have a good, steady, continuous insight into what's happening with your high achiever. Know something of his or her views and how your tiger relates with you and others. This changes fairly often and thus needs frequent review. Here's how you can avoid taking your tiger for granted:

1. Keep tabs on your achiever's general frame of mind. Especially watch personal likes, dislikes, exciters, motivators, and particularly any new and developing interests, skills, and talents.

2. Do not expect miracles of job dedication and performance. Many tigers pace around, roam about, and are not famous for loyalty. They often have all sorts of good and bad but flattering job offers from other firms—especially from competitors. In this respect tigers are a little bit like beautiful people who are highly attractive to the opposite sex. They are likely to get a number of proposals, both proper and improper. These are not necessarily acted upon, but neither do they generate a whole lot of dedication to the status quo.

3. Since tigers do have what is often a fierce dedication to their own projects and problems to solve and a dogged determination to achieve, you would be wise to take advantage of this feeling. Keep projects coming and you'll keep most tigers satisfied. Show appreciation and you'll build contentment that will overcome all sorts of outside temptations. As we noted earlier, the applause of even a single individual is often highly motivating.

AVOID EXCESSIVE FRUSTRATION

Frustration is probably one of the main reasons that high achievers leave. In this case, it simply means the almost total denial of action and progress—situations, orders, or conditions that prevent the achiever from being what he or she is: an achiever. Here are six typical causes of frustration that should be avoided:

1. Boredom makes the achiever become discontented. Here is a racehorse with no race to run. He or she is likely to trot off.

2. "Head bumping." In this case, your tiger is due to move up, but his or her way is totally blocked. A complete turnoff turns into a completely frustrated tiger—a tiger who starts looking elsewhere.

3. "Chicken" rules. This is the atmosphere in which nearly every action or proposal is met with a reason why it can't be done. Some could be sensible, sound, and valid, but most are petty and nit-picking ("We don't like red widgets around here, because red clashes with our orange logo"). This is guaranteed to discourage any achiever.

4. Impossible jobs. Sometimes high achievers are given jobs that nobody else has been able to accomplish. There's nothing much wrong with that. In fact, that's partly why your tiger is there. But

sometimes these are also jobs that no one, however talented, could reasonably do under today's prevailing circumstances. In short, impossible jobs. Too much is asked and expected. The high achiever may realize this right from the outset and be partly amused and partly discouraged. Or he or she may find it out later and be angered. Either way, your tiger may soon be lost to the company.

5. Broken promises. Sometimes a top manager agrees to provide certain resources such as time, budget, staff, or equipment and then, perhaps through no fault of his or her own, is unable to deliver. This can be highly discouraging to achiever and manager alike.

6. Rejection, criticism, or humiliation are elements that, for some reason, do not seem to motivate achievers very much. They tend instead to lose their enthusiasm and look to greener pastures.

Converting these six items to positive suggestions, you would be wise to keep your achiever busy, with opportunities to actually perform and complete his or her assignments, to move up, with promises reasonably well kept, accompanied by acknowledgment, respect, and appreciation for jobs well done. These simple things will go a long way toward retaining your high achiever.

RECRUIT TOP CO-WORKERS

Use quality co-workers to help you hold that tiger. Here we are talking about the well-known saying regarding birds of a feather. Talented people tend to seek out and be attracted to others like themselves. If this is true, then you will not be surprised to find that one tiger will tend to attract and hold another. One of the great advantages here is that the pattern is likely to snowball. One tiger attracts a second, together they attract a third, and so on.

A second advantage is that, with each new candidate, the intensity of the holding power is multiplied. And this does not just influence the last member to join, but all members. Even the first tiger is in part more firmly held because of the latest arrival. Your high achievers begin to look on themselves as sort of a "team of tigers." Another advantage is that you have to make less and less of a personal effort to keep the pot boiling. It becomes a self-perpetuating program.

Here's how you might get the snowball rolling. First, find your initial tiger. This gives you one more reason for going to all that trouble to recruit, screen, sell, orient, train, supervise, motivate, and promote that original high achiever. He or she will now attract others.

Second, you can use either a subordinate, colleague, or supervisor to the achiever to fill the role of the holding tiger. For example, a high-producing leader will often exert a strong stabilizing and retaining influence on similar people below him or her on the ladder of authority. Third, let the lead tiger know you encourage him or her to help bring in new high performers and hold others you may have. Be sure those others recognize the lead achiever.

U.S. Government Agency Starts the Ball Rolling

A major branch of a federal government agency was doing well in serving its community and had received favorable recognition in the local press and radio. But the director wanted to do better. He himself was well recognized as a high achiever, and he set out to find others. He had a key opening, and a major effort was launched to fill it. He was very particular about the replacement and, after many weeks of effort, finally found two good candidates. One took herself out of the running, and the director zeroed in on the remaining applicant. A strong selling program was used.

In the end, the high achiever was hired. He not only promptly won a whole series of awards, but he helped to attract several additional top people who also won honors. They in turn launched others in programs—others who then brought in even more recognition. The pattern had snowballed, and it is still going strong as of this writing.

ENCOURAGE SELF-TRAINING

Self-training has several advantages that help bond the achiever closer to you and to your unit. For one thing, he or she appreciates help, a leg up, and the opportunities that may or may not be offered by other organizations. Second, your tiger is not only appreciated by his or her associates for being selected to receive more education but also feels himself or herself growing in professional expertise. And we all tend to develop some emotional bonds wherever we have grown. Finally, further training gives him or her added recognition and respect from colleagues, supervisors, and subordinates. We usually don't like to leave a place where we are well regarded by people.

Here's how you can encourage continued self-training efforts. First, make programs of company-sponsored training available to the high achiever, who will usually enjoy seeing what might be had if he or she is selected. Second, pick 'em where possible, but only where it will really help the achiever's career and your goals. Be sure he or she sees the training as a privilege, an honor, and an opportunity—not as an obligation, a penalty, or an implication that he or she lacks skills. Third, encourage your tiger to pass along to others a brief, summarized version of the material. This establishes him or her even more firmly as a recognized authority. It also cements the tiger closer to the group, which is your goal at this point.

USE CHALLENGE AND RESPONSE

Famous historian Arnold Toynbee developed a major and generally accepted theory that human civilization grew largely because of the problems people faced and the way they solved them—with humanity doing a bit better with each passing century.

High achievers are particularly turned on by and tied to challenges. Most hate to walk away from a puzzle, because almost by definition, they are problem solvers. They want to face it down and find a solution. Surprising as this may sound, many an achiever was about to leave a group but then told those trying to recruit him or her, "I'm sorry, but I just can't leave at this particular time. I'm up to my neck in an important and exciting project that I simply must stick with and solve!" The project sometimes took months that ripened into years. Personal projects can sometimes outvote personal progress.

Here's how to see that this happens with your tiger: First,

assign problems. You won't get an achiever's excitement and enthusiasm unless you give him or her something to chew on. But don't just hand out busywork or challenges purely as a device to hold him or her. That's far too transparent. The problem should first and foremost be an important one that you and your unit truly need solved. As a strong secondary benefit, it will also tie your tiger more firmly to your group. Second, get his or her input and opinions. This not only gains you better quality results but brings your achiever still closer to your problems and your group and generates a deeper commitment to them. Third, get input from others. This further increases quality of results and also ties the achiever to the team. He or she feels even more a part of the organization.

FULLY UTILIZE YOUR TIGER'S SKILLS

Few things discourage an achiever quite so much as to have his or her ability unemployed or underused. This almost says that his or her potential is neither appreciated nor wanted or—what can be the unkindest cut of all—not even recognized as existing. But to most achievers, full utilization of their skills is warming and highly satisfying. They feel "at home"—a place they really do not *want* to leave. Here's how you can help your tiger feel that way:

1. Recognize and use his or her strengths and abilities. We mentioned earlier the wisdom of adjusting the job somewhat to fit the person. Here is another reason for doing just that: It helps you make your achievers feel they are where they want to be. And helps you hold that tiger.

2. Expand his or her duties, responsibilities, and authority. You might seriously consider shifting to your achiever some tasks now handled by others and even some of your own. As your tiger feels his or her status, importance, and involvement growing, he or she also feels more deeply committed and is less likely to leave.

3. Strengthen your achiever's position with management endorsement and appropriate resources. However, you will be wise to resist any temptation to make a new person of him or her or to cast your achiever in a different mold. He or she may be flexible, versatile, and adaptable, but tigers rarely change their stripes much.

Merck High Achiever Displays a Spectrum of Skills

A Merck Pharmaceuticals Company executive, speaking at a dinner meeting in Philadelphia, said, "In my opinion, the best way to get good people to stay put is to use not one but several appeals. I recall one department chief who had a prized achiever as a supervisory clerk in the computer group. She got fairly frequent offers of better jobs and, for a while, was greatly tempted. However, the department head made sure that this woman was permitted to attend available training courses. (Amazingly, she even walked out of one she felt was unsuited to her needs!) She was given many tough and challenging assignments, which she executed with outstanding quality and speed.

"Her supervisor also discovered she had excellent public speaking talents. Did he tell her to stick to her computers? No, quite the contrary! He used this skill to have her help train new operators and give public relations talks about the mysteries of computers, which she really enjoyed doing. The result has been a long-term employee. And believe it or not, in addition, she has ended up attracting, recruiting, and training a whole bunch of very fine, above-average people."

ENCOURAGE INITIATIVE AND CREATIVITY

Most people have all sorts of hidden talents, and high achievers are often especially rich in these assets. Recognizing and accepting such strengths further bonds the high producer to your group. Here's how you can tap the talents of your tiger:

1. Let him or her unfold, blossom, and expand. Many a clerk shows unexpected talents in a supervisory position, just as new justices on the Supreme Court often show fresh insights that were never expected. You can help this along by creating a nonthreatening environment.

2. Welcome creative new ideas. Let your achiever know this. Give each concept at least the dignity of a fair hearing and an objective evaluation.

3. If you get some creative ideas that are not useful, be careful

not to squash them with too much vigor, or you'll shut off the flow. (The very next concept might be a once-in-ten-years breakthrough.) Just postpone such brainstorms or modify the bad ones and use the better ones as circumstances permit.

4. Special creative talents may open new opportunities for you. Artistic abilities may be used in illustrating charts and graphs or making special visual presentations. Writing ability might be used for new and different letters, reports, speeches, or publicity press releases. All this tends to make the achiever feel far more fulfilled and attached to you and your group—willingly making an important contribution to your progress.

DELIVER ON YOUR PROMISES

Early on, during recruiting, selling, orientation, and training, you probably pointed out possible new projects, directions, and opportunities. That's fine—nothing wrong in doing this. But "possibilities" have a funny habit of being interpreted as "promises." And unkept promises have a nasty habit of being transformed into a feeling of betrayal. This in turn leads to the termination of a previously good personal and professional relationship.

On the other hand, keeping your word has many advantages, the first and most obvious being that the project goes forward. The less obvious benefit is the great feeling of trust and confidence and the bond of sharing that are established. Here is a powerful feeling and a mutual regard that can last a lifetime. Here's how you might generate this:

1. Be very careful about promises. As you point out prospects, possibilities, and opportunities, label these precisely as such. You are always wise to reinforce the point and protect yourself as well as your tiger by saying (perhaps with a smile), "We must remember, that's only a possibility, *not* a promise."

2. When you do make a promise, make it only when the odds are very high that you can deliver. The best situation is where you already have it quietly locked up, definite and firm. For example, when your tiger seeks a major expenditure, and you have already

secured and confirmed budget approval well in advance, you are pretty safe in making a promise regarding a part of that budget.

3. On the rare occasion when things take an "iffy" or uncertain turn—such as unexpected budget cuts—make every reasonable effort to deliver the goods, even if this means some horse-trading or substituting one program in place of another.

4. If for some reason circumstances beyond your control force you to renege on a promise, clearly explain this to your achiever. Be sure he or she knows and feels that you have a genuine and shared emotional disappointment. Also be sure he or she realizes that this was totally out of your hands, and that you went far out of your way to correct the matter and deliver as promised. This can snatch victory from the jaws of defeat by turning a nasty reversal into respect and bond building that help hold that tiger. If he or she is truly wise, your tiger will know that this same thing can happen to anyone, anywhere. Often your manner of handling the adversity has a greater impact than the problem itself.

GIVE RECOGNITION

Acknowledge and recognize but do not overpraise. High achievers know they are high achievers. They do not need recognition to tell them that. But they do need recognition for several other reasons. One is to reconfirm their own faith and respect—not in themselves but in their supervisors. If their boss does not give them recognition, they tend to feel that he or she is either so stupid as to be unable to see their ability or so unfeeling or jealous as to be unwilling to recognize it.

Other reasons high achievers like recognition are very practical ones: If they are held in high regard, then they have more influence with their own peer group and subordinates. They also probably feel fairly secure and hence might look for a long-term association.

And then there is just plain old-fashioned ego. Nearly everyone who does a good job likes to be told about it. So you tend to gain several advantages by acknowledging the achievers' high performance. You gain respect in their eyes, you reassure them of their prestige and permanence, and you make them feel good. Here's how you might accomplish all these good things that help to hold that tiger:

1. When you see a project especially well done, say so. Tell your high achiever what you see and why you like it. You will probably find that this has a behavior-reinforcing effect. He or she is likely to do it again—perhaps better and more often.

2. Don't overdo it. Tigers tend to choke on baloney. You can also hurt your achiever's position with his or her colleagues, who can get a little sick of too much adoration. Just state the facts and the reasons you feel the work is outstanding and how this will help everyone. Period. Don't hang fancy labels on him or her. Your tiger knows it is only partly true and doesn't want to embarrass you by denying it or embarrass himself or herself by accepting it.

3. Try for balanced recognition, neither faint and lukewarm approval nor thick and sickening flattery. Use your own judgment and let the praise fit the performance, person, and circumstances.

4. Think about expressing your acknowledgment with something more tangible than words. This might be some kind of financial award such as a bonus, pay increase, or stock option. Psychological motivators take the place of some money, but not all. An unexpected, unrequested income increase is a mighty sincere and powerful bit of recognition. It has also been known to hold a few tigers.

Carnation Exec Favors Moderate but Consistent Recognition

An executive from a Carnation Milk division gave an informal talk last year to a lunch group in Boston, where he said, "Yes, high achievers are certainly a challenge. You go to a lot of trouble finding them and bringing them on board. Then you can lose them to someone making a better offer if you are not careful. But I think that the greatest way to keep your best people is not necessarily financial. A friend of mine owns a medium-sized business that will soon be a big firm. It got that way because he gets—and more important, he *keeps*—good people. He not only encourages his production and sales people to use their initiative, he expects it. Frankly, it's a condition of employment. But he also sees that every contribution receives some sort of moderate recognition. He says minor rewards motivate just about as effectively as major ones."

MAXIMIZE AUTHORITY AND RESPONSIBILITY

Actually increasing the authority and responsibility held by your high achiever, or at least establishing the definite prospect of doing so, can be one of your most efficient and effective ways to hold onto your best people. This approach not only brings your producer closer to your team but often results in even higher productivity from your high achiever. Here's how you might use the prestige, promise, and promotion procedure:

1. Prestige is increased for the high producer when you expand his or her authority and responsibility. In this case, you might put your tiger in charge of several projects involving a number of people.

2. Promise further job improvements, such as a better office, increased staff, new equipment, favorable assignments, or perhaps special duty assisting you or one of the other managers. Most of all, hold out the specific possibility of a promotion, if this is truly realistic. You might even outline a career ladder program that could move him or her up several steps with a few years' work at each point. This can and does hold many outstanding people to their jobs. The realistic hope of future improvement is the engine that will drive a million achievers to work this week.

3. An actual promotion can and frequently does develop very strong emotional and financial bonds between a high producer and his or her organization. Your tiger feels important, wanted, needed, and an essential part of the organization. New horizons beckon, and new frontiers lie ahead to be conquered. You have sparked a fresh new spirit of enthusiasm. You have found your high achiever—recruited, screened, sold, oriented, trained, supervised, motivated, and promoted him or her. Now you will hold that tiger—and enjoy the productivity and achievement he or she will bring you, which can enrich your own personal career for many years to come.

TEN COMMANDMENTS FOR HOLDING YOUR HIGH ACHIEVER

1. Know what's going down with your tiger. Stay close and stay informed.
2. Avoid excessive frustration.
3. Use quality workers to stimulate your achiever.
4. Encourage self-training and self-improvement.
5. Apply challenge and response—problems and solutions.
6. Really use your achiever's skills and interests.
7. Encourage and expect creativity and initiative.
8. Deliver on promised opportunities whenever possible.
9. Acknowledge and recognize but do not overpraise.
10. Maximize your achiever's authority where practical.

Your OBI (one best idea) for holding a high achiever is to make your organization attractive to him or her and build bonds between you through mutual understanding, quality associates, few frustrations, ongoing training, intriguing challenges, opportunities to use creativity, kept promises, deserved awards, and expanded authority.

PART TWO
You as a High Achiever

Let's talk about you.

You have been reading this book about above-average people—how to find them and employ them to both your advantage and theirs. I think that if you are interested in high achievers, the chances are that you are almost certainly a high achiever yourself.

And you want to stay that way. You want to excel, to get others to perform, and get them to help you gain peak recognition, rewards, and job satisfaction. The rest of this book is aimed at accomplishing precisely those objectives. This is the flip side of the same coin, this time looking at you.

Here, then, is a career plan for you, an above-average person. First, we will outline a way you can get to know yourself through an "identity checkup." Then we can focus on career opportunities and personal goals. We will also look at how you can organize your staff and even your boss to help with your progress.

Let's start by taking a good close look at you.

CHAPTER 13
Do Your Own Identity Checkup

You are the most important person in your life. Naturally, others can become more important from time to time, but as you have grown up, received your training, moved along in your career, and met some defeats and victories, you are by definition the individual who has been center stage in your personal world.

And yet, do you know yourself? If so, how well? Most of us get a physical and dental checkup every year or so. But have you had an "identity checkup"? This year? Ever? Have you really stepped back for a few moments from your daily action, reaction, and interaction with dozens of people and the hundreds of problems you have to simply look at yourself introspectively? It's worth doing, and, done properly, it can be rather enjoyable.

The most important value of such an analysis is simply this: You reinforce yourself by gaining a good insight into your abilities and lack of abilities, your strengths and weaknesses. You will have taken careful inventory of your tools, supplies, and weapons—the resources that you have at hand and can call upon. Just as any athletic or military team must thoroughly know its strengths if it hopes to use them properly, so should you.

Leaders, fighters, or "resource users" occasionally see their tools and talents change, either moderately or drastically. They therefore check their resources regularly, and so should you. Note the phrase "check regularly." You should do this every few years, because you are a different person at different stages of your life—a student, shop boy, breadwinner, husband, father, professional, perhaps also artist, teacher, writer, pianist, skier, traveler, pilot. Further, you are different things to different people—to your wife, kids, boss, dog, neighbors.

As you can see, the identity checkup is not at all an exercise in conceit. Instead, it is almost entirely a matter of seeing what's present and what's absent, what you have and don't have. The key is accuracy. That means you should look carefully at both the pros and cons, strengths and weaknesses, halos and warts. We all practice a bit of self-deception occasionally. It serves a purpose. But now is not the time to kid yourself. Honesty will pay off big at this point.

Don't be afraid to judge yourself. The more accurately you do it, the better. Be brutally frank. Jot down a few notes. Don't worry about what people will think of you. These are "for your eyes only." Later you should destroy these notes, perhaps keeping just a key sentence or two outlining only what will be positive, purposeful, and productive for you.

There are lots of ways to do an identity checkup. The system suggested here seems to be one of the most effective.

DECIDE WHO YOU ARE

Your primary goal for an identity checkup is to decide who you are. This isn't always easy. Young people often have an identity crisis: "Who am I? What is my role? Where do I fit in this big, complex world?" Many people never do figure out who they are. Most never even think to ask. The whole purpose for making this analysis and reaching a conclusion is mainly to increase your power by a simple expedient: using your strengths and avoiding your weaknesses. But you can't use or avoid them until you know what they are.

How will you know when you have reached your identity-checkup goal? When you can say: "After a really careful review of my background and training, my strengths and weaknesses, likes and dislikes, *this is what I am,* at least right now. This is what I can honestly tell people I am and support it." Or maybe you just want to tell yourself. But it will be a statement you feel comfortable about, one you feel is as true and accurate as you can make it—a statement you can live with.

As a practical aid, you would be wise to take a piece of paper and title it at the top: "My Identity Checkup: Objectives." Then simply pick a couple of the goals mentioned above, like: "To find my strengths and weaknesses—things to use and to avoid to increase my power. To discover what tools and weapons I have and don't have. To know what to tell people I am—and what to tell myself." You will be in a much stronger position to sensibly plan your next few years if you know yourself better in this way.

Start with Your Parents

Think about your parents, as best you know them—not only today but in terms of what you may know of their early life activities and behavior. Don't be critical or complimentary, just factual. Maybe start with their physical descriptions—big, small, short, tall, heavy, thin, healthy, sickly, agile, clumsy, athletic, inactive, good-looking, ugly, and so forth. You will find yourself among these traits or a mixture of them (or the traits of your grandparents). And like it or not, this is the face you show to the world. This is part of your identity.

Now expand on your parents a bit. What about their activities? Were they social or withdrawn? Doing mainly brain work, manual labor, or a mixture? Consider their cultural or athletic interests. What were their early strengths and weaknesses? Were they stable, unstable, honest, crooked, drunk, sober, good citizens or bad, leaders or nonleaders? What about skills at reading, writing, math, music, art, public speaking, athletics, socializing, and so forth? What about their reputations? What did people think of them? What did they call them? How did they classify or identify them? In short, just who were your parents? Can you boil the description down into a few sentences?

Why bother with all this? Simple. You are the product of your heredity and your environment, and *your parents are both*. They greatly influenced, even firmly determined, who you are, or at least who you started out to be and who you can become. The original gifts you inherited from them—such as your physical, mental, and personal stature—plus their initial training largely established your life's potential. You'll never need to do this particular exercise again, although you may want to review it every four or five years.

Look at Your Early Childhood

Your early childhood is vital. Judge your activities in this time period properly and you will greatly improve your identity checkup.

Try to recall your three earliest memories, especially in your preteens. What were you like as a little kid—physically, mentally, socially, emotionally? What were your three best accomplishments? What were your best school subjects? Which did you like most? Least? How about music, art, athletics, friends, gangs, leadership, personality, games, likes and dislikes, successes and failures?

Pay special attention to what you can accurately recall about your mental skills, attitudes, creativity, imagination, dependability, and personality as well as personal relations with your equals, younger friends, and your superiors or authority figures. In later years, these relationships translate roughly into your colleagues, subordinates, and boss. Make particular note of those characteristics that not only were outstanding at the time but, in retrospect, seem to hold true even today.

Remember, too, that your first years were your "formative years." Your early childhood was by far the most influential period of your life in terms of shaping your future. As the twig is bent, so the tree is inclined. And as a twig, you got plenty of bending, whether you felt and remember it or not. It is here that your memory is very important. Let one experience remind you of others. Each episode has ten times as much influence during the preteen period as that same episode would have during young adulthood. By then, the die is cast. The melt has set in the mold. But with a preteenager, the mold is still forming, and every little wiggle, bump, dent, or scratch influences your entire life. (No wonder we are urged to use great care in raising our tiny kids!)

Look for your weaknesses, fears, and failures as well as for your strengths, successes, and victories. Bear in mind that you are totally blameless for your early errors. After all, at that time you were completely controlled by your home, school, parents, friends, and teachers. You could hardly classify yourself as very much of a free spirit, with an independent will and a capacity for self-determination. Your mistakes were caused more by others than by you—more so at this point than at any other time in your life. And they are important to recognize, because they are likely to show up again later on. Like right now.

Circle the half dozen or so main words or phrases that seem to best describe you as a preteenager. Again, boil these down to a sentence or so.

Consider Your Young Adulthood

Now review your teens and college years—your young adulthood. These are less important than your earlier years in one sense: Surprising as it may seem, this period is not as great or as magnified an influence on your potential as your childhood was.

But your teen years are a much greater indicator of a totally different factor—the way you were beginning to use and apply, unfold, develop, and enlarge your native, given early skills and traits.

In your younger years, your heredity and environment gave you your package of strengths and weaknesses. Your teen years begin to show you what you can and will do with that package. You are no longer a totally controlled little kid. You are now becoming a person in your own right, a free and partially independent spirit. Your basic personality developed earlier, but it is now being freely and clearly expressed as never before.

Take a good look at your school courses—what you liked and disliked, did well in or failed. How did you approach your assignments? How good was your work in terms of quality, quantity, and timeliness? How were your tests and grades? All these translate into handling assignments in the business world.

Note even more carefully the teachers you liked and disliked. How did you handle your relations with your instructors and parents? How about with your fellow students? The good and poor ones? The ordinary, average ones? How did you interact with friends outside your class who were older or younger? Your same age? Again, these translate somewhat into your bosses, equals, and subordinates. Not entirely, of course, but in a general sense. A person who always got along well with one or all of these groups in the teen years will probably do so for his or her entire life.

Now also look at how you judged these people. What did you look for, expect, or admire in authorities, associates, and younger people? This is a reflection of the values that you were establishing, born of earlier years, unfolding in your teen years, and staying with you now and always. These will change very little until you depart this world.

Naturally, you should list your basic educational training, with particular emphasis on any advanced, professional, or technical skills. These obviously identify and label you. You became a musician, mathematician, writer, painter, scientist, teacher, preacher, business manager, biologist, or sociologist.

Another important indicator of your teen and college age identity is what you did voluntarily with your spare time—your after-school time, your social life, cultural pursuits of music and art and science, athletics and games, team activities, politics, volunteer and charitable work, house chores.

Again, circle half a dozen or so key or most representative characteristics. But now you are really focusing very much more closely on skills or traits that you have today—things that people see in you right now—rather than characteristics that simply represent potential.

Check Hobbies and Early Jobs

In the realm of your hobbies and early jobs, we are now seeing proof positive of traits that developed in your teen years. Not a whole lot of translating is needed anymore to apply these patterns to your present abilities and personality traits. If, for example, your hobbies and early jobs were strongly oriented toward working well with people, that clearly is one kind of strength. If the pattern was one of working alone, that is another. The pattern could show either trait or both, giving us a mixed conclusion on identity. Some people truly are capable of working well both with people and in solitude.

An important clue regarding these early activities would be, Which did you *like* best and *do* best? These will usually be the same. We tend to enjoy most the things we do with greatest skill and vice versa.

Look at other abilities beyond the social ones—abilities such as math, communication, physical skills, work habits, attitudes, team spirit, and the roles of supporter, protector, or provider.

How about the first job? What did you do best and like most? Least? How did you relate to your boss, equals, and subordinates? What about your next job and the next? These should describe both your specific field of growing expertise (such as accounting, sales, social work, law, science) as well as the basic industrial classi- fication to which you belong (such as food, chemicals, cloth- ing, shelter, recreation, transportation, inspiration, politics, welfare, finance, energy, military, government, communications, manufac- turing, wholesaling, retailing, education, the arts, music, theater, insurance, real estate, medicine, or other services).

Notice a pattern? You should. No one is totally helter-skelter or unstructured. We all tend to be creatures of habit—using and displaying our skills and avoiding our weaknesses. Some of these patterns will have appeared in your parents, as well as during your early years and teen years. They should be fairly clear in your own first few jobs.

By now, you should have built up a pretty good descriptive picture of yourself. You know where you came from, what you did in your early childhood, teen years, and first few jobs.

Recent Victories

Now list what you've been doing best just recently. This should be a culmination of your early training plus your advanced training and experiences. Chances are that you had an image of yourself that you projected, or tried to project, to an employer. That employer accepted or partly accepted that image or identity and gave you a job assignment based on it. From there, you have prob- ably been given other duties. Some you did well; others bombed. But you know what you have done well and liked to do recently, and that tends to identify you in your immediate circumstances—right here and now.

Caution: What you are doing with your life right now is only one measure or description of your identity. It might be a good description. It might not. You and your employer may have distilled your training, experiences, and skills—and found the perfect assign- ment for you. Maybe. But few people are employed in a career that uses all their strengths or even most of them. Some people, trusting in luck and circumstances, have wandered by guess or by gosh into areas that hardly use any of their real skills. You may be clearly identified as a person qualified to perform a certain function in a certain industry, when in reality you are even better qualified for another function in another industry.

Don't worry. That doesn't make you a misfit or even misidentified. You may be very good at what you're doing and like it just fine. You may, in time, become far more qualified in your present position than in your other area of strength. Further, you may slide into another slot and be retrained and redeveloped. You could even discover new talents you didn't know you had—ones that, in early life, never gave you the slightest clue to their existence. (Some accountants who never led a team, played a note, lifted a brush, or penned a line become great leaders, musicians, painters, or writers.)

In fact, consultants say that we are likely to be reprogrammed into new careers at least three times during our lifetimes and that young people just entering the business world will experience even more major changes.

And so we see that your current professional label is one more important piece of evidence for your identity checkup. This is probably not your ultimate identity, but it may be an important indicator of it.

WHO DO PEOPLE *SAY* YOU ARE?

This one can be fun—especially if you are very honest. An easy way to cover who people say you are really fast is to take a page and divide it into three vertical columns, the first being rather narrow. In that one, list the five or ten most important people in your life, such as your spouse, your boss, your kids, your closest relatives, and your business associates. Include your best friends and worst enemies. Both groups know a lot about you—or think they do. Now at the top of the middle column write "Pros" and at the top of the right column, "Cons." In the pros column, just to the right of each name, enter the one or two key good things each person would say about you, assuming he or she were assured of total confidentiality.

DO YOUR OWN IDENTITY CHECKUP

In the cons column, list the negative things they would say. Come on, now, be brutally frank. You know pretty well what they think of you. They may be discreet, but they aren't professional actors. They can't help letting you know their opinion of you, either by direct statement, innuendo, or body language. And while you may not be a mind reader, you know darn well who likes you and who doesn't and how much. And maybe you know *why*, too. Don't hide anything. This is one place where the truth—even the ugly, awful truth—will help, not hurt you. After all, they will never see these quotes. (Just be sure they don't. That actually *could* hurt you!)

Naturally, some people will far overrate you on some things and underrate you on others. But overall, you can bet on one thing: As a group, these people have got your number. They pretty well know, or think they know, who you are. Or at least they know what face or identity you've been showing them—consciously or unconsciously—for some years. Remember, it is to our individual advantage (it has survival value) for each of us to understand the strengths and weaknesses of other people. And as a group, we're pretty accurate in forming such judgments. If everyone says that Charlie is "dependable," he probably is—even though they've never said precisely that to his face.

Look for things these people seem to be saying as a group—things they say fairly consistently. A pattern. Circle or mark the most frequent half dozen items, good and bad. Then boil this down into a sentence or so. Now you have heard the verdict of "a jury of your peers," and you didn't even need to ask them!

YOUR CORE DESCRIPTION

Now make your small ("net-net") list. Look at the traits and abilities you found in your parents, your own preteen years, early job and hobbies, your current job, and what others say. Look for repetitions—patterns of common points in each. Any item that shows up from most of those sources and during most of those time periods is almost certain to be a pretty accurate part of your identity. Look particularly for skills, likes, and things you did or do well. These represent key aspects of your positive or favorable identity.

Make these into a final list, then summarize them into a short sentence. It might be as simple as saying, "I am a numbers person. I like numbers and am good at them." Or you might describe yourself as a word person, people person, leader, follower, mechanic, team organizer, painter, artist, lover, athlete, politician, or student. Aside from occupation, you might express your identity in terms of your most notable personality trait—dependable, inquiring, independent, ambitious, determined, caring, organized, bright, social, a loner, active, careful, liberal, conservative, convincing, analytical, industrious, and so forth.

You may find you have indicated a small number of these traits, each having high intensity. So you might be "several" people. Some of these may overlap. One manager's traits not only overlapped but worked both ways. He concluded he was a "managed communicator—and a communication manager."

NOW USE YOUR ADVANTAGE WISELY

You have gone through the identity-checkup process just to get to a few descriptive words: your identity. Is it worth the hour or so it took you? Yes. For three reasons: First, you not only know who you are, you are fairly sure of it. You can document it. Your own personal satisfaction grows. Second, you are a giant step ahead of most people, who either don't have the foggiest idea who they are, or if they do have an idea, it remains in that foggy area. They are simply not sure. The slightest wind blows the fog one way or the other. You have something they don't.

The third reason is the most important: Your power has increased. You know exactly who you are. You know your strengths. It reinforces your own clear, calm, dynamic, and positive self-confidence. As long as you stay in that area and employ those strengths, you are using your resources in the best possible way. When you stray out of that area, you are becoming inefficient and noncompetitive, because your competition can outdo you. You are even becoming unsafe and possibly a little foolish—trying to excel where you have the least natural and developed skill. It's possible, but it will be an uphill fight.

Japanese Build Strengths Through Identity Development

The system of identity development that the Japanese use with their children has elements that are relevant for us. Both parents are usually alert to any early signs in a child that suggest basic or inherited skills. If this is noticed, the child is encouraged to develop them. For example, if a child is recognized as being exceptionally dexterous, he or she is given toys, games, and hobbies that will use, build, and develop that ability. The same goes for skills with numbers, words, pictures, or people. Second, the child is encouraged to get special training in related fields during his or her school years. Third, the child is informed of the skill—told "who he or she is." Thus, Japanese children have far less chance of going through the sort of identity crisis suffered by so many American young people. By the time they wonder who they are, they already know!

Some people may feel this stifles their creativity, cramps their horizons, or forces them into a pigeonhole. Four answers: (1) That is true, to a certain extent. (2) Like most of life, it's a tradeoff—in exchange for avoiding an identity crisis. (3) It's a good bargain. Far more is gained than lost. And (4) the child is not really stifled, stymied, or force-molded, because he or she understands that other interests can be pursued, too—just as long as the key skill is attended to first.

In later life, as the child becomes a young adult, he or she is encouraged to seek employment in that field. Teachers know of his or her particular strength and interest. As employers look for specific skills, they contact the teachers and discuss various students. Now the student knows, the parents know, the teachers know, and the employer knows. Identity and communication are complete. It started with an early check and continued with regular such reviews through the years. Result: a happy, productive professional person and a stable, prosperous family and career.

SUMMARY

Your best basic identity-checkup system is to follow these steps:

1. Set your goal—to decide who you are.
2. Start with a careful, honest look at your parents' traits and strengths.
3. Next, check your early childhood interests.
4. Now review the abilities shown during your teens and college years.
5. Examine your hobbies and early job skills.
6. List what you've been doing best recently.
7. Who do people *say* you are?
8. Make your "net-net" list—your core description.
9. Use your identity to strengthen your career.
10. Borrow some elements from the Japanese approach to identity recognition.

Your OBI (one best idea) for your identity checkup is to examine your strengths, likes, and abilities from the major periods and activities of your life and boil those down into a brief statement that clearly and simply, yet forcefully, expresses exactly who you are.

CHAPTER 14
How to Decide on Your Best Opportunities

In the previous chapter, we took a good, long, careful look inward at you—to help you identify your major strengths. Now we will take a good, long, careful look outward at the world around you. The purpose is to discover your best opportunities—to see places where your talents, skills, strengths, and abilities match up best with the wants, needs, deficiencies, gaps, and vacuums that exist in that outside world.

More important, we want to build a simple pattern or procedure you can use anytime—today, next week, or next year—that not only matches your inner skills with your world's major needs but shows which of these matchups will give you the greatest results per unit of your time and effort invested. The biggest bang per buck.

Looking for and at opportunities is nearly the same as considering your options—your choices, openings, or alternative goals. In the chapter following this, we will outline ideas for your career goal. But naturally, you would not want to take the step of picking your goal until you have first evaluated, checked into, and massaged your various opportunities. A person doesn't decide on law, medicine, or broadcasting as a career until he or she has considered a range of other alternatives, weighed their pros and cons, and then made an informed decision.

What has opportunity decision making got to do with career success? Everything and nothing. Nothing, if the perfect or near-perfect career is handed to you or is available to you for life. But everything, if your options are not quite so perfect—if your career is not handed to you or is not available to you for life. And most important, if you have a number of options—and you must make a selection. And that is very likely to be the case.

Let's look at some good ways to select your best—and often easiest, most pleasant, and prosperous—opportunity.

THINK BIG

Use "the-world-is-my-oyster" strategy. That means raise up your head and your eyes. Look at the green in your own backyard, but also look at the horizon. Think wide, think big, think deep. Don't be too parochial or shallow. Don't restrict yourself or your imagination.

Increasingly you can be nearly anything you want to be, if you want it badly enough and are willing to make the necessary effort—to do the things known to cause success. You already have an important advantage, a leg up on success, because you know who you are and what you can do well. You know your strengths. Most people never bother to learn this about themselves until it's too late.

Webster defines opportunity as "a matching of favorable circumstances." And that is exactly what we are doing here—matching your abilities with the world's needs, thereby creating a favorable circumstance for you. And the farther and wider you look, the more of the world's needs you will see to consider. If you look only at your own backyard, you may find only a few options. But if you look at a few dozen backyards, you will find a few dozen opportunities. "Lift up thine eyes and behold the glory that is here," says the Good Book.

Apply Simple Market Research

Get a little measurement of things: how much, how many, how big. If you are strong in a particular industry or skill field, then books, magazines, and professional associations will tell you the dimensions of this. Is the market huge or small? How many people are in it? What the five Ws (who, what, when, where, and why)? Is there anything like a qualitative measurement? How good are the companies, people, or groups in this field? Are you any better?

Worse? What are the trends: up, down, sideways, long-run and short-run, for quantity or quality?

Who does work like yours? Where do they come from? Are you as well prepared? Will you be later? Who uses people like you, with your skills? Who needs and wants your skills? Who are prospective employers? Can you identify potential customers or users of your abilities? When? Where? Why? Whom can you help? Who can help you?

Sure these are a lot of questions, and they are far easier to ask than to answer. But there are lots of resources, starting with your business reference librarian. And people do get answers—especially above-average people like you.

Even if you can't answer these questions, a thoughtful guess is better than nothing. A check of some sources such as an informed friend or two is even better yet. Research into printed material on your field may be the best approach of all.

Suggestion: Trade associations are organized groups representing just about every major industry, job function, and field of activity. There are over 4,700 such associations, and most publish monthly or quarterly trade or professional journals. Those often contain career articles. Books listing these associations are available at most major libraries. You can write to several associations and get all sorts of information free or at very low cost—especially if you mention that you are considering joining their association, which in truth, you might do. You just hit their "on" button, and they will usually help you.

DEVELOP AN "OPPORTUNISTIC" MIND-SET

An "opportunistic" mind-set means not only raising up thine eyes but thinking about what you are seeing. Think positively and creatively. When you notice a change in your world, ask yourself, "Could that be a new opportunity for me? Will someone need and want my skills now more than before? Who?" Avoid tunnel vision. Focus, find, and forage around in various directions.

Ask lots of questions—questions directed both to yourself and to others. Inquire. Let one answer lead to other questions. Again use the five *W*s but always in terms of Is this an opportunity for me? If so, why? How soon? How big? Where? Whom should I see?

True opportunists have a certain attitude, mind-set, viewpoint. Everything they see sparks a question in their minds: How can I use this to my advantage? "Time and tide are always on the side of the best navigator." Every wind blows such people some good, because they adapt to it and utilize it. This can be a pleasant experience, even fun, because you are learning things that may be helpful to you and perhaps stimulating and rewarding as well. And it costs you little or nothing. No rush, no push, no hassle.

You are becoming analytical. You are disassembling the situation, taking it apart to see if it has something you can use or someone who can use you. You are thinking opportunistically, and that means you are thinking resourcefully. "Is this an opening that I want or an organization that wants me? Is this a situation that matches my abilities?"

Even if things seem to shift in a negative way, there may still be opportunities for you. A revolting development may occur, but take heart. Every time one door closes, another usually opens. For example, if one project ends, you are abruptly thrust into an unhappy situation—and yet you have also suddenly been placed in the position of being able to apply for hundreds of other projects, from which you were previously barred. In fact, you probably now have new opportunities in large numbers.

Analyze Company Opportunities

Chances are that your most frequent opportunities will come from business firms—as you are looking at where you are or where you might want to be.

One professional consultant developed a simple company-analysis outline. He typed this on the back of a business card, covered it with scotch tape, and put it in his billfold. With this, he could quickly ask the right questions and easily analyze almost any company opportunity in relation to his career, occasionally amazing his friends and associates in the process. His analysis outline looked like this:

OPPORTUNITY CHECKLIST

1. History.
2. Key executive.
3. Products or service.
4. Sales volume.
5. Problems/strengths.
6. Competition/Government/
   Customers.
7. Market size and trends.
8. Goals: short-/long-range,
   quantity/quality. Image.
9. Strategy: products, price,
   promotions, publicity,
   packaging, people, pre-
   mium, policies, philosophy.
10. Schedule: Who does what,
    when, where, and why?
11. Fit me/need me.
12. Repute, *modus operandi*,
    future.

To this checklist you might add: What is my feeling—my pure, honest, deep-down gut reaction to the company's *modus operandi* and its managers' attitude toward me?

An easy way to use this list is to memorize the first two or three items and ask about them. Then glance down at the next two or three items and ask about those, and so on. Stay very alert for flaws in the responses. You will rarely sail right through the list, since most people become hung up on one or two subjects or involved in other side issues. But when you do get through it, you will have an excellent insight into your company opportunity.

Use People to Help

People can be wonderful and terrible as resources. Apply a few simple rules for using their skills properly and you open a gold mine of value.

1. Pick your people carefully. Select good resources.

2. Know what to ask each person. Some people are great for advice, some for projects, some can enthuse others, and some can recruit added resources. Try different small requests with each and measure the results carefully. Then use whichever of these resources works best for you.

3. Don't rush things. Take it one step at a time, because most people naturally resist pressure.

4. Almost anyone can be a sounding board for ideas and opinions. Sometimes the best personal opportunities are right under your nose or touching elbows with you on trains, planes or buses.

5. Judge people's reactions advisedly. If your question or need is far from their field—above them, below them or simply out of their line—take their replies with a grain of salt.

6. Value certain people above all others. Know how to pick the good ones. Especially valuable are those precious few people who have your best interests at heart, who gain from your success, and who are honest (even brutally honest) with you. Also identify people who have shown good, sound, sensible judgment in the past. Give their advice great weight and use that resource carefully.

7. Recognize expertise in a certain field. Every person you know has some specialized knowledge or information. Recognize who knows what and use that source when you need help.

8. Deliberately seek out divergent resources—people who have a much different viewpoint from your own, like cab drivers, retail clerks, or plumbers. Their opinions on such matters as company, industry, customer, or economic trends can be interesting and not always wrong. And nobody's smarter than everybody. A twist here is to predict their reaction and see how near you come. If you hit it pretty close, you know that you have a good insight into both the question and the respondent.

9. Don't hesitate to employ people as a source of direct assistance. Ask for help. It shows that you both respect them and place them above you in a certain ability. To many people, your request for help means you just gave them a pat on the back and a promotion. They like to do favors for others and are tremendously stimulated by your request. Sometimes they are especially honored that someone who is above average like you will not only recognize them but owe them a favor. They know you are advancing, and your debt to them is like money in the bank. Accept their help—and be sure to pay your IOU when you can, at least in a small way.

Consider the Competition

Consider what your competition is doing, whether you are looking at "competition" as another company or another person. It can be anyone shooting for the same target you are. These people are facing problems very much like those that challenge you. And here's the opportunity: Every one of them has solved at least part of the puzzle. If you can learn what part and how they solved it, then you have used a resource other people often ignore. Find lots of these solved portions, put them together creatively, and you have usually made major progress at very little cost to yourself. Why reinvent the wheel?

Another advantage is that your competitors have done some expensive and difficult testing for you. They have tried things and proved that they work. That saves you both heavy costs and heavy risks. Almost as important—these people have tried things and found out what does *not* work, thus saving you from other costly mistakes.

PEEK INTO THE FUTURE

Look ahead for a sign of the opportunities coming your way. Be alert and open-minded to judge and evaluate things that are developing. Remember Oscar Wilde's quip, "For most people, opportunities look much better as they are going away from them than they did coming towards them."

An easy step you can take is simply to watch trends—the growth, decline, or stagnation that you see in some industries, businesses, communities, resources, professions, or groups. If one field is booming and another is dying, those trends are telling you something. They suggest future opportunities, a bandwagon for you to ride. The proper move at this time might carry you along beautifully with little effort required.

Some trends are statistical or quantified, like the number of fast-food restaurants. Other trends are more emotional or attitudinal, like the need to avoid waste or preserve our environment. Some of these trends are predetermined and can be predicted with great accuracy—like the number of people who will be age 40 or age 60 ten years from now. Those people are here today, and we can be very precise in estimating how many will be alive in a decade. Other trends that are supposed to have statistical elements are, in reality, uncertain and unpredictable, like the stock market, interest rates, prices of groceries, or the number of compact cars that will be sold next year. Such figures can and sometimes do swing rather widely, even wildly.

Know which sort of trend you are considering, since that will tell you how probable your opportunity will be. A fixed trend is manyfold more certain than a fluctuating one.

Look at large-scale and worldwide trends such as the shortage of oil and energy. We all know that this will change our world in a hundred ways over the next few decades. Here is a fairly well established trend (as opposed to an uncertain and indefinite one), and one that is mainly statistical as opposed to being purely emotional or attitudinal. However, like most trends, it is partly a mixture of all of these. To make it work for you, ask yourself, "How can this particular trend become an opportunity for me—given my known skills and abilities?"

Also look at national, regional, local, community, and company trends. What is growing or warming up? When it's hot, it's hot—when it's not, it's not. Pick the right target and the right time to move.

Extend or extrapolate those trends from today into the next few years. Nothing is certain, but this can give you some very good indications of the opportunities that await you, just down the road.

Create Your Own Opportunity

Find yourself an opportunity, even in a less enterprising firm. "My company is dead. Dead on its feet. Dead in the water. Going nowhere, fast. And I'm trapped—locked below decks on the *Titanic*." That's what some people say or think. And yet true opportunists will see dozens of chances for development, growth, and improvement right there under their noses. They will see untapped markets, unused products or services, undeveloped people, and opportunities for leadership.

It's a little like the gag about the psychological experiment done with 10-year-old twin boys. One was an optimist, the other a pessimist. The pessimist was put in a roomful of new toys, the optimist, in a room three feet deep in horse manure. When the psychologists checked later, the pessimist was just sitting there frowning. The optimist was digging eagerly. When they asked him why, he said, "With all this manure around, there must be a pony in here somewhere!"

Here are three possibilities for finding that pony: First, the key to opportunity in a less-than-aggressive company is to learn, understand, and support the goals of those in authority. Those goals are often unspoken ones. Rather than sales and profits, the goals might really be company prestige, status, respect, and stability. If you help gain, secure, and increase those things, you could become a hero in your own backyard. You saw an opportunity, and you took it.

Second, even in a solid, staid, and quiet company, there may be a deep, unexpressed longing to try something exciting, dynamic, innovative, dramatic, and even downright risky—just as long as it does not endanger the major or basic establishment. The trick here is to look, listen, and *learn who has this interest* among the top people. A simple way to do this is to support some solid, conservative, prestigious effort during a top-level meeting but then add, "Of course, we could try a dramatic departure on a very small scale, in a separate division, so long as it can't reflect badly in any way on our basic company." Sometimes this taps a great opportunity. You might get put in charge. In some cases, a sleepy company has reacted with surprising enthusiasm—even overreacted—to a dynamic plan put forth by a live wire. It's even possible that half the management group may have been almost desperately waiting for just such a development.

A third opportunity is to flat out join, or even lead, a major thrust for new thinking, new directions, new progress, new products, new dimensions, new sales, and new profits—new worlds to conquer. To succeed, this effort should be carefully thought out, with many strong and influential supporters quietly enlisted—supporters who will act aggressively at the right time. Even then, this takes on the complexion of a palace rebellion. It can get quite exciting—even too exciting. It might cause you to long for the good old days, saying, "Sometimes we don't know what we have until it's gone."

SELECT THE BEST OF YOUR OPTIONS

Decide on your opportunity by using this 12-point decision program:

1. Protect yourself against "action freeze up" simply by reviewing the facts and making a small, safe decision on a part of the total opportunity.

2. Be both steely-eyed logical and soft-hearted emotional. Use each viewpoint—just know which is which.

3. Don't ignore the obvious. Many people disregard fine opportunities right at their fingertips.

4. Keep a cool head. Relax. It avoids tension, stress, and the rubber room.

5. Chop decisions, and then projects, into small bits if you can, and then take the bits one at a time.

6. Don't fly solo. Get other people's opinions. Consider these, taking the good advice and skipping the bad.

7. Play the odds. Choose opportunities where chances are strongly in your favor.

8. Use Maxwell Smart's "the-old-toe-in-the-water" trick. Meaning, try something on a small scale, such as a short-term test. Avoid diving in full force only to find the water is an inch deep.

9. Use the Brookings think tank "What if . . ." system. Plot out some hypothetical cases and step-by-step scenarios to be sure you can see what would happen first, next, after that, and so on.

10. Be ready to make a Mayday emergency selection from among your various options. (This happens sometimes.) One easy way—a little list: "If I had to decide today, here are the three key steps I'd take." This helps you to sleep well at night rather than lie awake grinding your teeth over alternatives.

11. Sometimes your best decision is to take no action and make no selection. That in itself is a decision—a decision not to act. But be sure you have a reason that will benefit you, then elect to procrastinate profitably.

12. "My God! What if I'm wrong?" Solution: Recognize it and take remedial action immediately. First, protect yourself. Then correct the situation if you can. There's an old German surgeon's saying that translates as, "The best doctor is not necessarily the one

who makes the fewest errors, but the one who sees his mistake quickly and corrects it immediately." This works with opportunity decisions as well.

Japanese Firm Does It Right

The Niko company, a very small food processor in northern Tokyo, produced a dry, precooked noodle and flavor package that became fairly popular a few years ago in Japan's capital city. Then its managers lifted their eyes to the horizon and began thinking of the export market. They did their market research using the five Ws and asked even more questions—particularly, "Where are our best opportunities?" After looking at various countries, they finally selected the United States and two other nations.

Niko carefully analyzed several major distributor cities and selected one in each country. Denver was chosen for the United States, partly because of its nearly centralized location and proximity to the growing "sun belt market." The Niko people used their distributor managers as key sources of advice. They carefully reviewed competitive product quality, prices, and promotions. And they looked at trends in consumer eating habits. Niko noted that some of its prospective competitors were relatively nonagressive.

Then Niko made the decision to act by starting a small test market in Chicago's north side, sending the product to market through its Denver distributor. Soon both sales and profits showed clear, and obviously favorable, trends. Niko managers also checked consumer opinions and found high product satisfaction levels—and repeat purchase patterns. They analyzed a number of "What if . . ." scenarios for national expansion and selected a program where chances strongly favored success. Within a few months, the Niko company reached a national volume of sales and profits in the millions of dollars—and is still growing as of this writing.

SUMMARY

The most effective program for finding and building on your best opportunity is:

1. Use "the-world-is-my-oyster" strategy.
2. Apply simple market research, like the five Ws.
3. Develop an opportunistic mind-set.
4. Use a basic company-analysis system.
5. Utilize people as a key resource.
6. Consider what your competition is doing and borrow ideas.
7. Peek behind the curtain of the future to glimpse trends.
8. Find or create opportunities, even in unenterprising groups.
9. Use a decision program to get yourself started.
10. Follow the Japanese pattern of looking at horizons, researching trends, and testing options.

Your OBI (one best idea) for finding a top opportunity is to lift your eyes, check around, have an opportunistic view, employ people as a resource, analyze companies, competition, and future trends, and make a careful decision. In short: Study, then act.

CHAPTER 15
Setting Your Career Goal

You have looked at your situation, meaning your own personal abilities plus the opportunities outside yourself. You now know where you might make the most progress with the least effort. Now you should set a career goal, something to shoot for.

Otherwise you are just a ship without a port. One direction becomes as good as another. Remember, Columbus didn't just sail, he sailed *west*. An African proverb says, "When you have no destination, any trail can take you there." As Thoreau said, "The mass of men lead lives of quiet desperation." They make heroic efforts yet aren't even sure of their own goal or purpose. "People often do not know what they really want and are willing to go through hell to get it," quipped Bennett Cerf.

Today, most successful companies and executives employ the concept of management by objectives: Every action is aimed at one goal or another. Little time, money, or effort is wasted. Every step and every day get you closer to your goal—if you have one. Said one philosopher, "The future belongs to those who aim for it."

Don't underrate the impact of this chapter. It may be the most important one in the book. Your goal selection will influence nearly every one of your future actions, including your joys and sorrows and levels of self-satisfaction and approval.

For that reason, in America, goal setting has become sort of an indoor sport in recent years. These objectives have a strange and wonderful way of becoming self-fulfilling prophesies. There are dozens of ways to set goals that are reachable, realistic, and rewarding. The system outlined here is one of those ways, and it usually works exceptionally well.

BE REASONABLE

Come on, now. You can fantasize about becoming president of General Motors or General Mills. But there are only 500 companies in the *Fortune* 500 listing and many thousands of good management candidates for those top slots. But consider this: There are over 10 million businesses in the United States. Add to that the nonprofit and government units plus operations in other nations and you have over 20 million. The point: Think about the giants but also consider many other areas where you are a lot more likely to reach the top.

Also, think in terms not only of the No. 1 position but of any one of the top ten spots in, say, the 1,000 largest companies. That gives you a pond to fish in teeming with some 10,000 positions you might catch. And most of these probably pay in the $100,000 to $200,000 bracket. They will pay a lot more by the time you reach one of them five or ten years from now.

And so we see that, even discounting some unlikely, pie-in-the-sky objectives, clearly you have a huge number of interesting and rewarding goal possibilities that are both reasonable and reachable. You can save yourself a lot of wasted time and saddened spirits in goal setting if you stretch but stay realistic. Still, reach for the stars.

You may not capture many stars, but by reaching toward the heavens, you won't end up with a handful of mud, either. Said Cicero way back in 80 B.C., "If you aspire to the top place, it is no disgrace to capture the second or third." So don't let the cold reality of numbers discourage you from making a major reach well beyond the next few levels immediately above you. After all, somebody's got to be president or get to the top of the heap. It could be you.

Look at Goal Makers' Goals

Goal makers' goals are the kind the professionals set. Besides being reachable, realistic, and reasonable, and providing a stretch or a real challenge, goal makers' goals have a few other terms and parameters, just to keep it interesting. These include: long-term, short-term, quantitative, and qualitative.

By "short-term," they usually mean where you plan or hope to be in the next few years. By "long-term," they generally mean three to ten years in the future. The "distant future" usually refers to beyond ten years. This makes for an interesting way to think about yourself. You can outline approximately where you would like to be in those three different time frames.

By "quantitative," planners are referring to a stated amount of money, the salary level, percent increases, the size of profit sharing, and other similar, measurable elements.

By "qualitative," they are talking about all the nonnumerical elements, the considerations other than income. These include life style, personal activities, location, and living habits.

Select Multiple Goals

Just as there is more than one earthly paradise, so there is more than one good goal. Very few goal makers select only one objective. About the only significant advantage to a single target is that it really does mightily focus one's total attention and resources upon a single hope. At times, this makes great sense. The disadvantage is that it becomes virtually an all-consuming obsession. It puts all your begs in one ask it. Your failure to reach the goal can become a devastating disaster.

While multiple goals have the disadvantage of spreading, rather than concentrating, your resources, this is usually far out-weighed by other advantages. Multiple goals give variety and spice to your life. Second, they permit you to use a greater number of your resources. Every resource you have may not necessarily be useful for a single goal. Third, they permit you to make much better use of certain specific resources, for example, your time. You may find that your progress toward one goal is temporarily blocked. While waiting for that track to clear, you can switch over and concentate on one of your alternative targets. Meanwhile, the person with only one goal must simply wait—and waste one of life's greatest resources, time.

A fourth advantage is that your best efforts may get you close but not actually enable you to capture your prime goal. Meanwhile, those same efforts might help you reach or exceed one, and possibly several, alternative goals. Thus, you have a chance of winning something and not coming up empty-handed.

A fifth advantage of multiple goals is that—as we saw in our identity checkup of you and your skills—no one presents the same identity every moment to every person. We change our identity and what we stand for from time to time—even from one circumstance to another. A young graduate just out of school, a seasoned executive with a company, and a retired citizen on a museum board may all be the same person at various stages in life, but in fact he or she has a different identity in those different times and places. Clearly, he or she should and will have different goals from time to time— preferably multiple goals.

DON'T GET SIDETRACKED

Don't be seduced by frivolous situations that come up occasionally, tempting you away from your primary goal. First, bear in mind that you selected your target only after a lot of careful thought, so it probably is a basically sound choice, worth consistent and steady pursuit. Second, you have an investment of time, money, and effort in your original goal, which could be largely wasted if you switch. Third, it is possible to go chasing after a will-o'-the-wisp, only to have the light flicker out, then chase another. There are people who do that and then wonder why they reach middle or old age and have little to show for it.

But Stay Flexible

Be alert for good "targets of opportunity." In training for combat, military personnel are taught to keep their eyes and minds on a primary objective but also to stay open to sudden, new, unexpected situations that can be taken advantage of to help them gain the goal. Infiltration training courses for riflemen often have pop-up targets that appear briefly and without warning. This is not the same as being seduced by a will-o'-the-wisp. Here, your primary target remains as such. However, sometimes a careful check on the new opportunity shows it has equal or even far greater value and is reachable with less effort. If so, grab it.

We have all heard of cases where a person labored for years

toward a tough goal, and then, suddenly, circumstances shifted—and a new and greater reward simply dropped out of the blue and into his or her lap. This is another confirmation of Machiavelli's belief that "half our future is through our own effort, half through pure circumstances." Don't ignore either half. Just make very sure that the new, fortuitous development is what you really want.

Aim High Enough and Low Enough

Aim high enough for your target to be worth shooting for—and also high enough to make you stretch a little. High enough to challenge you, so that reaching the goal makes you feel proud of yourself. But don't set the goal so high that you can't possibly reach it or you hurt yourself trying, and then, to add insult to injury, you feel seriously depressed when you fail.

Aim low enough so you can catch the brass ring. But not so low that there is no challenge, no stretch, no value in the winning, and no personal pride in the accomplishment.

PLAN YOUR INCOME GOALS

If money is important to you, it is worth planning for. It will be more vital at certain times than at others, of course. Also, the more money you get, the less valuable each additional buck becomes. For example, I have known multimillionaires who were never quite sure how many millions they had! A fluctuation of a point or two in the stock market over a few hours' time could gain or lose them several million, and they were never even aware of or concerned about it.

But getting down to your own few bucks and a goal for them—let's assume that you, as a high achiever, feel that your wage should go up an average of, say, 7 percent each year. (Use any figure that you feel is reasonable.) Now pick your best estimate for an average inflation increase. Let's say another 7 percent. That means, you target your total salary to go up an average of 14 percent per year as an income goal.

If you currently earn $30,000 a year, then at the end of three years (short-term) your goal would be to earn about $44,000. At the end of ten years (long-term), you would aim for around $110,000. In the longest term, let's say fourteen years, you would look for about $190,000. (You can use your calculator to estimate each year simply by multiplying the first year by 1.14 percent to get the second and so on.) A simple 10 percent increase would get you to $40,000 in three years and to $78,000 in ten years.

Don't be overawed at these numbers, for five reasons. First, and most important, it hasn't happened yet. This is simply a tentative goal. And second, even if it did occur, half of this growth is eaten up by inflation. Third, if it did happen, it would almost certainly not be in such an orderly way. And fourth, the "fortune factor" will influence these figures, perhaps cutting them in half. Or maybe doubling them! Fifth, you'll notice that the biggest actual dollar jumps occur in later years, simply because your percentage estimate of increase stays the same (14 percent), while the base gets bigger each year. You might be much more realistic to put that percentage growth estimate on a declining scale. Hardly anyone sees even a consistent 10 percent increase for ten to fourteen years.

Consider Quality of Life

Include quality of life in your goal list. Money is good, but by itself, it isn't good enough. You may also want to consider in what geographic area you hope to live, what management duties you expect, pressures, politics, working conditions, what sort of home and community you desire, your hobbies, outside community activities, friends, church, education, transportation, and culture.

You may want to think of what you wish to accomplish or achieve. Maybe it's to paint, write, join some group, act, sing, sail, travel, lead an organization, or jog X miles. Perhaps it's to achieve some level of recognition, reputation, or status. Man does not live by income alone. Other things are important, too, and these can become exciting, worthwhile lifetime goals.

Include Your Family

Ask your family to participate in the planning process and help them to be at least somewhat goal-oriented. This is especially plausible and feasible if they see and feel that they have something to gain in achieving the family goal. They can and will then be more likely to provide you with the spiritual, emotional, and physical support you need to help your progress toward the objective. This will add to your own fun and satisfaction, since getting there together is much more enjoyable.

Pick Your Dream

Decide on the nicest possible combination of things that could happen to you or that you could achieve. Ask yourself, if you could press some buttons and make it all occur, which buttons would you press? Now back off a little, find a reasonable level, and take aim. That is your aggregate, or package, goal. Dream a little, at regular intervals. But be careful: Never ask for something you don't really want—you might get it!

KEEP YOUR GOALS IN SIGHT

Use your goals as a self-fulfilling prophesy. You can do this by always keeping them either right up front in your mind or within easy arm's reach of your immediate thoughts. That way, deliberately or automatically, consciously or unconsciously, your goals will influence nearly all of your daily actions in a positive and productive way.

Set Priorities and a Schedule

Decide which goals you would like and reasonably expect to achieve first, then what's next, and so on. Write these down. Some goals may conflict, so that you can't reasonably expect to achieve them at the same time. This means you should decide which of your two options is most important to you personally.

SELF-SATISFACTION: THE ULTIMATE GOAL

In the end, be guided by self-satisfaction, because this, as the bottom line, combines income, life style, family achievement, personal accomplishment, status, reward, and contentment. It is probably a blend of many things, which varies at different time periods. But it can be the ultimate goal for you. It's also adjustable.

Go Easy on Yourself

Recognize that you may not reach all these nifty things. That's OK. You will be wise not to expect to get them all. Anticipate bombing out on at least one or two. That is another good reason for having multiple goals. Do not let any one goal become obsessive or overly possessive of your total inner happiness. If you miss a goal, be able to honestly say, "Well, even though I didn't make it, I tried. I wish I had succeeded on that one, but nobody bats 1,000. I'll enjoy the goals I did reach. Let's see. What's next?"

Replan Occasionally

As your circumstances, time, opportunities, and skills change, as you achieve some goals and bomb out on others, and as your values change from year to year—so should your goals. They should not be cast in concrete. Your goals list should be a living plan within your head. It should be hauled out and put under the microscope occasionally, say the first days of each year, for a midcourse correction. You may want to periodically redefine just what you really regard as "success."

Consider the Japanese Objective Matrix

The Japanese objective matrix works like this: Take a piece of paper and divide it vertically into three columns. At the top of the first, put "short run" (next three years). Next, put "long run" (next 10 years), and then "distant future" (beyond 10 years). Now divide the page into five roughly equal horizontal spaces, so the intersecting lines form fifteen boxes. Label these horizontal spaces on down (starting at the upper left of the far left box): (1) income, (2) family, (3) location, (4) quality or life style, and (5) key accomplishments. Add an extra line or two with other appropriate labels, if you wish.

Now jot down in each of the boxes across the first line, income. You might show $39,000 for short run, $98,000 for long run, and $165,000 for distant future. Now on the family line, enter who they are, number and what they might be doing in each of these time periods. Now your location. This might be a city, state, county, or community. Complete the other lines. Be brief, unless you wish to get into details.

You have just made a living career "objective matrix," combining accomplishment goals with the time schedule dimension, just as some major executives do in Japan. And you are a long way from where you were at the start of this chapter. You have peeked into the future and found it good, because you designed it that way. All these things may never happen, of course. But they are a whole lot more likely to occur now that you have identified them, visualized them, scheduled them, and planned for them, than if you had never even thought of them.

SUMMARY

The steps for setting your best career goals are:

1. Come on, now. Let's be reasonable.
2. But you can still reach for the stars.
3. Look at long and short run, quality and quantity.
4. Pick several goals.
5. Don't be seduced by frivolous attractions.
6. But do consider good, new "targets of opportunity."
7. Aim both high enough and low enough.
8. Plan your income goals.
9. Consider quality of life in your goal list.
10. Include your family.
11. Decide on the nicest possible combination.
12. Use your goals as a self-fulfilling prophecy.
13. Set priorities and a time schedule.
14. Use self-satisfaction as the ultimate goal.
15. Be kind to yourself.

16. Review, adjust, regroup, and replan occasionally.
17. Consider the Japanese living career "objective matrix."

Your OBI (one best idea) for establishing your career goals is to set reasonable, reachable, and pleasurable long- and short-term targets—with priorities and a schedule that can be adjusted.

CHAPTER 16
Plan Your Success

You have right in your hand a powerful system for insuring your success and increased progress. This book has given you the start of an effective personal program. It is borrowed from that used by the U.S. Navy in World War II. They called it SOS, or *s*ituation, *o*bjective, *s*trategy. Situation is where you are now. Objective is where you want to go. Strategy is how you plan to get there.

Those three easy and potent steps were used in many ancient military victories. Elements of them can even be found in the Bible. Since then, these steps have generated not only major military conquests but extraordinary corporate, financial, and personal successes as well. The system is used, in one form or another, by the most profitable and successful companies in America, Japan, Germany, and elsewhere, including firms such as IBM and Procter & Gamble, which some authorities have called the best-run companies in the world.

And you are already two-thirds of the way home: You have finished two of the three SOS steps, having completed the *S* and the *O*. In the first two chapters of Part Two, we looked at the *S*—your situation—first internally, in Chapter 13 (doing your identity checkup) and second externally, in Chapter 14 (identifying your best opportunity). Then we planned out some career objectives for you in Chapter 15.

Now we are ready for the last *S*—that is, your strategy. This chapter will present a general outline of your best planning procedures. Then the remaining chapters of this book will present a review of the many specific strategic steps you might take to reach your career objectives.

YOUR BEST GENERAL STRATEGY

You have a job. You know yourself pretty well by now, and you know your immediately prevailing circumstances. You came to work today, and you'll go to work tomorrow, and you know what faces you each day—good and bad. Plus, you have some goals—important ones. Here are ten general strategy steps you can take to reach those goals. We will look at these tactics briefly right here and then fill in a lot more specifics later, in the next few pages.

First—and this may seem to be a tired, dull, old approach, but it is still a perfectly viable option—you can *do a good, perhaps outstanding, job* right where you are. Your strategy, or at least your hope, is that this will pave the way and give you a leg up toward your goal. This may be a promising and reasonable option or it may not. It presupposes that successful performance of your present job will lead more or less directly to your goal. This is sometimes correct but more often is a debatable or unrealistic assumption. There may be no direct path from here to there.

Second, your general strategy may employ *additional education*. This answers the next logical question, "If doing a good job on my present assignment won't lead to my goal, what will?" Further specialized education may be the key.

Third, you could use the old *stepping-stones* system. You might feel you can't really get there from here—but you could get there from some other point of departure. This presupposes that you can reasonably get to one or more of these other points without taking half your lifetime. This general strategy has been and is being used successfully by millions. The more planning, care, and realism they employ, the better it seems to work out.

Fourth, your general strategy could employ *outside interests* beyond your immediate job. Here you have decided that on-the-job performance, education, and stepping-stones are not as effective as going toward your goal through other activities. These might be assignments that are supplemental to your present job or activities completely unconnected with your company. You may know people in your community who need some part-time help from you and who can be of direct assistance in your career.

Fifth, you may elect to play *the waiting game*. Here you decide that time is on your side. You know of something, perhaps several things, that are either definitely going to happen or are likely to happen—things that may or could help your career. You are waiting for the apple to drop into your lap. Just be sure that (1) the apple will, in fact, drop within a bearable time. (2) It will drop straight down, not sideways and into someone else's lap. (3) If and when the apple drops into your lap, you will, at that time, probably still want that particular apple.

Sixth, you may decide on *new worlds to conquer,* having concluded that the other major strategic options just won't do the job, and the track you're on will not lead to your goal. This means getting on a new track and learning a whole new operation.

Seventh, an important part of your strategy is how you go about it. The most successful planners and strategists *write it down.* Your simplest and easiest procedure is to use just three sheets of paper. On the first, outline your situation—a sentence or two on yourself, your problems, and your opportunities. On the second page, list your goals—long-term and short-term, quantity ($) and quality (life style). This is very important. Your goals will greatly influence your next page, your next steps—and the rest of your life. Then on the third page, outline your selected general strategy. Pick one or more of the items above or add some. Break them down into a few steps or actions. Now, you have a track to run on. You know where you are, where you are going, and approximately how you plan to get there. You are in the top one percent, because 99 percent don't know this.

Eighth, now select your *priorities.* Look at your various strategic steps and decide which is most important. Pick the top two or three. Now you not only know what you are doing, but you know what you are going to concentrate on this week, month, or year. You are much less likely to waste your time and effort on minor, unproductive activities that just spin your wheels, squander your energy, and get you nothing.

Ninth, your general strategy may be *flexibility.* Here you decide to play it as it lies, adjust from day to day, and take advantage of your opportunities. This is not a bad option. We all do this to some extent. Even the most structured or plan-oriented person should crank this into his or her program as at least one element of strategy. A good plan is fine, but we should all be alert for new and better opportunities. They do come along.

Tenth, your elected strategy may simply be *to stand pat:* "I'm happy as things are. Let's leave well enough alone and not tinker with the machinery." This is fine. Millions do it successfully. Unfortunately, this presupposes that things *will* stay put and remain as they are. But nothing does. All things change—slightly, perhaps, but a little every month. They drift. Even if you just drift along with them, circumstances will change. Perhaps in directions you don't wish. Either way you must control your life, or it will control you. Of course, none of us has absolute influence over our destiny. We noted earlier what that famous strategist Machiavelli said: About 50 percent of our progress is our own doing, and 50 percent is luck. The point is to be sure you effectively control your 50 percent. Your best bet is to move at least gently in some direction.

Let's take the rest of this chapter to look at the following selected six points in a little more constructive and helpful detail:

1. Education.
2. Stepping-stones.
3. Your outside interests.
4. The waiting game.
5. How to write it down.
6. Planning your next steps.

A seventh possible strategy, seeking new worlds to conquer, really refers to changing jobs. This is such a major, important, and complex step that it will be treated in detail in the next chapter.

GETTING MORE EDUCATION

Obtaining additional specialized education makes good strategy when the goal you want requires education you don't have—especially where the person holding the position you seek has that kind of education. (If he or she does not have that qualification, then you may not need it, either. But don't forget that educational prerequisites are going up steadily.)

Check around and do your homework. Get information about (1) whether this special training is really necessary, (2) where you can get this, (3) how good the training is, and (4) whether it all adds up for you, from a practical cost and benefit standpoint. In other words, if you put in the time, money, and energy to get this training, will it pay off? Occasionally, your company may give you business time for further training and pay all or part of the cost.

In a sense, there are two major kinds of specialized training: One is the kind that is of real value to you—providing practical, pragmatic, nuts-and-bolts, try-it-Tuesday type material. The second is training taken primarily to show it on your record. Your ideal program gives you both. (World-famous consultant Peter Drucker says that most modern managers must be retrained about three times in their careers, as circumstances and professional demands shift and change.)

Also, consider your competition. If he or she is getting additional education, you had better do the same, or you could be outgunned. In fact, it is you who should outgun your competitor, so have a look at what it takes to achieve higher qualifications.

If you already have excess educational credentials, as many managers do, then the added-education strategy is probably not your best route—unless it involves some specialized training that offers you either a practical or a show-type advantage.

USING STEPPING-STONES

Stepping-stones are one of the most frequently used career strategies. Here you feel that your present job will not lead you to your goal, but you believe that some other assignment is more likely to do the trick. Be careful about six things.

1. Do not plan for more than two or three steps, since each is naturally a little chancy or uncertain, and you don't want to compound your risks into almost impossible odds.

2. Check your time frame. If each step can be made in two or three years, your plan may be reasonable. If it looks like around ten years for each step, you might very well want to look at an alternate route.

3. Be sure this plan is practical and doable. Has anyone ever reached your goal by this route? And are circumstances roughly the same—or better—or did he or she have advantages you don't?

4. Try to arrange for some help from higher management, a boss, friend supervisor, or buddy or two who can give you a little boost. Talk it over with him or her and mention your hope for a next step. Be especially mindful that the person most likely to help you is not the one who owes you a favor, but the one who stands to gain the most from your move. That person will probably give you new, welcome, and wanted assistance.

5. Take things one at a time. Don't try to bite off the whole project at once. It won't happen like that, anyway. Also, as you reach each step, you may want to lift your nose up off the grindstone, look around, sniff the air, and make some midcourse corrections. Other, newer and better next steps may have come into view.

6. Don't fall for the old grass-is-greener-on-the-other-side-of-the-fence trap. It usually just looks that way. All jobs have advantages and disadvantages. Sometimes the positives are made to look much stronger than the negatives—or we talk ourselves into believing that. People often go to a whole lot of trouble just to find they've jumped from the frying pan into the fire—only then do they discover it's twice as hot. They experience a net loss. We don't always realize what we have until it's gone.

PURSUING OUTSIDE INTERESTS

Use your outside interests and contacts. These may be beyond your immediate job but within your organization, or they may be totally outside your company. Your best reason for selecting this strategy is simply because you do believe that other routes to your goal are not very good—and that this route is a better one.

If you are looking for further interests within your own company, your best system may simply be one of branching out and reaching out. Here you try to get more involved in diverse company activities. A good approach is to decide which of these would be most likely to help you toward your goal. Then offer part-time help in that area, even if it's only "grunt" work. At least it's a foot in the door. You make more friends who will think of you when openings occur. (Meanwhile, carefully hold on to your present job. You may need it.)

You also broaden your skills, which makes you eligible for a wider variety of assignments. This expands your options and your promotion potential as you sharpen abilities in such areas as public relations, accounting, advertising, production, market analysis, quality control, computers, public speaking, publicity releases, goal setting, plans writing, and learning new techniques and methods in other departments. This also reduces your boredom and expands your horizon of challenges, interests and excitement.

Pursuits totally outside your company might include work with your appropriate trade association; chamber of commerce; civic and service clubs; charities; volunteer groups; and cultural, educational, medical, religious, sports, political, and other organizations. Many a manager has put these activities to multiple use as a source of personal fulfillment and expanded contacts that greatly helped toward his or her career goal.

One caution: There is a danger that these activities outside the immediate job can become so interesting and demanding that they interfere with your primary assignment. Don't let this happen. It can hurt your reputation and your record, and thus do you more harm than good.

PLAYING THE WAITING GAME

The waiting game is good strategy when (1) there's no hurry. You have plenty of time. (2) You rather like what you're doing, so you don't have a burr under your saddle or a stone in your shoe causing you immediate discomfort. (3) You have reason to believe that the apple will drop into your lap—so it's just a matter of time. Good application of this strategy calls for constant vigilance to be sure things have not taken a turn for the worse. You should minimize your assumptions: Never take it for granted that you've "got it made."

Aside from simply continuing to do a good job—"keeping on with keeping on"—which may not be as easy as it sounds, here you are taking a passive role. You are letting circumstances move you along toward your goal. Circumstances, not you, are the active element. You should watch those circumstances carefully.

If you can control them somewhat and nudge them in a favorable direction, so much the better, because then you are sort of making your own luck. If you have little or no control over them, as is true for most of us, most of the time, then you had better have a lifeboat ready—some other viable option or direction you can take, should your apple begin to rot.

The bottom line is that you are watching carefully, nudging things where you can, and keeping that lifeboat in good repair just in case.

One final caution: Be sure you recognize success when it hits you in the eye. Sometimes it arrives so suddenly and so subtly, or is so well disguised, that it is not easily recognized. A simple way to avoid this problem is to have a crystal-clear definition in your own mind as to just what constitutes your personal success and what you need to get this victory. Then you'll be better able to know it when it appears. Remember, too, that *your criteria for success* at any stage in your life may vary a bit, from month to month or year to year, so it's well worth reviewing occasionally.

WRITE IT DOWN

Prepare a written plan. This is easy to do and has lots of advantages. The system presented here is one that the professional career planners find works especially well (this is a bit more thorough than the brief three-page version described earlier).

Get yourself a small loose-leaf binder. Put in about 12 to 14 divider tab sheets. Behind each of these, insert a couple of pieces of blank paper. Now label those tabs something like this (adjusting the headings to fit your own interests, viewpoint, preferences, and situation):

1. Personal identity checkup.
2. Present job situation—analysis of the pros and cons.
3. Job market—the trends.

4. Best opportunities—short-term and long-term.
5. Best resources—contacts and friends.
6. Career goals—short-term and long-term, job, salary, by year.
7. Education—why use it, or why not?
8. Stepping-stones.
9. Outside activities.
10. The waiting game.
11. New worlds to conquer.
12. Flexibility.
13. Standing pat.
14. Next priorities and schedule.

Now put down a few sentences under each heading. If you are *not* going to use some of those strategy steps, simply write down your reason for that decision. If you *are* going to use that step, then you should expand on it a bit. You may want to use the five *W*s (who, what, when, where, why)—and how.

This whole package might be called your "Personal Career Plan." Notice that this follows the SOS formula of situation, objective, and strategy. This written plan can be done in an hour or so, and it has a lot of advantages.

1. It gives you a track to run on.
2. It covers about all the bases, so you don't miss much.
3. It organizes and clarifies your thinking and planning. For example, a goal you had just sort of dreamed about becomes much more practical (or ridiculous) when you write it down and look at it. Planning sharpens realism.
4. It helps you to make better decisions about your career program and your best strategies.
5. It is a very flexible approach. You can easily take pages out or add new systems, methods, or procedures, almost at a moment's notice. It is a "living document."
6. It builds you a "lifeboat" of viable alternative options.
7. It's comforting to know that you have it at hand. Now you know, as of today, just what you can reasonably expect out of life— and what you need to do and to put into the program to reach your goals. Your world will take on a new, vibrant perspective of realism.

8. It can be rather fun to do, because you will see your own "grand plan" unfold before your eyes, devised by your own hand and brain, for your own personal lifetime of satisfaction.

Caution: Don't keep this plan at work, where people can find it. Keep it tucked away at home. This is for your eyes only or for selected other eyes—not for just anyone's.

PLAN YOUR NEXT THREE STEPS

The next three steps in your strategy may all be in one area, such as "education" or "outside activities," or each may be in a different part of your strategic program. The advantage to picking these three activities is that now you can focus your time, effort, and other resources exclusively on these steps. By bringing your total power to bear on them, you make maximum progress. You also avoid cluttering your mind with all those other considerations and options. You put those on the back burner, for use only if and when needed.

Now you can put these next three steps in priority, plan them in detail, and move forward with execution and performance. As you measure your results, this can influence your schedule and your program. Unexpected trouble may suggest that a cutback is good strategy. Unusual speed could indicate a need for acceleration.

Your time schedule should cover your total program in general, but your next three priority steps in particular. This may be simply a half-page list of action steps with approximate dates. Basically, it should show you who does what, when, and where. There is great psychological value to a schedule, because it begins to set time benchmarks and targets to shoot at. It almost automatically sparks movement.

The most common error in scheduling strategy is setting unrealistically short time frames and expecting too much to be accomplished. This leads to "the tragedy of excessive expectations," disappointment, and disillusionment—all because of bad scheduling. The key: Give yourself a realistic time frame and then allow a little extra to account for unexpected troubles.

As you list each step and element, stop and think about the

procedure. Imagine that you are actually doing it. Think of the various problems you will face and a couple that probably won't happen but might. All systems can fail. And as one version of Murphy's Law goes, "Anything that can go wrong will go wrong—at the worst possible time and in the most unexpected way."

You may be far-above-average as an achiever, but you, too, can and will make a few mistakes. If you budget some time for these, then the occurrences won't be as disruptive and may cause you no setback at all.

For I. G. Farben Executive, Planning Is the Key

A top executive from I. G. Farben, the giant German conglomerate, speaking at a dinner last June in New York, said, "Planning strategy is a major cause of our well-known success, and this is true for any really progressive and prosperous company or manager. Personal career planning is only just now becoming popular among top executives, although I strongly suspect that our best executives have been secretly using careful strategy plans for years.

"As a German, I feel a little strange quoting one of your own American astronauts to you Americans, but one of your space pilots was asked what he would do if he were told that a major crisis had occurred during a mission, and he had only ten minutes to live. He said he would plan, recheck, and communicate for nine minutes and act during the tenth. That illustrates how he feels about planning. And remember, the U.S. space program is one of the most successful ventures on, and beyond, our planet."

SUMMARY

Here's how you can plan your success:

1. Use the easy, effective situation-objective-strategy formula (SOS).
2. Just doing a good job is often your best base plan.
3. Specialized education is effective if it fills a gap.
4. Stepping-stones work well if executed with care.

5. Use outside interests when these lead to your goal.
6. The waiting game works if the apple will drop into your lap.
7. Go conquer new worlds when other strategies are ineffective.
8. Write it down into a "Personal Career Plan."
9. Select your next three steps. Set priorities and focus on them.
10. Stay flexible. Use new opportunities.
11. Stand pat when you like things as they are.

Your OBI (one best idea) for planning your success is to use the SOS formula, good performance, education, stepping-stones, outside interests, the waiting game, new worlds, a written plan, priority steps, flexibility, and standing pat. Employ each strategy as circumstances suggest its usefulness.

CHAPTER 17
Your Search for
New Worlds to Conquer

The objective of this chapter is to give you a couple of hundred constructive and proven suggestions for finding a new position. At this point, you have concluded that other strategies are not effective—and that a new job is your best move.

LOOKING ISN'T LEAVING

Looking just means checking around. Also, there's a whole lot of groundwork and preparation you can do before you actually contact any prospective employers. One of your best guidelines to looking is to *do it soon enough*. Better to be a little early than a little late. The advantage to you is that an early start gives you enough time to take all or most of the right steps that will help you reach your goal. If you wait too long, you may be rushed, need to skip some steps, and it won't work out as well for you.

When should you start looking? There's no sure-fire rule. But a good policy is to begin your search when you are pretty certain you have a serious problem—and when other strategies simply are not working. On the other hand, if you have stayed only a year or two on your last few jobs, you won't be very attractive to most employers. They may feel you're a job hopper. Weigh these factors and balance them against each other.

START YOUR SEARCH EARLY

The advantages to lead-time scheduling are numerous. An early search lets you operate at your own speed, perhaps even casually. And you still have a job and an income. You feel no urgency or pressure, or at least this is less than it would be under emergency conditions. It also gives you a stronger bargaining position—you look much more attractive than you would if you were in a panic or without a job.

The "sub rosa seeker" can actually have a little fun, since he or she is playing a game of great potential reward at little or no cost. With reasonable care, the chances are very small that you will be discovered by your employer. Oscar Wilde once said, "You can get away with almost anything if you don't talk about it." So watch your conversations with associates. Don't fear that prospective employers will reveal that you contacted them. They get hundreds, perhaps thousands, of such contacts. Many could be from employees of your own company—maybe even from your boss!

Make a Plan

Use the situation-objective-strategy, or SOS, formula we discussed in the first few pages of the last chapter. You know your situation—the problems and opportunities, the strengths and weaknesses, of your job and yourself. You know your objective, or goals. And this chapter will give you many strategy suggestions.

Make your selection and choices from these strategy options. Write them down. Take a good look at them. Think about them. Decide if this is really the program you want and if these are really your best steps. A written plan will make you much more careful, accurate, thorough, and effective. But keep it fairly simple—a few pages. One page may be too few, fifty too many.

Pick Your Objective with Care

Since your objective will greatly influence your entire set of strategy steps, which is the heart of your program, it should be selected with special care. Also, be sure you really want the goal you pick. Will Rogers used to say, "Be careful about asking for something you don't really want—because you might get it!" Your goals should probably be short-term, like this month, and long-term, like six to twelve months. Many good searches take that long. Certainly, three of your short-term goals should be (1) to start soon enough, (2) to get a *better* job, and (3) not to endanger your current position.

Another important set of goals should include the approximate type of job you seek, industry, function, and perhaps location. Definitely include salary range and possibly some conditions of employment, such as staff, surroundings, hours, future, and fringe benefits. Better to be a bit fussy, specific, and detailed. That way, you'll know the perfect job when you see it. And you can always compromise or trade off some of the items later, if necessary.

A final important objective is certainly to *get several good job offers,* so you can pick the best.

Identify Your Prospective Employers

"I can't understand it! Nobody wants me! I applied to ten companies and didn't get a single job offer!" This is a very common complaint. The person making this sort of statement has not yet developed a feel for the situation, the market, or the ball game he or she is playing in. This isn't like applying to some college for entry. The college is selling education, and *you* are buying. In the job market, you are selling your services, and *the employer* is buying.

One of the most important things to know is that *you are playing the odds*—and the odds are *stacked heavily against you.* You may be a beautiful, attractive, smart, well-educated high achiever. But at any given moment, most companies simply do not have an opening for your particular type of person—no matter how wonderful you are. A good working estimate is that about 5 percent of the firms you contact may have an opening for you. But 95 percent do not.

However, knowing that gives you an important advantage over the unknowledgeable novice. It tells you that you must *look to your numbers.* The novice hasn't caught on to that yet. It means that if you apply to twenty companies, only about 5 percent will have a possible opening. That means one company! And that job may not be anything at all like what you are seeking—or the department head with that opening may never even see your application. You don't know about that department head, and he or she doesn't know about you. Yet you are both seeking each other. It's a little like two blind people groping for each other in the dark.

The message is simple! *Get the numbers on your side*. How? Use lots of numbers—lots of applications. If you send to 100 firms, the odds are that about 5 will have openings for you, and 2 or 3 may show an interest. One may make you an offer—maybe. Conclusion: Apply to a couple of hundred. Even 500 to 1,000 contacts is not at all unusual—unless you have a particular skill that is in very high and frequent demand by nearly every other company in town.

How do you find 500 really good prospective employers? It's easy. Decide on your criteria for such an organization—size, type, location. If you will relocate to any place in the United States, or at least to a major portion of the nation, then ask your business reference librarian for *Moody's Manual* or a similar listing of American companies. *Moody's* lists about 35,000. You can scan these, comparing them against your criteria, and pick out 500.

If you want to stay in your city or one of a few specific towns, check with their respective chambers of commerce. Those organizations can usually sell you, for a few dollars, a listing by size and type of the major companies in the town.

If you only want to work for a specific type of company, such as food, clothing, cosmetics, or construction, again your business reference librarian can help you. There are several books that each list over 4,000 trade associations. Every one of these organizations, of course, specializes in a particular industry. Write to a couple in the category of your choice asking for a list of companies and addresses. These should cost no more than five or ten dollars.

As you can see, there is a lot of homework you can do before you have seen the first prospective employer. It may take a month or so just to complete this much groundwork, if you are doing it part time.

Or you may simply wish to just contact a few employment agencies, major management consultants, or executive recruiters at this point. But before you do, you should at least scan the rest of this chapter, so your actions are as productive and effective as possible. Remember, in many cases, you get only one turn at bat with the prospective employer, so you want it to get you the best possible results.

PREPARE A RÉSUMÉ

There are all sorts of opinions on résumés, and a lot of this is a matter of your own tastes and preferences. But an easy way to start is to look at the purpose of such a document.

The objective of your résumé is to help you reach your goal (to get a job—a better job); to do this by summarizing you (your training, experience, achievements, and abilities); to show your best face in the best possible light; to capture your prospective employer's attention, interest, and preference, and to make you look better than your competition. (Where there's a really good job, there will be other people looking for it.) To achieve these objectives, your résumé should probably follow these guidelines:

1. Put it on one sheet, both sides.
2. List your name, address, zip, phone with area code.
3. Include a small, passport-size picture. (It personalizes, captures attention, puts you a notch above others, and shows that you don't have two heads. It starts a friendship.)
4. List your last few jobs—company name, duties, achievements.
5. Show education and specialized training.
6. Include any special activities or honors.
7. Give a few reference names and phone numbers.
8. Mention height, weight, health, family, hobbies.

Be very factual. Use a telegraphic style and few adjectives. Let every item you select speak well for you and tell your story. Have the résumé quality printed on a good grade of heavy paper. Spend a little extra here. It will be a good investment. But don't go overboard into anything like a deluxe folder. This could hurt you more than it helps—unless you're an artist.

A few exhibits can be a low-cost and very effective way to give you a good edge over your competition. The ideal such items are just one page each—clear, strong, simple, concise, dramatic, self-explanatory, and directly pertinent to the job you seek. For example, if you completed a major or especially constructed project in sales, production, accounting, or administration, you might select a one-page sample. Ideally, you should have two or three of these. This can be a very impressive, useful, and effective selling tool.

Exhibits should be used right along with your résumé and handed out again during an interview or at any other opportune moment. It provides a few extra arrows for your bow and gives you a competitive edge over other candidates.

Your Cover Letter

A plain résumé landing on an executive's desk leaves him or her a bit cold. It opens almost as many questions as it answers. The recipient wonders, "Is this for me? What kind of job does this person want? Pay? What does he or she want me to do next?" Chances are good that the résumé will hit the round file.

Your cover letter is a short note that accompanies your résumé and keeps it from hitting your prospective employer cold. It can accomplish a lot of things very quickly and pleasantly. It says hello. It introduces you. It greets your potential employer. It dignifies your résumé and gives you a good chance to say what you are looking for in terms of duties and salary, to explain why you sent your résumé, to offer a few highlights of your abilities, and to "ask for the order" (or at least for an interview). Here's an effective format for the cover letter.

1. It's on one side of one page, on quality paper, with your name, address, and phone number printed at the top.

2. Mailing list companies say not to even try addressing it to a specific person. People change jobs so rapidly that most lists are 20 percent to 50 percent out of date within a year. You are much better off to simply *send to a given position,* like the president or the vice-president of sales or production. Generally, it's the present holder of the position you want to contact, not any one special person. If you have identified some particularly good companies, you might be wise to send to several positions at each of those firms. You could bomb with three people but hit with the fourth. Again, you're getting numbers, and the odds are on your side.

3. The letter can be printed. It need not be individually typed. If you have what they want, they could not care less how the material is produced, as long as it's neat and readable.

4. It can start off generically, "Dear Manager." He or she doesn't really care.

5. Talk first about the manager and his or her interests: "If you are looking for a sales manager of xyz (or in abc town), then perhaps you would like to consider me."

6. Then mention some of your most recent major accomplishments: (1) supervised ten representatives, (2) launched four new products successfully, and (3) exceeded annual sales goal by 80 percent."

7. In giving salary requirements, indicate a range, from 10 percent to 30 percent above your present salary. More than that will turn off most employers. You can also add, "I will relocate anywhere in the United States" or indicate a few specific sections, but the pickier you are, the smaller your chances get.

Run Your Mailing Program

At this point, you have your résumé, prospect list, cover letter, and exhibits. Put them together and send them out.

You should consider mailing to 50 or 100 management consultants or executive recruiters at this time. Again, see your business reference librarian or friendly local consultant for the list called *The Directory of Executive Recruiters*. Bear in mind that head hunters don't normally find jobs for people—they find people to fill job-search assignments. They are working for and paid by the employer. You might do this in batches, but usually your letters can all go at once.

Allow two to eight weeks for answers. About half or more will never reply. Some will send you a "thanks, but no thanks" or "so sorry" letter. Some will reply, " we have nothing, but if you happen to be in town, we hope you will drop in and say hello." These are mostly companies that really do not have anything, but that like your résumé and may hire people like you occasionally.

Some of them are understating and actually do have something but, for various reasons, cannot bring you in to see them. Generally, put these people on a B-priority list, to visit if and when the opportunity arises.

The letters you are looking for are the 5 percent or so that will say something like, "We received your résumé and were very favorably impressed. Yes, we do have an opening much like the one you described, and we would like you to come and visit with us at your earliest convenience. Please call me at this number." *This is a hot prospect*—an A-priority. Phone him or her immediately. But be prepared. Sometimes, for ego or other reasons, the person has grossly exaggerated.

In any case, keep careful records of replies. This will prevent serious foul-ups and help you move more efficiently toward your goal.

Use Personal Contacts

Along with your mail program, you might make a few personal contacts. This could be through your own friends or their friends, suppliers, and other good associates. This is called networking. A good approach is to give each of these people a few envelopes containing your résumé, cover letter, and exhibits. Be careful to whom you give these, since some may feel even greater allegiance to your boss, and your material could end up on his or her desk!

Respond to Ads

Answer "help wanted" ads and special display ads, such as those found in the daily *Wall Street Journal,* as time and convenience permit. Those particular ads can be very attractive and often pull several hundred applicants (who are rarely acknowledged!).

Be Ready for Phone Calls

Within a week of so after you mail your material, the phone may start ringing. These are often your *very best A+* opportunites. They saw your material, liked it, and *they want action right now*.

Encourage other members of your family to hold their phone calls to a minimum in number and length. You don't want your caller to get discouraged and contact the second- or third-choice candidate instead.

Have a note pad at the phone and start writing the minute the person says, "My name is Smith, with the XYZ Company." If you aren't sure what the caller said, ask him or her to please repeat, so you get it right. He or she will be glad to. There really is a big difference between "General Motors" and "General Movers."

The chances are that they will ask you to come and visit them. Accept this, unless you have a very strong reason not to do so. Even if you don't know who they are, they might offer you an opening that would amaze you. And if it was a wasted trip, at least you probably learned some interesting things and made good contacts. And sometimes most inportant, you kept occupied. The worst times you will face are when you have no action. You badly need to keep busy. It will help lift your spirits, which could be pretty low at this stage.

Tack up near the phone a little list of key points to discuss such as (1) company, (2) caller's name, (3) the firm's address and (4) phone number, (5) basic facts, and (6) who pays for the trip? (Most will pay and will promptly say so. If not, get it clear—or you could get stuck. If they want you to pay, you might schedule the trip for a week or two away and then reschedule or cancel if something better comes along.)

Double-check time, place, and date of the visit. Confirm these points in a short thank-you note. You have an important opportunity. You will only get a few, so you don't want some mix-up to ruin it.

Look out for phonies. A certain percentage of your calls may be from people who want you to "buy into our franchise distributorship" or do door-to-door selling or telephone solicitation, perhaps on a part-time basis. Unless this is what you really set as a goal for yourself, thank them and bow out gracefully. The experience will do you good. When you are in the search mode, it is important for you to know how to tactfully decline invitations.

TRAVEL WISELY

If your prospective employer offers to make hotel/motel and/or flight reservations, record these carefully and accept them, since the firm's staff may move people in and out a lot and know what to do and what not to do. Perhaps more important, you are establishing a *vital dialog*. They are advising. You are consenting. You are getting to know each other. There's nothing wrong with taking five or ten minutes to make plans. They know this is an unusual experience for you (or they hope it is), and you become better friends.

When your travel plans (hotel and flight) are set, then reconfirm these in a note to your host, if you have not already done so earlier.

As you travel, keep an accurate record of your legitimate travel costs. (Hotel, plane, cabs, and meals are the main ones.) Don't pad. Spend moderately and wisely. It gains you points. Some otherwise very bright applicants hurt themselves by submitting expense reports that look like a sheikh's holiday.

If for any reason you are delayed or must change the date, phone your host at the earliest possible moment. Managers don't like last-minute surprises. Explain the problem and ask for an alternate appointment. But try to avoid this, because they may have juggled a lot of schedules to set up your meeting—such as arranging for the key manager to be there. They might not be willing or able to do this a second time.

INTERVIEW EFFECTIVELY

Interview so you come out as the best candidate. Take every reasonable step you can think of to make a good impression.

Arrive rested, well dressed, and a little ahead of time. If you are early and have a few minutes to chat with the receptionist, compliment her if you can and have a few simple questions handy. You may be amazed at what she will know and might tell you.

Greet your host with his or her name and a smile. Be alert, pleasant, interested, and moderately relaxed—not a bundle of nerves. Don't try too hard and don't try to be a joker. Have a short list of questions that are general and easy to answer, at least at first. And give your host every opportunity to talk about himself or herself and the company. He or she will usually be delighted. Listen carefully. Ask permission to take a few notes. Don't interrupt. If offered tea or coffee, accept it. You're building friendship.

Answer his or her questions in a clear, brief, businesslike but friendly manner. Expand on these points if your host seems at all interested. Have some extra résumés to give out. Then pause. Come up for air. Don't hog the conversation. Briefly cover the most important points in your background, then steer the visit back to your host. Remember, he or she has seen your résumé. Show a lot of interest—even a tad more than you may really feel. It never hurts. People will nearly always be interested in you if you first show a strong interest in them. Keep using your host's name fairly frequently.

If you have some brief, pertinent, and significant exhibits such as reports, charts, pictures, slides, products, or flip charts, wait for an appropriate time and then present this material. It will often put you well ahead of your competition. If a good time opening doesn't occur, then make one by simply saying, "I have several exhibits *that you* might find interesting," and then go right into it.

Be superpolite and accommodating 90 percent of the time, but you may find that, in the other 10 percent, you must be just a little assertive. Try to brag without seeming to do so. A good way is to simply and briefly mention accomplishments and let these facts speak for themselves.

If you are asked about your company or boss, resist *any* temptation to provide confidential information or to "bad-mouth" them. If your host doesn't like those folks, you won't be telling him or her anything new—and if your host does like them, you'd be making a big error. And he or she *won't respect you* much for revealing any confidences. Your best approach is to say, "Well, those people have some strengths and weaknesses." Few people will be offended with that. And your goal is to make a friend, not give a management analysis.

If the interview takes a negative or abrasive turn, try to get back to pleasant subjects. Your interviewer may be testing your tolerance. Don't get angry. Keep cool and keep trying. Sometimes just plain ornery interviewers will turn around completely and become most pleasant.

Try to always end on an upbeat note. Thank your host and express a strong interest in the company and the hope that you will meet again.

SELL YOURSELF

Here's how to sell yourself with some *extra* devices: During the interview, show not only interest in the firm's problems but, if possible, a true *understanding* of them. Be careful. Do not presume to know the solutions. But do ask about actions your host and his or her staff have taken or options they have eliminated.

Focus in on *their immediately upcoming project,* if they have one. The chances are that this may be the very reason why you are being interviewed. You would be making a serious error to treat it lightly. It's probably very important and pressing to them. Listen very closely to their problem, as *they* see it. If you show a keen interest in their problem, this makes it seem almost *as if you are already working for them*—the ideal approach. More important, this makes you look better than your competitors. You may even appear better than some of their own employees! Also, be alert to their *goals* and objectives, if you are lucky enough to hear these. Jot them down.

Now, here's a very strong card you can play. If and when you are interviewed for a job you especially want, ask your host if it would be all right for you to send or bring in an example of your planning. Few interviewers will reject this offer. They won't feel they will learn anything about their business, but they figure they will learn more about you—and they are right.

Then when you get home, send your host a thank-you letter strongly expressing appreciation for the interview and promising a "simple plan" within a week or so. This gives you a chance to make another contact with the interviewer—a very important one—that can let you really sell yourself.

Your plan can be pretty simple. If you asked the right questions, then, without realizing it, your host practically handed it to you. You can simply look at your notes and, on a page or two, outline the firm's problem, exactly as your host gave it to you (and as you wisely jotted it down). Then cover the objectives, again as they were stated to you.

The strategy can be a list of the firm's own steps—and why these were satisfactory (just as you were told). Add some reasonable, sensible, logical, and somewhat middle-of-the-road additional suggestions. Be very careful of extremes, either way. You are sailing on unknown water. You could be flying in the face of your prospective boss—unless you are lucky enough to know his or her preferences. If you have any contacts in the field involved, you would be very wise to get a few suggestions. Don't get too complex or overpromise.

Be sure your plan is typed neatly. Bind it in a simple paper folder and send copies with a short cover letter to all those who interviewed you. This will usually knock their eyes out. Not one in a hundred applicants thinks to do this—and it's really quite easy. You go to the head of your class and to the top of the list. (I have personally seen this work with remarkable success.)

How to Handle the Psych Tests

Your interview went well. They like you. Now, they are willing to invest big bucks to get an independent, third-party expert opinion. An invitation is extended to you, and you have accepted. Why not? You have nothing to lose. You won't get the job without taking the psych test. And a date is set. This is a very important hurdle. Bomb here, and you're out. Do well, and you're 90 percent home.

The secret to success with most psych tests is surprisingly simple: It is your attitude, or mind-set. This will greatly influence your answers, since the tests are seldom really trying to measure your technical skills. Your best policy or strategy is simply to imagine yourself to be the "ideal" candidate and then *play that role*. These tests can be fun. Use that attitude, too, as part of your mind-set. Think positive.

Move carefully. Read all instructions. Do the best you can, while you constantly *play your role*. If you run into something you don't understand, don't get hung up and waste a lot of time. Skip it and go back later, rather than taking the chance of messing up a section. Further sections may clear things up.

The test may try to trip you up by "proving" that you have strange, violent, obsessively sexual, or perverted ideas. A favorite device is sentence completion. You will be asked to complete such sentences as, "My secret desire is . . . ," or, "The one thing I don't dare tell people is . . . ." Your best strategy is to keep right on *playing your role*. Say something like, ". . . to do the best possible job I can," or, ". . . to be a better professional," or ". . . to be the best manager in the country."

Another common test involves showing you pictures and asking you to describe what is happening. Again, *play your role*. If you are shown a man clinging to a vertical line, say, "Here is a man climbing a rope" (going up), never "sliding down a rope."

CHECK OUT THE COMPANY

While the company is checking on you, you should be checking on the company. Your purpose is to be sure you are reaching your objective and not getting back into the same situation as the one you are leaving—or worse. (It happens all too often.)

Read the company's annual report but take it with many grains of salt. Check company write-ups in your library (*Moody's* and others). If you possibly can, *get other people's opinions*. Talk with customers, suppliers, current and past employees. You may be amazed at what they know and say. The company officers showed you mainly their best side, just as you did to them. They checked you for problems, just as you are doing. Don't take only one person's opinion, but do consider the answers in total.

Look for the company's reputation in the industry and in dealing with people, especially with employees. Check pros, cons, sales, profits, reorganization, job security, salary levels, competition, turnover, ownership (family held?), location, duties, kinds of employees, kinds of top managers, policies, future, and the compatibility of your goals and style with the company's.

Evaluate and Negotiate the Company's Offer

At about this point, you are likely to get an offer from perhaps half the companies you've been visiting intensely. Don't accept instantly, unless you are desperate. But do sound enthusiastic. Say, "May I reconfirm a few points with you?" Be certain of the salary and fringes like bonus and profit sharing. Those are occasionally treated vaguely in earlier visits. Recheck duties, location, responsibility levels, whom you report to—and your plain gut feel about the whole situation. Things sometimes change during detailed discussions.

If everything looks like gangbusters and roses, accept right there. If you'd like to think about it, say, "It sounds great. May I call you tomorrow with a firm commitment?" Most will have no objections. If they hesitate, accept the job, firm things up, and make plans. It will still take you and them some days or weeks to get working together, and that's plenty of time to compare on a point-by-point basis other offers you may get.

Occasionally, you will get an offer paying not as much money as you expected. A 10 percent to 30 percent jump over your present level is reasonable. Perhaps a bit less if you are unemployed. You may even need to take a cut—but sometimes it's good strategy to go down one step to eventually go up two. If the offer is a bit too low, stall them until you see what your other prospects bring. In the end, you might take the low offer.

You really won't be invited to bargain very much. By the time they make you a proposal, they know the exact job they want to offer and what salary they want to pay. The original proposition may be modified a bit by that time.

It is well for you to remember that the offer may be strictly limited by ranges and the salary structure they are paying others. A change of just $1,000 could cause all sorts of ripples and static through a big part of the organization. This at least partly ties their hands and limits their willingness and ability to bargain. Your best bargaining points are on other conditions that are far less structured and more flexible—like duties, responsibilities, staff, location, office, and reporting date.

If you do bargain, do it in a friendly, relaxed, almost casual way, since you want to start your new job on a good note, not under a cloud.

Adapt Job Search to Your Needs

You can shorten or lengthen this whole job search program. Upon reading all this, your initial feeling may be, "Oh, wow! I don't want to go to all that much trouble."

Fine. You can easily adjust this system to be a lot simpler. You might just wish to check around, apply to a few firms, make a few phone calls, and that could do the trick. On the other hand, you might want to take a long, leisurely year to check out many more opportunities than outlined here. This plan gives you maximum flexibility for adjusting to your own wants, needs, time frame, and life style.

SUMMARY

Here are some practical guidelines for your most effective search program:

1. Looking isn't leaving—just checking.
2. You get lots of advantages from looking early enough.
3. Make a simple plan: SOS (situation, objective, strategy).
4. Select your objective with special care.
5. Make a large list of prospective employers.
6. Prepare a résumé of your background, plus exhibits.
7. Write a short cover letter.
8. Run your mailing program.
9. You might make a few personal contacts.
10. Answer "help wanted" ads as time permits.
11. Be ready for phone calls.
12. Travel wisely, with very careful spending.
13. Interview so you come out as the best candidate.
14. Sell yourself with some extra devices.
15. Handle the psych tests largely through attitude.
16. Check on the company, just as the company checked on you.
17. Evaluate and negotiate your job offer.
18. Shorten or lengthen this plan, according to your style.

Your OBI (one best idea) for a successful search is mainly to make— and then act decisively on—a fairly complete SOS plan covering your situation, goal, prospects, résumé, cover letter, exhibits, mailing, interviewing, and final selection.

CHAPTER 18
Organizing Your Staff for Outstanding Performance

As an above-average person, you have now either decided to stay and gain high achievement and fulfillment with your present position, or you have gone to a new job. Either way, you probably have at least a small staff. Even if this is only one or two people or half a dozen, your staff represents a great opportunity for you, because, properly organized and utilized, they can help you take giant steps toward your goal of company progress and your personal gain. And if you do it right, this will require only a minimum of effort on your part. The objective of this chapter is to look at how you can accomplish this.

MAKE YOUR STAFF YOUR NO. 1 TOOL

Your group represents a great opportunity and potential for future success. A disorganized, confused, unstructured, misused, or underused staff is highly inefficient and counterproductive. It is even harmful. We all know the old saying about idle hands being the devil's playground. Such a situation can actually destroy them, your company, and you. If you are to save yourself and reach your achievement goals, you really have no choice: organize progress or perish. How can you make your staff into a "major tool"? Several ways.

First, look at the situation and the problems facing you. Select a couple of challenges and issues to be resolved. Pick ones that will respond to and be corrected through the specific efforts of your staff. Avoid projects where you and you alone must carry the key

234 YOU AS A HIGH ACHIEVER

burden. Second, encourage your staff to understand your group planning process. Get them directly *involved*. As you study problems and look for solutions, bring staff people into and encourage them to become a part of the process.

Third, use your staff to help set objectives, so that *your* goals become *theirs*—so that they know the name of the game and why they are really there on the job. Fourth, outline steps that divide up and parcel out projects to every staff member. Each new one has his or her own resposibilities and "territory." And everyone knows this. They all feel a certain pride and some obligation, not just to you, but to themselves and to their fellow workers.

Focus the power of your organization on your problems, like sun rays through a magnifying glass. Your staff members have dramatic, and even amazing, potential power, but you must turn it on. Concentrate their attention. Treat your staff as something you value and care about as a master tool, and it will rapidly become just that.

Discover—and Employ—Their Strengths

Everyone has certain good abilities. If you find these and put them to use, you will greatly strengthen the power of your organization and your staff's morale and maximize your own personal progress. It is truly a sad sight to see executives struggling mightily, trying to do a job by themselves, when they have people right there in their organization who could easily do that same project—as well as the managers, or even better.

How do you find their strengths? Stop, look, and listen. Stop long enough to study and analyze people just a little. Look at what they are doing, what they like to do, and what they do well. They are trying to tell you that they will serve you better in those fields, if you will just take the time to notice. Listen to what they are saying. They are expressing interests. Ask them about their work and hear them when they answer. Most people like to do the things they do well and thus are not slow to talk about these things. In reality, you are taking a personal and talent inventory.

Praise these people for what they do well, and they will do more of it. Famous organization specialist Frederick W. Taylor said, "Listen, learn and laud."

Let people try their wings and stretch their abilities. Discover and apply *all* the good that is there. After all, you are paying for the whole package.

Discover—and Avoid—Their Weaknesses

To protect yourself, you must also learn about your staff's weaknesses. Even good managers have a bad habit of forcing projects on people who really can't perform them very well. This hurts everyone. The strong organizations use people's strengths but avoid their weaknesses. In that way, every assignment that comes along goes to a person who is skilled in that activity rather than to someone who may let the project crash to the ground. You can learn about weaknesses right along with your search for strengths. Note both at the same time.

These inabilities may also come out as you let people try new things and stretch themselves. Some will overreach and fall on their faces. Switch such a person to some other task and remember the sad experience, so you avoid making that type of assignment again in the future, unless you have no other choice. And discourage other people from giving that person similar projects. In short, protect him or her, your organization, and yourself from the weakness.

Generally, you will be wise and expand the power of your group by avoiding any excess criticism. You might simply say something like, "Don't worry too much about it. We all have our weak spots. Avoid these and work where your best strengths lie." Just make sure the strengths really are there and really are used.

MAKE AND USE A "PHOTO CHART"

A major problem with many organizations is simply that people are often not very clear about the hierarchical layout—where they stand, who's above, who's below, and who's on their same level. And who does what. Outsiders looking in are even more perplexed.

The solution is to develop some sort of organization chart or diagram, with titles and people's names in boxes or circles. Done properly, this solves the confusion and also has lots of other advantages. People not only know where they stand, but they know where everyone else stands, too. They know who's on first and who's on second—who gives orders, who gets ordered, and who does what. And it's all right out there in front of God and everyone. There will be fewer people sneaking around acting like bosses when they are not (skim milk masquerading as cream). People see the lines of authority. A secretary can see that he or she really only reports and is responsible to one or a set number of people—not to everybody. This avoids a lot of trouble and boosts spirit and morale, as well as building a stronger, more effective organization.

How do you draft an organization chart? So many top people don't know how to construct a simple, yet highly useful, diagram such as this that we should look at one of the procedures. Here are eight suggestions:

1. Do a messy rough draft with pencil, just to get the feel of it and familiarize yourself with the general pattern.

2. In doing this draft, start with the group head. Put that person's name and title in a box near the top of the sheet. If it's you, put your name in there.

3. Under that supervisor, put a horizontal row of boxes. These are the second-level people, those who report directly to that group head—or whom the group head supervises directly.

4. Put people's names and titles in those second-level boxes. Now draw a horizontal line over that row of second-level boxes. Then connect each of those boxes upward to the horizontal line and put one line up from there to the top supervisor.

5. If there are third-level people who report to one of the second-level positions, put them in. Same for fourth and fifth levels. When completed, a good organization chart usually resembles a pyramid.

6. Avoid dotted lines, curved lines, wiggly lines, and two lines going to the same box. These are usually symptomatic of a schizophrenic, paranoidal uncertainty as to just who is really in charge. It also suggests that some games are being played, in which one person has two supervisors or two managers are told that they each supervise the same person or group. This can cause all sorts of confusion, trouble, conflicts, bad feelings, and inefficiency.

7. Use photos or head shots of individuals in the squares.

After all, positions are not boxes; they are living human beings. A roll of high-speed black-and-white film without flash will usually do the job quickly and at low cost. Crop the photos to show just the head or the head and shoulders. This will really humanize and warm up your chart. Those shown on it will take a much greater personal interest in your organization.

8. As a couple of "extras," you might use a variety of brightly colored felt pens to put wide borders around each box. This will add further drama, brightness, and excitement to your photo chart. You might also use little sketches (such as state, national, or world map outlines) or little gears to show "We mesh together with other groups" or to show how you work. They might be labeled "resources, action, results." In short, use any simple step that clarifies the action of your organization without getting in the way.

In the end, you will impress other managers, including your boss. But most important, in a unique and powerful way, you will have educated, sold, unified, and enthused your own organization.

BUILD MUTUAL RESPECT

Building mutual respect among team members means fostering a regard for one another and an appreciation for what each can do. There are many advantages to such a system, attitude, and environment—all of which add up to increased service to your company and to your own personal goals.

First, it pulls people together, unifying and focusing their efforts so that they get more done as a group than they ever would working individually. Second, it improves morale, spirit, and that "can-do" attitude that pays off in giant dividends. Third, it attracts more good people as well as awards, outside respect, recognition, promotions, and salary increases.

Here's an effective, well-proven method for building high organizational morale: First, level with your people about your goal and your strong desire to reach it. You might even say something like, "We have a good group here. A good organization. I am proud of our group, and I am proud of each of you. I respect you. Each of you, each of us, has strengths, and we are using these. I want us to have high morale. It makes life a little more worthwile. It makes getting up in the morning something to look forward to and makes our day more fun. I need your help if we are going to get and keep a good spirit around here. I need your help, but in the end, this will help both you and me—all of us."

This may be a little exaggerated but should never be a total untruth, or don't say it. However, such a statement can become a self-fulfilling prophesy.

Second, lay down the law: "Here's one thing I really want us all to do. When we talk to others about our group, *always boost the team*. Never knock it. In fact, take every chance you get to give the group a plug and a lift. Pretty soon, you'll find our reputation and our spirits going up. Others aren't often smart enough to use this device. Let's work smarter—and feel better about ourselves."

Third, make sure *everyone knows everyone else's strengths*. It's amazing how many people work with someone for years without realizing that he or she has some very strong job-related ability. But the boss knew. He or she *should have said something* about this— and said it often. It builds morale, mutual respect, and a stronger, more powerful organization to better serve the boss and the company.

Plan Assignments for Maximum Effectiveness

The advantages to planning and assigning both group and individual goals and duties are quite simple. Everyone often then feels a certain factual and emotional obligation to reach them. Your organization becomes stronger and more effective—and you achieve more.

Here's how you can do this: First, set a team goal and make sure everyone knows it. This is your reason for being, and each member of your group should be well aware of it. Second, work with each key member of your organization to set personal goals. Do the same with their methods, systems, or strategies for reaching these goals. Such steps are basically their job description and duties.

Third, share this information with everyone. Job descriptions should not be a secret. Make summaries of each of the key ones and pass them around. Now everyone knows not only everyone else's strengths but their duties as well. This means the proper assignments and the proper credit or respect are given to the right persons. And your organization is strengthened—doing more work and better work in a happier climate.

Use the "Rule of Ten"

The "rule of 10" is a span-of-control guideline that says that a manager should supervise about 10 people. Possibly a few more or a few less—but not 3 or 30 or 100.

If two managers are each supervising three people, this usually indicates a structure that is top-heavy with management—too many chiefs and not enough Indians. The organization could be much more efficient if the better of the two managers supervised the six people. The other manager might supervise some other group or be made staff specialist—or become one of the Indians! If, on the other hand, one manager is trying to directly and personally supervise 30 or 100, his or her span of control is spread hopelessly thin. The manager can't really control, serve, supervise, or advise this many people. He or she is hoarding power—power that should be shared.

The long-ruling Roman military used the "rule of ten" for all its successful legions. And even Jesus Christ had only twelve disciples. Most effective military and business units in our modern world use this same "rule of ten," though not always consciously.

The advantage to this guideline is pure and simple: It provides effective control. Three people with one manager are oversupervised. Thirty people with one manager are undersupervised. In both groups, control is faulty. Efficiency is low.

Among less professional, more routine operations and groups, a manager can effectively supervise or control more than ten. In more professional, nonroutine operations, the manager is more effective supervising less than ten. And as education and technical training increase (half our high school graduates now go on to college), there is a trend toward professionalism and thus a need for smaller groups per supervisior. Here is how you might do this:

1. Where you have only a few people reporting to a supervisor, try to arrange for these same people to report instead to some

other, underutilized manager. This frees up the first executive for other important assignments.

2. Where you have too many people, perhaps thirty, reporting to one manager, break these into several groups of maybe ten each, and appoint someone to act as subleader, spokesperson, or supervisor for each of the three groups.

3. If the three groups do similar work, consider encouraging a bit of moderate and healthy competition between them. This makes activity more interesting, spirited, exciting, and fun and your organization more productive.

SELL YOUR TEAM

Your team will need to be sold to themselves and to others. First—now that they know the members' abilities, duties, and goals—remind them of these points occasionally. People forget all too quickly. Second, insist on mutual respect and the "boost-don't-knock" philosophy mentioned earlier. Check to be sure this is followed. Third, emphasize how you, as a team, are working together to help the company and themselves—while winning a good and growing reputation.

Fourth, talk to other leaders and groups. Explain how your group is put together. Show them your organization photo chart and explain that you want to cooperate, work with, and help other groups as best you can. Perhaps even volunteer to provide some service or take on a project for others.

Such an approach helps to build spirit, reputation, pride, confidence, and a high-performing organization.

ORGANIZE YOUR GROUP'S TIME

Many a fine, strong organization operates far below its potential for one, simple reason: Its members waste great quantities of time. They are wasting their lives and yours. Here are ten ways to correct this:

1. Demonstrate your own sense of time and urgency.
2. Encourage your people to start each day with a list of to-do projects—*more than can easily be done*. Stretch a little.
3. Urge them to set priorities for the projects, so they do first things first.
4. Suggest that they do difficult jobs at their best time of the day.
5. Avoid wasting much time on unimportant projects that are easy and largely fun.
6. Select projects carefully, since 80 percent of your progress comes from 20 percent of your projects.
7. Multiply yourself by using the phone, job delegation, notes, and short meetings. Put travel time, waiting time, and spare time to good use.
8. Avoid boredom by switching the projects' order around.
9. Reward yourself. Do a tough job, then an easy one.
10. Avoid long-winded phone calls and meetings. Make an excuse and cut out, back to more productive uses of time. ·

In short, don't waste time, any more than you must. Time is your life—and your money.

Consider the Toyota Quality Circles Method

Some of the Japanese methods just recently being tested by several of our largest American corporations are definitely worth considering. In one branch of Toyota, the executive director (equivalent to an American executive vice-president) said, "We deliberately organize our people in ways that increase their productivity and their morale. We consider our staff to be our most important investment. They decide our future. Of course, we all know one another's abilities and duties. Mutual respect is a way of life for Japanese people. This strengthens our organizations.

"We have a system that some people call 'quality circles.' Here each supervisor brings his or her entire team, of about eight to twelve people, together twice a week. The objective of the meeting is quality control and quality improvement. They sit in a circle, and each has his or her turn to speak a minute or so. He or she is expected to suggest some steps to improve quality. If the person has no suggestion, he or she is expected to comment on someone in the group who has helped maintain or improve quality. You may correctly conclude that as a result of the 'quality circles' program, these people are constructive, dedicated, hard-working high producers."

SUMMARY

Here's how you can organize your staff for outstanding performance:

1. Make your staff your No. 1 tool for progress.
2. Learn their strengths, to employ them.
3. Discover this weaknesses, to avoid them.
4. Make and use a photo organization chart.
5. Build and insist on mutual respect among the team.
6. Plan and assign group and individual goals plus duties.
7. Use the span-of-control "rule of ten."
8. Sell your team to themselves and to others.
9. Organize your group's time.
10. Consider trying some ideas from the Japanese "quality circles" method.

Your OBI (one best idea) is to know your people's strengths and weaknesses, build mutual respect, use a photo chart, follow the "rule of ten," establish group and individual goals, and ensure productive use of them.

CHAPTER 19
How to Get Along With and Influence Your Boss

There's a hard way and an easy way to achieve your success goals. The hard way is to buck the boss. The easy way is to get along with the boss—even get him or her to help you.

To accomplish this, there are hundreds of things you can do. But that would be a book in itself. The objective of this chapter is simply to provide you with a few dozen of the best guidelines.

TEN BASIC TYPES OF BOSSES

Once you know yourself, the next most important thing you can do is to know and become compatible with your boss. By studying your boss and understanding his or her type, you will know how to adjust your approach. Obviously, your supervisor may be a mixture of several types and may switch and slide between all of them, depending on the problem he or she faces—just as you and I do. However, the suggestions here will help you recognize each type and give you some effective tactics for dealing with them.

1. *Ms. Participative* is democratic; listens; gets people involved in decisions, goals, and programs; trains where there is a weakness; and uses existing strengths. To get along with Ms. Participative, get involved. Contribute. Play a role—maybe several. Suggest. Help. Participate and cooperate. Also, appreciate her. She can be one of the easiest and most productive personalities and styles to work with.

2. *Mr. Bureaucrat* is very much concerned with the rules or system. He is anxious to keep things going properly, and wants to

avoid damaging delays or confrontations. He has a good record and intends to keep it that way. Getting along with Mr. Bureaucrat is fairly simple. Know the same rules he does. Understand them thoroughly. Show him that you are doing those things. Discuss new regulations as they come along. To Mr. Bureaucrat, this is "mother, God, and apple pie," and you will be his best buddy.

3. *Ms. Identifier* is an example of what Machiavelli meant by saying, "Many a prince imitates someone he admires." A sure sign of the Identifier is frequent reference to a specific leader as an obvious role model. This might be followed by clear efforts to adopt the leader's policies, philosophies, or methods.

To get along with Ms. Identifier, first be sure you have hung the right label on her. An occasional quote from some individual is hardly enough for your boss to qualify as an identifier. If the role model has written a book or made speeches, get a copy. Pick up key points and occasionally mention them to your boss. Try to apply these ideas. You might find some concepts worth putting to work for yourself.

4. *Mr. Achiever* will be someone that you should have little trouble recognizing. It may be a little like looking in the mirror. He mainly seeks accomplishment and values people in almost direct proportion to their contribution toward his objectives. To get along with Mr. Achiever, simply help him reach his goals. You can't really help, however, unless you know him and his key targets. Ask. Let him know you are on his team and want to help him. This won't ever hurt you. He is looking for assistance, just as you are, and won't forget those who provide help, just as you won't forget such people. Advise this boss of opportunities and dangers you see for him.

5. *Ms. Entrepreneur* is a lot like Mr. Achiever, but a bit more narrowly focused upon winning and profits. She wants, needs, and expects the same sharp concentration on financial return. To get along with Ms. Entrepreneur, give her just such a concentration of your attention and effort. Adopt this boss's goals and let her know it. Let your actions show this. Make suggestions occasionally when you see chances to improve sales and income, cut costs, or raise profits. Do what you can to help the enterprise prosper and make progress.

6. *Mr. Controller* is a bird best identified by his loud call ("I'll

run it! I'll run it!") and feathers of a sort of Blue Jay blue—blustery, brassy, bossy, boisterous, and bullish. He flys around squawking, "Do this. Do that. No, no, not like that—like this!" While interested in your help toward his goals, such a boss is often equally concerned with *how* you do it. He gets a big kick out of manipulating people.

To get along with Mr. Controller, let him either control you or at least feel like that is what's happening. Listen to his requests and take careful note of them. Wherever possible, respond favorably, promptly, and positively.

7. *Ms. Fire Fighter* is probably in over her head. She is constantly preoccupied with short-term brush fires. Employees are mainly "things" that you stuff into holes to stop leaks. She is disorganized; unpredictable; loves you one minute, hates you the next; and is just a bit dangerous.

To get along with Ms. Fire Fighter, don't get frantic. This type doesn't really want you to crowd into the panic along with her. Your boss is enjoying it too much all by herself, and merely wants some-one to hold the hose—to exclaim how brave she is to have conquered that blaze. Come to such a boss with little fires and let her spray on them. Ms. Fire Fighter likes little problems, so she can trot out the fire truck and exercise the equipment.

8. *Mr. Crisis* is often dangerous. He is usually in a state of high anxiety, desperate, capricious, and unstable. This type differs from the fire fighter in that Mr. Crisis is either in a frenzy or frozen stiff. Such a boss is negative, fearful, and feels inferior. He often is inferior. Pathological panic prevails.

Getting along with Mr. Crisis can be a real challenge. He doesn't really know what is right, so anything you do can be called wrong—and usually is. This type wants someone to blame. If at all possible, convince him that you personally have the support of his boss. That will impress Mr. Crisis. Show him how he can avoid problems. "Could we shift this impossible project over to the Western Division?" Solve part of a problem but let him lay on the last licks and take the credit.

9. *Ms. Fight* takes almost everything as a signal for combat. The gong for round one. "Those rotten SOBs, they did it to us again! Let's go get 'em!" Everything is an affront that she is ready to answer. This type may be doubting her power and trying to prove it.

To get along with Ms. Fight, don't fight back. Play it calm, cool, and quiet. If you do the opposite, then you become the adversary, and you don't need that. Bring her news of victories. "You sure showed them, chief." Also, use her to make some of the tough confrontations that you have been reluctant to handle personally. Give this warrior someone's name and say, "Go get 'em!"

10. *Mr. Flight* is vice-president of ducking out, a master of evasion, shifting responsibility, finding scapegoats, neglecting or abandoning the project—the multi-martini lunch, then resignation. This type doesn't really know what to do, so he concentrates on not doing *anything*—or sliding out of it.

Getting along with Mr. Flight is perhaps the most difficult challenge of all. He's so shifty, tricky, slippery, and mercurial. You can play copilot and navigator to this boss's flight captain by showing him ways to delegate and then slide away from projects. Volunteer for things you like to do and can do well. Mr. Flight will appreciate the help, and you will gain a good and growing reputation with him and with other people as well.

LEARN YOUR BOSS'S REAL GOALS

Your boss will not always state an objective, or the one he or she gives may not be the real one. He or she often has reasons for less than total frankness. And goals change with time. How can you discover the secret target? Here are five steps that work well:

1. Be sure you know who really is boss. Drucker says your boss is the one who hired you and can promote or fire you. Be very sure just where the real power lies.

2. Ask your boss about his or her key objective. This gets surprising candor, at times. Even if it doesn't work, it tells the boss something: You want to know his or her goal. This implies strong support, and he or she likes that.

3. Take his or her reply advisedly. Your boss may be telling you only part of the answer. Look, listen, and learn the rest. Always keep on the alert for new indications. They come in all sorts of circumstances. For example, what are his or her favorite projects? Now—why is your boss doing these? Does the reason tell you his or her goal? Maybe.

4. Stay flexible. Your boss is, and you should be, too. Remember, a goal cast in bronze this month can be melted down and recast into a whole new signpost next month.

5. Get on the boss's side each time he or she shifts. He or she will be amazed at your adaptability and your support. You may not like all the changes, but then your boss might not enjoy this, either. Use the CPA formula (Calm-Positive-Action). It works well.

DON'T BE EXCESSIVELY AGREEABLE

Being overly accommodating can lead you into trouble, like agreeing to something you can't possibly do or overpromising. You can get swamped with work and ultimately become a doormat.

Your best strategy: First, agree with most requests and do so with sincerity. There is a saying in the U.S. Congress: "To get along, go along." Second, if an assignment is going to cut into time on another of your boss's projects, mention this casually and ask for priorities. The reply may be, "They are both A-1," but he or she got the message and will usually give you a clue. Third, if some parts of the project are a problem—or not too practical—develop a better alternative. Show how the old approach will hurt progress toward his or her goal, but the new plan will help. Fourth, be sure the boss sees that you are accommodating and supporting his or her position.

Keep a Positive Attitude

A good level of enthusiasm covers a multitude of sins. Important note: You can even disagree, mildly and without damage, if you retain a strong level of positive, loyal spirit. The boss almost can't dislike someone who is strongly behind him or her and rallying support in his or her behalf.

First, keep an open mind. You may be somewhat underwhelmed, initially, by your supervisor's project, but as time unfolds, more advantages may appear, and you don't want to close these out. Second, think up, not down. Specifically and aggressively search for the positive points. You may be surprised at what you find. Third, rally resources behind your boss's project. Get your staff and others working on the program and, if at all possible, enthusiastically supporting it. The boss may value a person who shows enthusiasm, but the individual who brings together a small army in support of his or her project is very nearly "the indispensable person."

Accept Responsibility and Blame Wisely

Your supervisor will like, appreciate, and value you with increased intensity when you show a willingness to shoulder a portion of his or her project as your duty. But don't suffer: Be sure it's doable. Say, "I'll take the responsibility for this part of the project, and I'll take the blame if it isn't done properly."

Your stock just went up 100 percent. In this day of personal evasion and always blaming the other guy, your boss will be pleased, amazed, and even shocked. In 30 years of executive work, I have seen many people fired, but not one for offering to share the load and then not keeping his or her promise. But many were let go for not being willing to accept responsibility in the first place. Those who did accept this frequently became highly valued by their superiors—and were promoted. It's a strong route upward.

If the project does become flawed, and you did all you reasonably could, show this to your boss and indicate where and why it went wrong. This is often because someone else dropped the ball. Don't take the heat for that. Analyze and demonstrate where the errors occurred and identify ways to correct them in future efforts. This will quickly remove the curse of blame and dramatize to your boss that you are still playing a responsible role. You win the boss over emotionally and logically.

Plan to Survive the Clash

Make plans to survive the clash on policy and personality. This is almost inevitable. Sometime or other, you are not going to see eye-to-eye with your boss—and you will get tired of always being agreeable. This means a collision—a crisis. It's no good for me to advise you to "avoid" the crisis. You've been doing that. But you can't do it forever.

Your objective now is to get through this unscathed and hopefully in better shape than ever, with respect to your boss. Here's how: First, never confront. This becomes a situation of "the boss or me." You'll lose. The boss has got you outgunned, and for emotional and social reasons, he or she cannot let you win. Even if you win, you lose. Sometimes you are wrong to be right. Instead of a direct confrontation, use a roundabout or indirect approach. You might even "quote" others, for example, as asking about flaws in the proposed plan—or suggesting several better programs.

Second, don't forget that while the boss may be wrong, he or she is still the boss. He or she still pays your salary, thus buying your services, which means your willingness and your abilities. Your boss is still personally responsible for the success of your unit. And he or she may have more experience than you do, so it is just possible his or her approach is not all bad.

Third, if you remain convinced that the boss is wrong, and that you must say something, treat the matter as a mixture of logic and emotion—but *mostly emotion*. Appeal to the boss's heart and mind. Show that the plan may harm or cost him or her more than it is worth. Offer other alternatives that the boss can select as his or her "own" plan. Let the boss save face. Bosses choke if you try to force them to eat crow or humble pie. Your best and most attractive option will usually be one that is basically emotional but sounds logical.

Duck No-Win Projects

If you don't evade the boss's hopeless projects when they collapse, you will be found guilty-by-association and tarred by the same brush. Your objective is to appear to support the boss while actually standing apart from and unconnected with any hopeless project. Then it can crash to the ground without seriously cutting you with flying glass. Here are some strategies for steering through this tricky terrain:

1. Discuss the project with the boss. Be sure you understand it and can clearly see any fatal flaws.

2. Indirectly mention these flaws as possibilities and try to sell some modifications. Recheck to see if the boss is really committed to a hopeless course. Allow time for any midcourse corrections that may be possible.

3. Do a little research. Gather additional data, especially if these will help you prevent problems. See that these sift in to the boss.

4. While showing mild reservations, let the boss know that *he or she has your full support*. This is vital. If your boss thinks you are working against him or her, you're a dead duck. He or she might even set you up to be the patsy or fall-guy if and when the project fails.

5. Test a part of the program. Get it started. Really give it a more than fair trial. If it works, admit you were wrong, get on the bandwagon, and go full bore. You may have an unexpected winner.

6. But if it is clearly a loser, then try to back off a little. Let the boss know the facts of the test—not your personal conclusion. Allow the *boss* to make that on his or her own. Begin dragging your feet. Work hard on the boss's other projects and show progress. Your major effort now is directed toward surviving and coming out of the crash in as good condition as possible. Stand ready with some correctional or recovery procedures that just might help turn a lemon into lemonade.

A Little Extra Never Hurts

Find some extras to add to projects assigned. The advantage here is that when you have completed the project, the boss will see that you did just a little bit more and a little bit better than other people. He or she will appreciate you more than ever.

First, listen and watch for extra opportunities. These might be small, simple things, and yet little steps are the ones that can often spell the difference between mediocrity and excellence. Michelangelo once said to the Pope, "Trifles make perfection—and perfection, my Lord, is no trifle." Second, note especially any particular wants, needs, and preferences that the boss may have in relation to the project. There's not much sense in doing an "extra" that is disliked!

Third, get help, ideas, suggestions, and active support from your resources. The wise members of that group will recognize that extras done *by* them will mean extra credit *for* them—possibly at very little added effort *from* them. How tough, really, is it to put the cherry on top of the sundae? Fourth, be sure the little extras actually get done—and that the boss sees them. Don't overdo the point that you got this accomplished. Your boss will figure that out.

ALWAYS MAKE THE BOSS LOOK GOOD

If you really want to get along well with your boss, about the best thing you can do is to see that he or she gets credit, honors, and glory. The worst thing you can do is to bring your boss dishonor, disgrace, and disaster.

First, decide to do everything within reason to help your boss with his or her projects and goal. Then do just that. Second, make sure everyone knows the product is basically his or hers, not yours. Be especially sure of this if it is a success. Under no circumstances should you try to hog the credit. You can bask in the reflected glow. Your rewards come mainly from the boss, *not* from the onlooking audience. And your boss will usually make it a point to know who helped out, because then he or she can ask again. Third, if and when the project fails, do what you can to help the boss disassociate himself or herself from it. Assign the blame where it belongs. Spread the responsibilities among others who were to see that the project succeeded.

DO IT RIGHT AND ON TIME

Deliver reliably and promptly and you'll make a real friend of the boss. He or she will value your services above nearly all others. Here's how to do it:

1. Be sure you know what it is your boss wants to do and whether he or she has preferences as to *how* the project should be done. (That can be almost as important, suprisingly, as reaching the goal!) Double-check the five Ws with him or her. The boss will rarely object, since he or she will see that you both have the same goal—to get the job done right. And you'll avoid a lot of false starts, wheel spinning, and wasted effort.

2. As soon as you get the project going, get into the habit of

making brief but frequent progress reports to the boss. He or she will appreciate being kept informed. Bosses hate people who keep them in the dark.

3. If you run into trouble, promptly let the boss know this and, most important, what you plan to do about it. Managers want solutions, not riddles. Your boss may have some further ideas or sources of help that you don't know about. This gets and keeps him or her closely involved with the project and closer to you. The two of you become a team—one that can better live through both success and failure. If the time schedule needs revising, get this done when you see it is necessary. That way you are sure you will be on time. You simply move the goalposts and due dates to fit the situation.

4. Your boss probably wants quality *and* quantity. He or she will rarely settle for just one or the other. The boss paid for both and expects it, just as you do. Your two best hedges for getting those is to adjust the program and change the time frame.

5. Don't get hung up on the old management saw (or dilemma) about responsibility needing to equal authority ("He gives me the responsibility, but not the authority!"). This is usually not really true and is sometimes total nonsense. If you are responsible, then you almost automatically have the authority. Assume it. Take it. Act on it, until and unless the boss tells you otherwise. Just take the simple precaution of telling the boss, in an asking sort of way: "This is what I plan to do. *Is that OK with you?*" Bosses don't like surprises. They do like people who clear their action plans ahead of time. This also gets the boss behind you and in a supportive position, not one calculated to pull the rug out from under you.

SUMMARY

To get along with your boss, influence him or her, and achieve without suffering, consider using all or most of these guidelines:

1. Know the ten basic types of bosses and how to work with them.
2. Learn your boss's real goals, if you can.
3. Be agreeable, but not excessively so.

4. Display a high level of enthusiasm.
5. Accept some responsibility and blame.
6. Make plans to survive the clash on policy and personality.
7. Duck the boss's hopeless projects.
8. Find some extras for enhancing assigned projects.
9. Always make your boss look good, never bad.
10. Get it done right and on time.

Your OBI (one best idea) for getting along with your boss is to understand how to handle the various boss types: know and support his or her goals; and be agreeable, enthusiastic, and responsible. Learn how to survive a clash, duck hopeless projects and enhance good ones, get it done fast and well, and always make the boss look good.

CHAPTER 20
Motivating Average and Below-Average People

Nearly all successful managers know how to motivate *ordinary* or *below*-ordinary people. This is often the secret reason for their success—they manage to move even difficult people.

By yourself, you are only one person. But if you can motivate people, you can eventually command a small army—or even a large one! You multiply yourself. You leverage your ability and build your power. You move rapidly toward your own personal success.

Back in Chapter 8, we discussed motivating above-average people. While the approach presented in this chapter has a few similarities, it also has three major differences. First, in the next few pages, we will not be talking about the high achiever, who is already self-motivated. We will be considering very average or even troublesome people, who may be greatly undermotivated. That's a whole new ball game, as we will see. Second, we will be talking about pragmatic, practical, nuts-and-bolts systems and steps you can take aggressively, right now. Third, this chapter is directly aimed at increasing your immediate personal power through greater and more constructive control of all your staff people, not just one high achiever.

ATTITUDE IS VITAL

Never underestimate the power and importance of attitude. Top recruiters value people who are both willing and able. But a highly motivated average person can usually far outdo an able person who is negative. Recognize the average or below-average employees' attitude. It is rarely one of great enthusiasm. Know how they feel. The advantage to you is that a problem well defined is half solved. Knowing your situation will often suggest the most effective strategies you might employ and your best use of time. This can often be the key to your progress and your power. Here's how you can analyze your employees' attitude to your mutual advantage:

1. Study your people but use a plan. Consider the LLAD program (*l*ook, *l*isten, *a*sk, and *d*iscuss).

2. Try to learn the pros and cons, the good and bad, in their attitude. This will tell you where your priorities should be—what needs immediate attention and what can go on the back burner. It will show you some good strengths to use. (For example, the team may be negative toward their jobs but turned on by their country, state, city, company president, marketing spokesperson, or ad slogan.) Find out about this and put it to use.

3. Look for common ground and mutual beliefs, where you both agree strongly. This will bring you and your employees closer together. It also gives you a chance to show your support of their views and demonstrate that you are interested in them and care how they think and feel. When they know you care about them, they tend to care more about you.

4. Keep an eagle eye out to find their "on" button—the one subject, hope, dream, or interest that really turns them on and lights their fire. Get into their heads and under their skins. Don't prejudge or preguess too much. You might shut out some good possibilities. Remember, money isn't always your employees' big interest. If it were, they would probably have studied business. Money is usually important, but other factors are often nearly as vital—sometimes more! Man does not live by bread alone.

SET MUTUAL GOALS

Encourage goal setting by mutual agreement. This has many advantages for you. It saves time, because once goals are set, action usually occurs fairly soon thereafter. Goals help you concentrate your effort and that of your employees on making progress rather than on wasting energy. Once again, you work smarter, not harder. Goals even suggest the kind of strategy or plans that might work best: Small goals may suggest small steps; major goals need stronger programs.

Goals or objectives have become another one of modern management's magic buzz words that people increasingly accept, use, and even live by. Goals often become a reason for being and even a crusade, boosting worker spirit, challenging and stimulating them—and controlling them.

First, use the MBO, or Management By Objectives, formula. Be sure that nearly all resources, especially staff efforts, are used only to reach goals. MBO is a hot subject, and employers are becoming responsive to the idea.

Second, find mutual objectives, so you can honestly say to your employees, "Your goals are the same as mine, so they are *our* goals!" Third, let them know what happens—that is, what reward to expect—if they hit those goals. Perhaps it is simply that they get to keep their jobs. Or perhaps it is a thank-you award, bonus, raise, or promotion. At the very least, they should believe that you will give them some enthusiastic recognition. That is often all they expect. And finally, if you see someone wasting time, a practical and effective use of objectives as an "instant motivator" is simply to ask, "What is your goal today?"

Show Respect

There exists a great hunger, want, and need for respect. Smart supervisors use this centuries-old, powerful motivator almost continually—especially today, when a "respect gap" exists. Most employees *demand more,* while managers all too often *provide less.* They foolishly miss a great opportunity to control and to enlist help toward their own goals. Respect, shown up, down, and sideways, can almost become a self-fulfilling prophesy of action in your behalf—action that is worthy of your respect.

First, to work well, respect must be genuine. That really isn't difficult. Almost everyone deserves respect for something. Take a few minutes to find out what. It will pay off for you. Second, show your respect in a sincere, full, strong, and emphatic manner. Anemic respect is almost an insult. And never allow it to be contrived or phony. Third, pick the right time—when people have done something worthy of respect and are attentive and receptive to you, not distracted with chores.

An excellent indication of respect can be such simple words as, "I'm listening to you. I have confidence in you. And I am proud to be working with you." Some workers will nearly devote their entire careers to the supervisor who says that. And it costs you nothing!

Hold Participative Meetings

Use participation, discussion, and comments in meetings. This usually guarantees "good" meetings, because they result in constructive decisions and move people. And that both saves you time and work and brings you closer to your own personal objectives. Here's how you can motivate people through productive meetings:

1. Have a reason for the meeting. This will start people's juices flowing, right from the beginning. Don't hold meetings just because it's "Tuesday meeting time" or because you're lonely.

2. Plan ahead. Do a little homework. "Prior preparation prevents piddling poor presentations," says the U.S. Marine Corps. Use your five Ws to decide who, what, when, where, and why (plus how) you want to hold your meeting.

3. Be especially careful to check out simple, old-fashioned mechanics, facilities, and logistics. These may seem like boring and mundane considerations, but excellent accommodations can almost save a poor meeting, while bad facilities can ruin a good meeting. Check such things as light, heat, air conditioning, noise level, PA system, chalk boards, flip charts, wall plugs, phones, security, chairs, tables, carpets, drapes, coffee facilities, rest rooms, elevators, and if appropriate, barrier-free halls for wheelchairs and a storage room.

4. Use a good invitation letter along with a detailed agenda. Assign topics to many specific people. Do this singly or in groups. It will stimulate interest, involvement, participation, and enthusiasm. Be careful whom you invite. Have a reason for asking each person: participant, approver, producer, worker, stimulator. But not just a chair filler.

5. Start with the problems but convert them to *our problems,* our challenges, and our opportunities. Show where these lead—to *our gains* and our rewards. A meeting takes on new meaning when participants see where *they benefit* from the program.

6. Encourage and generate personal participation. Get everyone involved. Ask questions. Talk directly to nonparticipants and invite their comments. Stay on the subject but don't run things so tight or brittle that there is no room for flexibility, or even some fun. This often gains more value than the time it uses.

7. Have the discussion lead to concrete decisions, plans, and strategy. And those steps should point to who does what, when, and where. Such an action/time schedule has remarkable motivating effects.

8. Close with a recap. "Here was our problem, and this is the plan we have decided to follow." Send each participant, and other appropriate people, a short written summary and action plan. This provides added motivation. It also lets you editorialize and emphasize key points.

APPEAL TO BOTH LOGIC AND EMOTIONS

Use the AIDA formula (*a*ttention, *i*nterest, *d*esire, *a*ction) to win your employees' hearts and minds. People are governed by their emotions and their logic, but in the end, primarily by emotion. It rules the world. Want evidence? Read and judge your daily newspaper, item by item, including sports, politics, and economics. Recognizing this gives you a great advantage. If you know the universal "on" buttons, then you know something most other managers do not. You can use creative thinking (emotional logic) to stimulate constructive motivation. Here's how:

1. Establish a fairly permissive atmosphere. Let thoughts and feelings flow. Allow things to boil and bubble.

2. Set certain limits—some reasonable guidelines—so suggestions can bounce around freely, but within broad boundaries.

3. Challenge people. Even the most sluggish individuals will often awaken to a dare—a positive expression of your confidence or a question of their ability or their personal resolve.

4. Let one idea lead to another, with the first door opening a

second. This will happen if you allow some strange and wild ideas. Be careful not to rain on their parade and turn the creative flow off at the tap. Note: Even average people can be surprisingly creative if you let them. Harry Truman said, "The world is run by 'C' students!"

5. Record ideas and suggestions. Adjust them a bit to fit reality, then grade them into some sort of rank or priority.

6. Use the AIDA formula to stimulate group and individual motivation. Design a statement, visual, drawing, or move that will accomplish each of the AIDA steps. Result: You will motivate massively in a major way, nearly every time.

Motivate Through Work

"People hate work!" you say? Surprise! People love work—*if* it's "meaningful," that is, helps them reach their own personal goals. In such a case, they hang onto their work for dear life. (Just try to take it away from them and see what happens!) The way to use work as a motivator is:

1. Be sure the work you assign really is a meaningful path toward the employees' personal goals.

2. Take care that the workers see that—and don't simply look on their assignments as drudgery. (Far more absenteeism occurs from boredom than from illness.)

3. Allow your employees to do the job. A strange suggestion? Workers report that supervisors "won't let them" complete their tasks in an average of 23 percent of assigned jobs! Executives interfere, chat, digress, interrupt, redirect, change, and reassign far too often. Many managers not only fail to provide a solution—but they are part of the problem!

4. Give your employees work they are trained for and can do. When you do this, you almost automatically motivate them to move, because they are programmed and reflex-conditioned for action when given such an assignment.

5. Challenge them—but also show your own personal confidence in them. "Here's an interesting and exciting job. It's pretty tough—some people say you can't do it. But I believe in you, and I think *you can* do it."

6. Get a commitment. "What do *you* think? Can you handle

it?" "Good! Now, can we beat that goal?" As long as you have your employees rolling, challenge them further with a little stretch, search, and reach. You will often get a surprisingly well-motivated person or group.

Delegate to Get Action

Don't be greedy or hoard all the assignments. After all, why should you carry it all on your back? Be generous: Divide up and parcel out your jobs. You'll lighten your own load and free yourself up to handle selected, personally profitable projects. You can troubleshoot other key and perhaps more valuable activities. Let people "specialize" on a project and thus give it more time, effort, and perfection than you could. In short, you are motivating people to help you get greater progress at less cost. Here's how to do this:

1. Ask yourself, "Can I delegate this safely? Is the person willing and able? And is it proper, reasonable, and right for me to give this person the task I have in mind?"

2. The time to delegate is when you have more to do than you can handle properly—and others have free time or are doing lower-priority work and could do the task as well as or better than you.

3. For maximum motivation, don't dump everything on others; instead, share the project. Say, "You do this part, and I'll do that." You now function as a team. It becomes a matter of honor for the employee to do his or her part. Your subordinate will if you will.

4. Beware of delegating tasks only because you are unable (insufficiently skilled) to do the job. That can cause disaster. Also beware of delegating too much, too fast. Delegate with care, selectively, a bit at a time, to make sure each project "flies."

5. For maximum motivational value, give proper praise, thanks, and recognition. This will often result in a doubling of effort in your behalf—which would not happen if you remained silent.

USE THE "EX-DEM-PRA" FORMULA

"Ex-dem-pra" (*ex*planation, *dem*onstration, and *pra*ctical work), can be the key to fast motivation. This is the basis or beginning of coaching, which comes into full flower when one or more vital ingredient is added—the "we" spirit. This is the attitude of learning together and working together as a team to teach, develop, act, and accomplish.

The great advantages to this system are that it works rapidly and works with a team of any size, from one to thousands. It motivates enthusiastic, constructive action and does so at a very small investment of time, money, and effort. That makes ex-dem-pra a pretty good strategic tool. Use these steps to make it work for you:

1. Explain the project you want done. Outline the problems, opportunities, goals, rewards, and especially the steps to a solution, success, or victory. Be sure the employee understands each point you make.

2. Demonstrate these steps. This might be through a personal demonstration—or through drawings, diagrams, sketches, cartoons, models, role playing, photos, slides, recordings, movies, or similar devices. Try to use some sort of visual material.

3. Practice these steps. Encourage the employees to experiment a bit. Let them make little mistakes. We learn a lot from our errors made on a controlled, safe, small scale, and we do so at very low cost.

4. Show that you are personally interested in their success—that you care, you believe in them, and you expect results. Avoid the put-down.

5. Don't overcoach—but do follow through. Watch, listen, guide, suggest. Eternal vigilance is the price of success.

USE HONESTY AND CANDOR

Be straightforward, open, and level. In this day of personal evasion, the shock alone motivates people! But season this with discretion, restraint, and good sense. It creates credibility and believability. Bare-faced facts and hard problems don't scare people. It shows you trust them. But flat-out deceit and trickery can enrage them.

First, use the KISS formula: "*Keep it simple, stupid.*" Set up one basic problem or one major action to take. Don't get all tangled up in your underwear of complex issues. This rarely motivates much more than wasted motion. Second, don't try to get tricky, clever, evasive, or manipulative. People quickly see through this sort of thing.

Third, pick a favorable occasion when possible. If necessary, hold back, wait, bide your time until the moment when a real opportunity or goal exists and the employee is receptive, not distracted. The ideal time is when your credibility is on the rise—when you have just been proved right about something, so the stage is set—not after a failure or some mistake.

And finally, try to have your honesty and candor directed toward or lead logically to some obviously desirable action that the employee should take. "Since we have such a serious problem (or excellent opportunity or worthwhile goal), here are the steps we must follow." Let this evolve into a constructive action plan. Candor will then have produced important motivation.

EMPLOY AWARDS PROPERLY

Properly used, awards can double your motivation. Recognition comes in all sizes and shapes, from a big gold trophy on down to a simple smile. And sometimes the smallest things have the greatest impact. But they all have power, because people have a basic, almost instinctive, need for appreciation. We all like compliments. Don't ever underrate a person's appetite for recognition.

The advantages to you are that when you fill this need, you generate a nearly priceless spirit, enthusiasm, and constructive action in your behalf—at very little expense. In fact, it's kind of fun, because you are making others feel good—and some of that rubs off on you. Here's how to give recognition effectively:

1. Begin by taking a close look at the recipient of your award. Know his or her wants and needs and know what the person did or did not do that deserves praise. Also know what it is you are trying to accomplish—to build spirit and enthusiasm, leading to increased or better performance.

2. Be especially careful in your selection of the act of accom-

plishment to acknowledge. Be sure that the recipient and his or her associates would agree with your citation. If not, you lose impact and believability.

3. State your compliment or citation in a fairly plain, flat manner that avoids exaggeration or flowery adjectives. Don't sound like a snake-oil salesman, or you'll have little credibility. Use a sincere, spontaneous approach and tone of voice, not a contrived, slick, phony, or manipulative style.

4. Smile. Use the recipient's name several times. It is a beautiful sound to him or her. Cite the reasons for the recognition and (this is important) *show why* this action helped him or her, others, and the organization itself. Give your worker a reputation to live up to—and he or she is likely to do it.

5. Pick a good moment, a time very soon after the event, not months later. Make a special, serious, important occasion of the recognition, unless it is a very small matter. And still, be basically serious, at least briefly.

SUMMARY

The following is the best strategy for motivating your average and below-average people:

1. Recognize the employees' attitude.
2. Encourage goal setting by mutual agreement.
3. Show respect, and people will respond dramatically.
4. Use participative meetings to generate action.
5. Employ the AIDA (attention, interest, desire, action) approach to win their hearts and minds.
6. Use meaningful work as a powerful motivator.
7. Delegate and get productive performance.
8. Remember: Ex-Dem-Pra—(*ex*plain, *dem*onstrate, *prac*tice).
9. Use honesty, candor, and the KISS formula. ("Keep it simple, stupid.")
10. Employ recognition and awards to double enthusiasm.

Your OBI (one best idea) for motivating average or below-average people is to know their attitude; set goals; show respect; hold participative meetings; and use the AIDA formula, meaningful work, delegation, Ex-Dem-Pra, candor, and proper recognition. (Then step out of their way, because they are going to move— dramatically!)

CHAPTER 21
Above-Average People—
Above-Average Presentations

As an above-average person, you will probably be called upon to make talks or presentations. Your audience and your boss will both expect these to be of extra high quality.

And this is a great opportunity for you to look good, sell your plan, proposal, or yourself and make major progress. Or you could bomb out. And we are all aware of those possibilities. That's why the thought of making a speech can fill us with anxiety, even terror, and we ask, "Why me?" The answer, of course, is that since you are above-average, people feel you know something useful. They want to hear about it.

Here is a plan. It includes a summary of about one hundred suggestions for the easiest, most effective preparation and execution of your presentations. Good coaches know that the game is often won (or lost) long before the team hits the field.

PLANNING A SUPERIOR TALK

Start by preparing for the talk by getting a very clear definition of your assignment. This is essential, but it is not always easy. Your assigner will sometimes be a little hazy and vague. This can destroy you, because you might shoot a beautiful arrow at the wrong target. Get a clear assignment as to subject and—almost as important—how *long* you are to take. (Ten to twenty minutes is usually ideal.) Also find out who your audience is, what they already know about the topic, and what they want to know.

Learn the purpose of your talk. Generally, there are four possible objectives: to entertain, instruct, persuade, and inspire. Chances are, your talk should do some of each, but executives are usually asked to instruct or persuade.

Prepare thoroughly. Do your homework. The better work you do now, the fewer problems you will have on the podium. Of all those who sweat bullets on stage or bomb out, 95 percent simply did not prepare well. Once you know your subject and the purpose of your talk, then get some facts and some background information. Ideal sources are company files, your library, current magazines, books, and other above-average, knowledgeable people.

Make a simple outline of your talk. A good presentation has a title, an introduction, several key points, a summary, and a close. The introduction is important, since it makes a first and lasting impression. It sets the tone. Use it to introduce your main idea in an attractive way. Audiences usually make up their minds about their receptivity during the first minute or two. Your key points should develop your main theme, factually and emotionally—mostly emotionally. Aim every sentence at your objective. The summary should recap these points and close with your one basic idea.

In general, tell 'em what you're going to tell 'em. Tell 'em. And tell 'em what you told 'em. Then, instead of only 10 percent remembering your talk, perhaps 30 percent will.

Have something worthwhile to say. Most of your audience will appreciate your courtesy in helping them use their time profitably. Use short words and short sentences. Avoid long jokes. Use quotes if pertinent. Keep it simple, or it will be misunderstood. Don't waste many words. Get to the point fairly promptly.

DELIVERING A SUPERIOR TALK

All too often, *what* you say is not nearly as important as *how* you say it.

Let's look at some things that you should definitely do or strongly avoid:

1. Don't mumble, shout, drag, scold, repeat, or speed frantically. Don't use sarcasm, too many gestures, strings or "ands," or hackneyed clichés.

2. Walk up to the podium in a calm and confident manner, with a smile on your face, looking right into the audience's eyes. Be thinking of your good, strong, memorized first sentence. It should be about the audience, if at all possible.

3. Wait a moment for attention. Then speak loud and clear. Work from an outline and memorize only the ideas you will cover, not the exact words. Always speak to the people in the last row, or they will not hear you. Try to pick out two or three friendly faces and talk to them.

4. Relax, Smile. Talk at a moderate pace but vary it a little occasionally—first fast, then slow. Use pauses. Look at your audience's eyes most of the time. Speak in a warm, friendly, almost conversational manner. Watch your grammar, and use only words you understand. Don't get stuffy or talk over their heads or down to them.

5. Don't shuffle papers or hide behind the podium. Step out and away from it. Use visuals if possible: You'll double your impact.

6. By all means, rehearse your talk at least four or five times. Do the first few before a mirror or a friendly critic who will tell you the truth. Time yourself carefully. Don't run over.

Shooing Away the Butterflies

How do you end the jitters? As the shrinks say, "It's all in your head!" The problem is to *control* your head.

The secret solution is really twofold: first, become *comfortable* and thoroughly familiar with your talk, and second, develop an *attitude* of calm, confident assurance. Luckily, both of these can come from one source—rehearsal, as mentioned above. When you have run through your talk over and over so many times that you are almost tired of it, you will note that you now have very little reluctance or fear about giving it. It almost becomes second nature. Butterflies disappear. Frightened people usually didn't practice.

Polish it up. Check yourself on all the dos and don'ts listed above. You might use a tape recorder. Get so comfortable with the talk that you can even make small errors and easily recover. Try doing this a couple of times. Now your presentation is no longer brittle, but fairly flexible. It is also probably a much warmer, friendlier, and better speech.

Don't try to give the talk in exactly the same way every time you practice it. Vary it a little. That will make you feel even more comfortable and still come out just fine. Also practice your use of visuals (discussed in detail below), so they are smooth and easy.

Don't fear your audience. Generally, most are your friends, and most are pulling for you. The larger the audience, the easier they are to address, in many cases, because they are more varied, more willing to respond, and there are likely to be more friendly faces. If you pick out a few of these people, as mentioned above, and talk mainly to them, you will also find yourself feeling more relaxed. As you relax, your audience feels more friendly, and your jitters melt still further.

Professional speakers often use the simple trick of showing extra friendship and respect to their audience. Within moments, the audience tends to return the attitude. They get on *your* side. Soon everyone feels pretty good. And some will leave saying, "That really was the best speech I've heard in years!" You accomplished your mission.

SPECIAL DELIVERIES

Here are some professional techniques that will add sparkle, the extra, dramatic touch, a "plus," and give you that competitive edge of superiority you want and need. (The methods were used by one speaker in winning an award for top presenter in the State of Illinois.)

1. Let yourself be a little afraid. Surprised? It stimulates you. Learn what other speakers will talk about and tie in your subject with theirs. Start off strong, perhaps with a provocative, eye-opening, pertinent rhetorical question. Get your audience nodding and saying "yes." Get them "with you"—in accord and agreeing.

2. Favorably mention several people or groups in the audience. Smile. Add interest by moving around a little, when appropriate. This shows you're at ease.

3. Sell. Use the AIDA formula (*a*ttention, *i*nterest, *d*esire, *a*ction). Encourage the audience to "reach" a little for ideas. Employ the dramatic, pregnant pause. Use honesty and sincerity. Con-

stantly try to make the audience feel comfortable. Ask them to do something, take some action, or just think about a particular point.

4. Make small, harmless verbal mistakes, deliberately, then calmly correct yourself. It makes you seem human.

5. To gain personal impact, if you are giving a slide presentation, stand and move about *right in the light* of the projector, at least some of the time. You become almost a part of the visual on the screen.

6. To get applause, close with a compliment to the audience (for instance, "I'd personally like to thank each and every one of you for your fine interest, attention, and courtesy"). Give them time to think, appreciate your words, and react. You might even *applaud them!* That usually works.

7. If possible, hold a question-and-answer session. Ask the first question yourself, if you must. Then answer it. Compliment each "asker," and you will please the audience. Answer pleasantly and courteously. As you end, thank them again. Give them a one-page summary of your talk as a handout.

GIVE THE AUDIENCE SOMETHING TO LOOK AT

Use visuals, pictures, or graphs. Why? First, they hold people's attention. Second, 80 percent of what we learn enters through our eyes. Third, it makes a lasting, favorable impression. Just think about some of the best talks you ever heard.

A good visual can be almost any graphic that helps you make your point. For example, a chalkboard lets you write a few key words. Yes, words on a board are certainly a graphic. They are a device that has focused people's minds for thousands of years.

Small, hand-held, lettered flip cards made on plain sheets of typing paper can be even more effective. They might be in striking colors; they can say more than a chalk board; and they can be prepared ahead of time and easily arranged for maximum flexibility, as a fast or slow, short or long, presentation. They are also easily made, easily carried, and easily used, and thus are one of your best graphic tools.

Large flip charts on an easel are ideal and often dramatic when used for big groups. Lettering can be large, and charts, numbers, tables, graphs, and diagrams can be employed. A disadvantage is that these charts take more time to prepare than small flips and are more awkward to carry and use. But the advantages often far outweigh these drawbacks.

Color slides in a tray and a projector are unusually effective and flexible. They permit a wide range of subjects—anything that can be photographed, high speed or low—with vibrant color and very large images from two to twenty feet in size. It is best to use a remote control with a long cord and stand up near the picture, so you can see your audience and they can see you. This system usually needs a screen, which can be cumbersome, but slides can often be shown on a light, smooth wall.

A variation on all this is the flip chart that has been photographed and converted to slides, perhaps with other photos of people and objects interspersed.

Overhead projectors permit page-sized transparencies, in volume, to go up on the screen. Preparation is easy. Major error: Presenters all too often use long, typed, wordy material that cannot be read at any distance. Use few words and make them large enough. This technique is best for small groups and offers good flexibility. You can easily switch back and forth between pages. You can also make charts and diagrams. It is easy to point to them personally from the projector—but more dramatic to do so right up there at the screen.

Movies and TV tapes are fine and permit professionally prepared material. However, they are much less flexible in terms of time and room size and tend to take the presentation out of your hands (which, at times, may be just where you want it!). These can be ideal for a short, two- or three-minute segment of your talk.

Other devices, such as boxes, building-block gimmicks, and personal role-playing sketches, can also be good visuals if planned and used carefully. A handout summarizing the visuals or ideas in your talk can greatly increase your impact.

Be sure to check and double-check your materials and equipment well before your appearance—in time to take corrective action.

These methods were used by several executives in successfully presenting many millions of dollars' worth of advertising.

"JUST SAY A FEW WORDS"

Here is where you are called upon without any notice to make the "little," "instant" speech. But you are still expected to excel and shine. (Your promotion may depend on it.) A simple solution to this tough situation was devised by the famous management consultant Frederick W. Taylor. He kept his "instant speech ticket" in his billfold. It was a business card with the following letter on the back:

Intro: Happy to visit you fine people.
Situat: Problem & opportunities.
Obj: Cut prob, use opport—get more $ & fun.
Strat: Prod, price, promos, PR, pkg, people, policies, & philosophy. Next step.

You can surely think of a problem facing the group—plus some possible ways of solving it.

A good alternative, when it is appropriate, is to say, "I was unaware that I would be asked to speak, but let's review a neat and handy way you can use the modern plans matrix and put it to work for you today, just as it serves many top executives. One easy system is called SOS." Then, again go through your card—and give it to *them* as an "instant speech" they can put in *their* billfolds. They learned something. You looked good. Your mission is accomplished!

THE "SALES CALL" PRESENTATION

From the president on down, nearly everyone is selling something—a plan, product, service, system, proposal, or themselves. *Your objectives* here should be to make a good impression, convince, close the sale, and open the door for later business activity. *Your emphasis* should be on benefits to the listener. If you are to succeed, then the heart of your presentation must, above all, focus on how your plan helps your prospect. Here are some proven techniques for landing that order:

1. Your preparation is most effective when it makes good use of your facts and tools. Facts include your prospect—his or her wants, needs, interests, and "on" button. If you know this last ele-

272 YOU AS A HIGH ACHIEVER

ment, your sale may almost be made. Your tools might be an out-line, small flip charts, slides, samples, case histories, and a purchase plan.

2. Rehearse. Run through your sales presentation several times to a constructively critical audience. Correct, polish, and improve it.

3. Make an appointment with your prospect to meet at a convenient time and place. Reconfirm in a short, pleasant note the five Ws. Include a brief agenda. Recheck all equipment and exhibits before you go. Get there a little early.

4. Begin with a few warm, friendly comments and a brief preview. Get your group's attention. Use their names frequently. Make them feel comfortable, or the sale is lost.

5. Keep a good pace in your presentation. Don't drag, speed or "snow" them. Make five or ten key points. Watch their eyes. Get them involved, with questions and discussion. Build desire by showing how your proposal *helps them,* not you.

6. End with a summary and warm thanks for the meeting. Give them a handout recapping the material presented. Then ask for the order or for their decision.

7. Follow up with a thank-you letter, highlighting a key point or two from the meeting. Again, ask for the order. Phone them in a few days and plan next steps.

(These steps were used by a corporate president in selling millions of dollars in franchise contracts.)

THE "TEACHING" PRESENTATION

To teach effectively, you must know your data, facts, and audience and be certain just what it is you want to accomplish. Then outline a dozen or so key points to reach this goal and marry these items with some visual tools, like flip charts or slides.

Boil your talk down into a one-page outline of easily read key points. Use sentence fragments, not long statements. These are for your eyes only.

Use your audiovisuals with a certain degree of flair, enthusiasm, and fun. It's contagious. Include a few case histories as proof and demonstration of your points. Also, consider enlisting some of the audience in a role-playing skit. But arrange this well ahead and coach them carefully. This has impact. An old Chinese proverb says, "I hear, I forget. I see, I remember. I do, I understand."

Encourage questions, discussion, and audience involvement. Answer each question clearly and pleasantly, never with a put-down. You might even give your audience a short, self-graded oral quiz to reinforce their learning. Close with a one-page summary handout and a clear statement of suggestions as to "where we go from here"—followup, next steps, assignments, or action they should take.

(These methods were used by instructors at two universities in Chicago: Northwestern and DePaul.)

THE WRITTEN PRESENTATION

Writing presentations can be both important and fairly frequent assignments—especially for the above-average person like you. This type of presentation is long on words and short on personal delivery techniques. What it lacks in such personal elements must be made up by effective organization, good appearance, style, readability, and devices that develop interest and acceptance. Here's how:

1. Start by being quite sure you understand the problem, your assignment objective, and your readers' likes, wants, and attitude.

2. Get your facts—do your research and your homework. If your goal is to explain a sales, production, or accounting proposal, break this down into nine or ten parts or points to cover—just as we are doing right here. (Notice how easy it is for you to follow and understand these items.)

3. If it's got to be a "one-pager," start with an introductory sentence, to build attention and interest. Then list your ten short points. Close with a conclusion and a call for action.

4. Use your AIDA formula (*a*ttention, *i*nterest, *d*esire, *a*ction) if the presentation is long enough. Think of a simple item or sentence to fit each of those four letters.

5. A title sheet and short introductory page can have excellent

eye appeal and impact. You get readers' attention. Then you develop interest with your introduction by telling them a little of what they will see.

6. Use short words, short sentences, and short paragraphs. Don't get wordy. Get to the point promptly. Your readers and your boss will appreciate you all the more.

7. As you make each point, use personal words like "you," "they," and "we" to generate desire and acceptance. Talk about how your proposal benefits your readers, not you.

8. Close gracefully and forcefully with a summary of your points. Express these in such a way that your readers can believe them and use them in the near future.

9. Ask for the order or the decision. Suggest, "Here's where we should go next."

10. Dress up your presentation with some charts, graphs, diagrams, tables, or photos and a simple binder, if appropriate.

(These approaches were used with outstanding results by a White House staff member in preparing material for President Ford and his cabinet.)

THE "ELABORATE" PRESENTATION

The "elaborate" presentation is the one where you want to pull out all the stops and go full-bore. Even a big presentation budget may seem tiny compared to the expected results. You may want to use some of the following techniques to beef-up your basic talk with exciting, even dramatic, visuals.

A combination of flip charts and slides can give you lots of flexibility and control while you please the audience with variety. You might switch back and forth a few times between these tools.

The "double-slide" projection program lets you put huge pictures up on one side of you and large photos of the flip charts on the other side, with you standing between the screens—holding the remote control buttons. This calls for considerable preparation and rehearsal but can be one of your most effective, *personal,* showcase devices.

"Multiple-slide" projectors give you large, dramatic, changing,

color visuals on three to six different front- or rear-projection screens. Here the verbal portion should be taped, perhaps with background music, and run through a computer properly programmed to time and control everything in correct sync. This is relatively expensive. The equipment can be rented, but preparation should be done professionally. Your advertising agency will know of sources.

Role-playing skits permit several players in costume and with props to dramatically demonstrate the points you have talked about in your speech. These could be interspersed with your comments. Your audience's attention can be controlled by shifts in spotlighting.

The two-person presentation has people up front switching and exchanging media between them. One does a voice with slides, then the other a short, personal talk. Then the first comes back with flips. Then comes overheads, tape-recorded movies, or videotape.

The "dog and pony show" is a name used for almost any elaborate presentation but is usually an extension of the two-person talk. Generally, each part of the set program is handled by a different person or group. This can involve a very wide variety of thoughts, visuals, personalities, and viewpoints. Done right, it is highly flexible, dramatic, and effective.

The "extravaganza" is a combination of all these devices plus others. A speaker, flip charts, overheads, multiple-slide projectors, role playing, various presenters, a "light show" of colored abstractions with sound effects and background music. Plus professional actors, gimmicks (like building blocks or working models)—even magicians, singers, bands, horses, wagons, cars, trucks, airplanes, and fireworks!

SUMMARY

Your route to above-average presentations for above-average people might be:

1. Write the program from a practical outline.
2. Rehearse, then give the talk in a clear, relaxed, friendly manner.

3. To abolish jitters, practice until you get very familiar with your talk.
4. Use "special deliveries," like addressing people directly and using the AIDA formula (attention, interest, desire, action).
5. Use visuals. These can be almost anything—just let people "see" something.
6. For an "instant speech," use the SOS formula (situation, objective, strategy).
7. For sales presentations, rehearse, be friendly, and use a good pace and summary.
8. For teaching presentations, use an outline, visuals, participation, and summary.
9. For written presentations, know your goals and facts. Your format: intro, items, conclusion.
10. For elaborate presentations, combine people, flip charts, slides, light, sound, models, bands, even fireworks.

Your OBI (one best idea) for doing a superior presentation is to know your goal and facts; have an outline; rehearse; present in a clear, friendly way; use convincing visuals; and summarize forcefully.

CHAPTER 22
How to Get That Promotion

The purpose of this chapter is to give you ten proven steps to getting your promotion. If you are to move up, two key circumstances must exist: a factual or practical one and an emotional or psychological one. The first is the simple reality that there has to be an opening for you or one must be made. The second is that your boss must say, "Yes, I want you in that new position!"

If you wish both these things to happen, you might depend solely on luck. You could wait around for lightning to strike. Meanwhile, your competitor may be taking positive action and is likely to attract and get most of the good things as they come along. You need a plan, a program, a hard-nosed, realistic campaign. And that's what we will outline here.

You will also need some patience, some time, since these things won't happen in a day or a week. And you'll need some effort. You can be almost anything you want, if you really try. Your secret formula for promotion success is PEP—*patience, effort, program.*

REVIEW YOUR PROSPECTS

Take a good look around you, at your situation. Look for your next logical step up, or even for a not-so-logical, but still conceivable, new and better position. In short, isolate and identify your options and opportunities. If you are on anything like a programmed "career ladder," your next step should be clearly known. If you do not have such a plan, check with your boss to see if something like this can be set up, even informally.

Be sure to let your boss know that you are interested in a promotion. That can make a giant difference in his or her evaluation of you. He or she will usually respect your interest. After all, your boss was like that and maybe still is. He or she will also now see someone who can be utilized more fully.

If there are problems to moving up, such as no slot or a person in the slot, can steps be taken to resolve this? Like creating a new position or promoting the incumbent? Know your strengths. Armed with this information, you may find that you are much better qualified than one or two other people in other slots. You just might be able to "bump" someone out. Also, take a look at how other people in your job moved up—the path, route, or stepping-stones. Find out what happened to the best of the last few people who had your job.

Measure and evaluate the trends in your position. Is it going up, down, or in a sideways drift? Are you on a sinking ship, a melting ice floe, a desert island, or a rising star? Sometimes you will like where the trend is taking you, and you need only hang on and ride along. The chances are, however, that you will want to choose a better direction.

Understand the Game

Learn the rules and procedures that must be used if you are going to move on up the line, but don't buck the system if you can possibly avoid it. You are much smarter to *use the system* to your own advantage. Find out how it works. It usually has both momentum and authority, hence power. Put that power to work for you.

One of the best ways to do this is to get to know one or two company personnel officers, if you are in a large organization. Find out your best procedure for moving up. They will often know some important dos and don'ts—the right forms to use, the proper things to say in an application or cover memo, the right people to address, the proper time to take action, and even the most fertile and promising company divisions to consider. Personnel is their business. They live and breathe the very facts that can help you tremendously. Cultivate these people.

If you are not in a large company, make an acquaintance with people in the personnel business, such as in agencies or officers in

other similar companies or related trade and professional associations. Level with them. Tell them you want to go up in your field and
would appreciate their advice as to ways and means. People usually
like to be asked for their opinions and may give you lots of good
suggestions.

KNOW WHO'S REALLY BOSS

Be sure you know who can really promote you. Even in
medium-sized operations, this can be a little fuzzy or hazy, since
more than one person may be involved. Or there could be a key
person, but he or she may listen to opinions from other people.
Know who these "opinion makers" are.

If you have any doubt as to just who is your boss: He or she is
the person who hired you and can reward you, promote you, demote
you, and fire you. That's your boss, and that's the main person you
should impress. You should not waste your time on any other
targets. That may be fun, but it is nonproductive wheel spinning, not
managing by your objectives.

However, sometimes the most effective route to your boss's
conviction is through the suggestions of his or her close advisers. At
times, this is the only route. If this is the case, then single out a few
of these people as your primary targets. The important thing is to
know who you're trying to impress and why.

Know Your Competition

If there is a worthy position open or soon to open, then you can
be fairly sure that someone else also has an eye on it. Your competitor may have taken many quiet steps to get the assignment. He
or she may be way ahead of you. Your best strategy is to assume
that by the time you learn about the position, he or she has a reasonable, but not an unsurpassable, lead.

If you learn that, in fact, your competitor does have "a lock"
on the job, you are usually wise to look for more promising options.
But keep your hat in the ring. Foregone conclusions don't always
happen according to the script. Also, sometimes the person who
comes in second gets a compensation prize that is actually better

than the blue ribbon. In addition, the winner doesn't always work out, and then your name becomes prominent in the boss's mind.

Know your competition inside and out, his or her strengths and weaknesses—especially the flaws. Watch him or her. Study, note, and record those weaknesses. That is the area or the spot where he or she is vulnerable to your superior performance.

Hone Your Competitive Edge

Know what it takes to exceed, outpoint, outdo, or outscore your competition—to offset his or her weaknesses and to zig where your competition zags. Avoid or minimize his or her strengths in the eyes of others—especially of your target people. Excel in the areas where your competition is weak.

Learn your boss's wants, needs, and feelings. Pay particular attention to his or her emotional reaction to your competitor. How? Ask him or her. Discuss your competitor. But don't be too obvious about it: Stay casual. Ask, first, about your boss's likes and preferences. Don't bring up your competitor directly or in relation to the job you're seeking. Lead with a very mild compliment about him or her and carefully measure your boss's reaction. If the boss is highly favorable, you may want to back off a bit, regroup, rethink, and replan. But if your boss is less than enthusiastic, then comment a little in the opposite way. Again, check the reaction. Your boss may be telling you something, consciously or unconsciously.

Be very slow to bad-mouth your competitor. This can boomerang badly and hurt you. Your boss could be leading you on. He or she might *like* the person or repeat your words to someone who does—such as your competitor—just to watch the sparks fly.

Your major effort at this point should not be to *give* information, but to *get* it—to learn how to outdo, outcompete, and outscore your competitor.

GET ALONG WELL WITH YOUR BOSS

To get ahead, you must get along extra well with your boss—or with the person who can say yes or those who influence that person. Preferably all of them.

Make that extra effort and go that extra mile with these people. Especially do this with all of them if you have any doubt as to exactly who makes the decision. In this day of dispersed and diverse authority, it might just *be* all these people.

And in any case, by building a good, strong, favorable reputation for yourself, you cannot help but gain. The effort is rarely wasted. Reputations tend to flow, seep, trickle, and permeate through an organization. And a good reputation can help you in many ways besides getting you promoted. It might help you *keep* your new assignment, by providing a little help and support here and there. That's why you are wise to build good relations from the lowest individual on up to the top.

To make your best impression with your boss, approach your tasks and his or her requests with a positive, agreeable frame of mind. Show a feeling of enthusiasm, yet responsibility. Come to the boss with solutions, not problems. Do your job right and on time. And above all, make him or her look good.

Don't argue. That's usually kid stuff from the pseudosophisticated nonprofessionals. You can't really expect your boss to exclaim, "Wow! He really told me off and made me look foolish! I guess I'll promote that guy."

Find Helpers

Seek out other people who can help you and enlist their aid. The best, most effective, people are probably those one or two levels above you. They may not have a direct influence on the man or woman who can promote you, but that person is likely to listen to such people—*especially* if they have or can have favorable or unfavorable financial impact on your boss.

Talk to others who went up. Ask their advice. They know how it was done and may have some good suggestions about contacts. They may also be willing to help you, perhaps by putting in a good word for you at the right time and place.

Get support from your staff. Most of them would like to see you promoted for at least two reasons: This would give them a friend in high places who, in time, could help them, and it would immediately open a position that could lead to musical-chair shifts upward for them. Be sure they understand that if you get promoted, they could gain. It builds their support and performance, and this improves your reputation, increasing your chances for promotion.

Most people are usually willing to help a high achiever, since they feel he or she will move up anyway, and if they help, then they may one day be rewarded.

DO GOOD DEEDS IN PUBLIC

Excel where people can see it, not privately. Don't hide your light under a bushel. When you accept an assignment in a positive, enthusiastic manner, be sure your boss sees this—especially if it is a tough task. If your boss's supervisor notices your positive attitude, you just gave yourself double points. When you work out a solution, don't just grind away at it behind the closed door of your office— merchandise it! Romance it!

Go to your boss and say, "Chief, you'll be happy to know that we found a solution to that bad problem in Toledo. It was a sticky one, but we worked together as a team and designed a new program that solved the matter in less than a week. The manager there says he will be writing you a letter expressing his personal thanks to you and your people."

Your boss may not even have known about the nasty little problem in Toledo. But you didn't come to him or her with a problem, you came with a solution. And you didn't make a big deal of it. You just explained the facts, briefly and succinctly, yet completely. You also didn't act grabby about the credit—"We (not I) worked it out. *You,* boss, will get the recognition." President Reagan is reported to have a small sign on his desk that says, "We can accomplish amazing things if no one cares who gets the credit for it."

Have your own *personal marketing plan.* You know your situation and your objective. Now, have a list of merchandising strategies to reach that goal. For example, be visible. Be sure your performance is, too. Compliment others. They will often return the favor in kind when talking about you. Display your potential for bigger things. Provide little extras as a "sales plus," like superior talks and presentations. Take steps to be seen and appreciated, without overdoing the matter. Use the advertising AIDA formula with your boss for *a*ttention, *i*nterest, *d*esire, and *a*ction toward your promotion.

PROMOTE YOURSELF

Use the "great progressive plan" strategy. You have probably developed a personal marketing plan using your *SOS (s*ituation, *o*bjective, *s*trategy) formula. So you know how to design a practical and progressive program. This in itself is a real skill. It can also be a source of power.

Now consider using this ability in an even more direct strategy for getting a promotion. Prepare a progressive business plan featuring you in a prominent position and present this to the person who can approve and promote you.

Here's how you might do this: Your ultimate goal—or next major position—might be to head up a key unit or organization. And so you should make a plan, not just for getting there but for functioning as head of that unit. You know the situation, your problems, and the opportunities of that job. You know the objectives of your new role. And you have some operating strategy steps in mind. The more qualified you are to fill this role and reach this goal, the more complete your program is likely to be.

The major advantage: You can present this business-building, goal-reaching plan to those who can give you this major assignment. Unless you are excessively unqualified and premature, this generally can't hurt you. The worst that can usually happen is that they won't let you try. Or if you do try, it may not work out. But even then, you will have learned a lot, experienced a lot, perhaps reached a goal, enhanced your record, and possibly made a strong and favorable impression. Your competition probably has not even thought to do this.

But here is the key: Authorities find that a *person with a plan becomes, psychologically, almost irresisitible to people with power.* Top managers have a nearly compulsive urge to try a well-thought-out plan.

In short, if your goal is a certain job, assignment, or promotion, then take your time and make a very thorough, well-considered, written action plan showing you in that role. Cover the situation, the objective, and several elements of strategy for performing the job, including a reasonably easily reached time schedule. Be sure it sounds practical, reasonable, and doable. Get some help. Review the plan with some knowledgeable and sympathetic people. Then present this plan to the person who can say yes—and you may have reached your goal in just one, swift master stroke! Just be quite sure you can deliver, or you could wind up back on square one, with egg on your face.

TIME YOUR MOVE

As you analyze your prospects, your game, boss, competitor, and your plan, timing can often spell the difference between success and failure.

Plan your schedule, your calender, your dates, and your steps. Just the simple act of setting down such a program has a certain magic: It helps to make it happen, because you now know what you want to do next. Your attention begins to focus on that particular step and on that particular date. It becomes far more probable and and likely to happen than would be true if you had no schedule.

Circumstances have a way of changing. Suddenly, doors can open that had long been closed. Be ready. Be well prepared. Wait. Watch. Bide your time. Use patience. Not long-suffering, wait-forever-type patience, but enough restraint to sit tight until conditions are most favorable—when a small or moderate effort will get you big results.

Chairman Mao of China taught strategy thusly to his highly successful socioeconomic and military forces: "They attack, we retreat. They stop, we stop. They sleep, we attack." Eventually the time will be right. Then strike! Move! Take action now! All your thought, planning, and preparation will pay off. You have the right proposal, the right program. Now present it to the right person at the right time. And do it in the right way—a pleasant, constructive way—one that is not totally self-seeking but is also aimed at helping the group, the company, and the boss. Do this, and the boss will *want* to promote you.

And don't be discouraged by a turndown. Keep asking—at decent and discreet intervals. Use the drip-drip-drip-drip tactic. It wears down the hardest rock.

SUMMARY

Your most promising strategy for landing that promotion is:

1. Review your prospects.
2. Know the game you're in.
3. Be sure you know who can really promote you.
4. Know your competition.
5. Sharpen the competitive edge.
6. Get along extra well with your boss and his or her boss.
7. Enlist help from others.
8. Do good deeds where they can be seen.
9. Promote yourself! Use this "great progressive plan" strategy.
10. Time your move.

Your OBI (one best idea) for getting that promotion is to know your prospects and your competition, get along well with all your bosses, enlist help, do visible good deeds, and promote yourself at the right time.

CHAPTER 23
Stress Without Distress— to Avoid "Burnout"

Above-average people are likely to experience above-average stress. In fact, stress might be called "the achiever's sickness." Is this surprising? Not really. Achievers almost invite stress, for at least two reasons.

First, by definition, achievers solve more problems than other people do. When trouble and difficulty block most people, achievers move forward, push, and apply themselves. They take on Shakespeare's (or Hamlet's) "slings and arrows of outrageous fortune . . . *and by opposing* end them." They try, dare, strive, push, fight—and win. They can't win them all, of course, and often say so. But they don't expect to. And win or lose, they inherit some stress.

Second, now that they have achieved, they have also gained a reputation for accomplishment. Therefore, when a new problem assignment comes along, guess who gets the job! Managers have a slogan, "Responsibility gravitates to those who can." And it surely does.

As an achiever, you are expected to take that new assignment and solve it. You are probably asked to manage your affairs and perhaps those of others, to correct things, and resolve difficulties. Yet you are expected to do this peacefully, calmly, sweetly, and serenely, without ruffling your feathers, rippling the waters, or dumping the apple cart!

At times, you may be painfully reminded of the skeptic's remark, "If you can keep your head when all about you are losing theirs—maybe you just don't understand the situation!" But whether you understand the problem or not, for your own sake, you should follow another management axiom, "Learn to complain without suffering." This chapter gives you some ways to achieve that.

RECOGNIZE AND UNDERSTAND STRESS

Stress is usually a function of time. It generally occurs when you have more to handle (or are ambitious to do more) than you have time to do it in. Stress often occurs when people deluge you with problems or take you away from your important, goal-oriented activities. We have all seen the sign, "When you're up to your knees in alligators, it's hard to remember that your original objective was to drain the swamp!"

Stress is caused primarily by overload, but also by mistakes (yours and others'), bad luck, misfortune, adversity, criticism, frustration, worry, anxiety, conflicts, threats to your job security, and just plain, unvarnished anger. One serious negative can color other things, until your whole personal world seems to fall into a deep shadow of despair.

Stress can come from physical illness, injury, or exhaustion. It can also *cause* all sorts of physical problems, such as headaches, backaches, stomach upsets, and even high blood pressure. Psychologically, stress often comes from threat, fear, uncertainty, change, or loss (such as death in the family, divorce, jail, or loss of your job). Emotional problems are harder to solve than physical ones, where mechanical or medical remedies are better understood and more easily administered.

Many physicians define stress as "serious wear and tear." There is more of it today, because our lives are subject to hundreds of extra pressures, tensions, complexities, and problems. In some ways, *more* performance is demanded of each individual, especially achievers. Yet today individuals receive *less* help and personal support from such previously strong influences as church, school, community, family, personal codes, inner direction, and stabilizers. Achievers are victimized by a contradictory trend that compounds and thus multiplies stress—more demands, less support.

Welcome a Healthy Level of Stress

We all need and can effectively use *some* physical and emotional stress. It gets us out of bed in the morning. It stimulates us, hypes us, gets the juices flowing. It can provide the spice of life.

We even experience some stress connected with happy events—a stimulating dinner, vacation, shopping trip, movie, game, sex, success, trip, honors, or a pay raise. These all cause pleasure, enthusiasm, and excitement, which bring on stress as a companion. Generally, these are healthy, pleasant levels of stress. So we can easily see that there is good stress and bad. There are healthy, moderate, nondestructive levels—and the opposite.

Psychologists largely agree that the key question is not, "Do you have stress?" but, "What kind, how much, and most important, *what do you do about it?*" These pages will give you some answers.

Know How Much Is Too Much

We all know that the mind and body work together very closely, each affecting the other. Your brain reacts to stressful problems by stimulating your hypothalmus. This in turn activates your dynamic little pituitary gland, which produces a powerful chemical, adrenal cortico-tropic hormone, or ACTH. ACTH stimulates your adrenal cortex to release steroids and adrenaline. This activates your heart and lungs, increases blood flow to the power muscles in your arms and legs, and cuts blood flow to your digestive muscles. Now you are ready for flight or fight.

If you can't do either but must hold still, sit, and take it all with calm composure—this can cause great stress from internal conflict. Your body really can't stand too much of such stress for very long without reacting. The obvious symptoms of excessive stress are painfully tight neck and back muscles, headaches, irritability, insomnia, chronic fatigue, depression, overeating, overdrinking, and so forth. This can lead to serious physical illnesses, such as gastrointestinal upset, high blood pressure, stroke, asthma, ulcers, colitis, and heart attack. This is "burnout" at its most extreme. Excessive stress shortens life.

Obviously, to say, "It's just in your head," is correct, but only partly correct. Your problem is real. Your brain, emotions, and body are real, and they have reacted in a real way. If stress is too much, the reaction is too great. Those who say, "Just go to a movie and forget it," mean well and are partly right. But you clearly need a much more comprehensive program, as described here. You need to back off in a great many ways. Perhaps like the guy who said, "I've enjoyed about as much of this as I can stand!"

Know and Like Both Yourself and Your Team

Understanding and accepting both self and staff is a good way to start backing off from stress.

Begin by writing down some of your problems and negative thoughts. Then try to separate what is real from what is imagined or what *might* happen. Try not to borrow things to fret over or worry about things that have not happened—especially those that are very unlikely to occur.

Don't look at rules as demanding absolutes, or a matter of life or death. They are rarely that serious—notwithstanding the teachings of school, family, church, military, job, and society to the contrary. Unfortunately, some of those teachings are "overstressed" to make a valid point. But above-average persons, high achievers, *soak it all in* and become exactly that themselves—overstressed. Be a little tolerant of yourself. Take some things with a grain of salt. Don't drive yourself up the wall.

The same attitude should be used with your group. Their mistakes or problems should not be magnified, but seen in the light of common sense, hopefully with a positive view. Try to see the good in people. Recognize their accomplishments and be proud of them. This will build their spirit, certainty, security, and confidence—a belief that they can handle problems in an orderly, constructive way, with a minimum of fuss, fights, frustration, and fear.

Building your group's peace of mind enhances your own. Their calm, successful performance reflects well on you—and it also helps you to back away from excessive stress. It's good preventive maintenance.

AVOID STRESSFUL SITUATIONS

Don't invite needless stress. Duck high levels of noise, crowds, congestion, traffic, hassles, and conflict when possible. You are not being cowardly, just smart. You can absorb only so much stress before it starts damaging you. Save your capacity for when you need it, and your planning will pay off.

Thousands of good people fight traffic, swear at drivers, crowd into coffee shops, half run to the office buildings, fight for space in elevators, and arrive at their desks in a state of nervous tension, with sweaty palms and a churning stomach. Then they wonder why they can't handle more stresses later in the day. Go out of your way to avoid such a rat race. Give yourself a little extra time for each project. Develop smooth, simple systems and procedures for calmly resolving problems.

If you're trying to do too much, set priorities. Reassess. Decide what's really important. Do those things first. Do the rest only if you have time. This alone will reduce your internal pressure.

Strongly discourage fights among staff members. Explain that they are expected to get along with one another. It is "a condition of employment." If necessary, call in the feuding persons and knock heads together. Criticize both parties. Emphasize the damage they do to themselves, to others, and to the company—and the advantages they can enjoy through teamwork.

However, handle correction of such problems without becoming excessively involved or personally distressed. As we noted earlier, learn to complain without suffering. Approach problems in as calm and friendly a manner as possible. And try to stay that way. Handle the issue, then forget it. Try to let most problems roll off you like water off a duck's back. And follow Caesar's ancient Latin dictum, "Illigitimus noncorborundum!" ("Don't let the bastards grind you down!").

When you face a stressful situation, don't sit, stew, boil your brain, and grind your guts. It's a battle you can't win. Learn the cause. Cure it, duck it, get around it, or leave it. But one way or another, learn how to handle it decisively.

See the Silver Lining

Make a distinct and specific effort to see the bright side of things: the barrel that is half-full rather than half-empty—not in order for you to be a phony, self-deceptive, unrealistic Pollyanna, but in order to relieve you of some stress. Optimists rarely suffer the pressure experienced by pessimists. Optimists tend to look for the positive and accept what exists. Churchill said, "Optimists may be wrong in the short run, but they are always correct in the long run."

We have all heard the old familiar prayer, "God give me the courage to change what I can, the patience to accept what I cannot change—and the wisdom to know the difference." The last two phrases help reduce stress: "patience" and "wisdom," particularly the "wisdom" to know the difference. How many times have you seen people become stressed and distressed over things they simply could not possibly change (like taxes or foreign countries' activities)? Their anger or frustration is not only damaging to them personally but is a total waste of time and effort. God apparently did not grant them "the wisdom to know the difference."

Psychologist Dale Carnegie says that even if you can anticipate a serious development—a production error, lost sales account, late report, or even the loss of your job—try to avoid or correct the problem. But remember that if it does happen, "It won't kill you." You will wake up the next day. The sun will still rise. You may have to adjust your life style or hear some harsh words, but you won't die. And it's almost never really worth suffering damaging, excessive stress over the matter.

One of the nation's leading consultants says, "Use the CPA formula: calm, positive action. It may be corny, but it works. It also reduces stress. Life is hard by the yard, but life's a cinch by the inch."

Get the Monkey off Your Back: Delegate

When your boss gives you an extra project, your first reaction should be something positive like, "OK, chief, I'll take care of it." But your very next thought should be "Whom can I give this to?"

Don't fall into the terrible trap of trying to do everything yourself. And don't "nice-guy" yourself to death by letting your foxy subordinates lean on you for things they should be able to work out all by themselves. Still more important, don't let them shove stuff uphill and onto you.

One executive used to come in to work in the morning, greeting every person as he passed his or her desk. But each one would say, "Oh, by the way, chief, will you call Mr. Jones about the XYZ project?" (or "check the ABC report" or "write to the ACME Company about its inquiry"). They kept putting monkeys on his back so that by the time he arrived at his desk, he was tottering under the weight of the crowd of chattering primates—already overloaded and in a high-stress situation before he could even sit down.

One morning, he simply walked back through the office and handed each of his monkeys back to the requester or other appropriate person. Then he went into his office and read the newspaper.

In other words, don't take on more than you can properly handle. Delegation is an overload reducer. It is also a safety valve. Use it rather than put yourself in an overstressed situation.

If your boss gives you more than you can handle, then use two simple steps. First, accept willingly. That's very important. It strengthens your next or second step: Ask for the tools—time, budget, people—to do the job. Your boss may have just promoted you, without saying so. If it can't properly be done with available resources, then ask him or her to give you priorities—tell you which item is first. Learn to say no by saying yes. "Yes, I'll gladly do each of those, but to do them both at the same time would dilute my work and reduce the quality of my service to you."

TWENTY-ONE ANTISTRESS TECHNIQUES

Here are twenty-one antistress techniques that can help you by reducing the tension level in your personal life:

1. Allow several specific times in the day to deliberately relax. Ideally, this would be at breakfast, lunch, and supper—at least.

2. Do some occasional deep breathing. Seriously. Walk up a few flights of stairs.

3. Take a nap on both Saturday and Sunday. Cats do.

4. Exercise moderately for a few minutes, twice a day.

5. Be sure you get enough sleep—a little extra if you are under high stress.

6. Loaf a little, every day. Plan some time each day to be quietly alone.

7. Get into a hobby—one that's *not a chore,* but just for the hell of it. *Don't "work at it,"* as achievers often do. It's important for you to play a little, laugh a little. These melt stress.

8. Eat and drink moderately. Any excess hurts very seriously. Don't take this lightly.

9. Get regular checkups on your teeth, eyes, and general physical condition.

10. Don't take on or borrow other people's troubles (like all the starving refugees in the world, as shown on TV).

11. Don't keep your pressures or anxieties all bottled up inside. Get your family to help you (after all, you help *them* in many ways) by letting you get things off your chest. You'll feel better, and it won't hurt them if you don't overdo it.

12. Don't feel guilty. Many of our fine institutions teach you that you should be perfect. ("I thought I made a mistake once, but I was wrong!") This is unrealistic. Don't overreact to their admonitions.

13. Do what you reasonably can, but accept your limitations, deficiencies, and faults. You are not perfect and are not likely to become that way any time soon.

14. Leave your work (and your anger) at the office. Don't bring it home. It will make you and your family less than happy.

15. Get socially involved: bowling, bridge, archery, teaching, gardening, fishing, music, civic work, art, plays, swimming, singing. Just get into something—anything.

16. If things are still piling up on you, recheck your priorities. Ask yourself, "Is this project really important? How important?" Put things in a priority order.

17. Decide what matters to you. Should you redefine "success"? Is it money? How much? Why? Are there other things that are more important (like your life, health, happiness, family, or future)?

18. Should you set new and easier goals? Maybe nicer, personally more pleasant goals?

19. Are people using your ambition to manipulate you into higher performance? Perhaps for their own personal gain?

20. If you can't handle things yourself, get professional help early. Soon enough so the problem can be solved. Check with your doctor, church leader, or therapist.

21. Try to "forget it" and put things into proper perspective, if you can. Use time and growing a little older as an important aid.

IF IT'S TOO BAD, GET OUT

Change things. Eliminate the problem or condition causing you stress, if you can. Suffer along with it as your cross to bear, get used to it, duck it, or forget it. But if none of these measures works, and if you and your family begin to see that stress is having a noticeable negative effect on your life—it is time for you to take some decisive action. Bite the bullet. You must make some kind of major change, for the sake of your present life and future health and for the good of those you love—and who love you. If you have your health, you have everything. If you lose your health, you have nothing. No wage is worth your health—or your life.

You may need a different job or at least a reshuffling of your group's assignments. You do not have much to lose by talking it over with your boss. He or she may understand and be able to help you. Your boss may very well have felt the same way himself or herself many times. It is no disgrace to ask for relief. Rather, it is a sign of intelligence, maturity, and good sense. OK, so you may not get that promotion this year. So what? Maybe next year. If more people adopted this attitude, there would be fewer ulcers, heart attacks, divorces, and suicides.

If you think you need help or counseling—then you do need it. Ignore help only if you are sure you can handle it on your own.

Use Your Own Antistress Plan

Your antistress plan should start with an awareness of just what stress is all about, what it can do to you, and how to recognize it when it hits you. Keep an eye out for causes. You can sometimes bring a quick end to stress when you know what created the trouble. You can often either solve, reduce, minimize, or get away from it.

Take specific steps to avoid stressful situations—to build a life style of conditions with little or no strain and pain. Then keep watching. Keep a sharp eye out for opportunities to avoid and prevent stress even before it has a chance to start and thereby eliminate it. Also be aware of key changes that signal improving or worsening trends. Keep everlastingly at your antistress plan. Just as you strive to accomplish and achieve, so, too, you should strive to get relief from damaging stress. It is a project and crusade well worth your long-term commitment.

Finally, if your program is not working, then change the plan, try something different, or get help. And do it early enough so that new treatment has a good chance of working. Don't wait too long. You'll just make matters worse, and your recovery will be longer and costlier.

SUMMARY

Here's how you as an achiever can handle stress without distress:

1. Recognize and understand stress.
2. Welcome a certain amount of stress.
3. But know how much is too much.
4. Know and like yourself, like your team.
5. Avoid stressful situations.
6. Use the "power of positive thinking" and the CPA formula (calm, positive action).
7. Delegate, to get the monkey off your back.
8. Take some antistress steps in your personal life.
9. Get out, if it's too bad.
10. Use your own antistress plan.

Your OBI (one best idea) for resolving stress is to understand it; avoid it; find ways to handle it on the job and at home; and commit yourself to an ongoing, long-term antistress program.

CHAPTER 24
Job Satisfaction— Even in a Quiet Company

Politics is often called "the art of the possible." That same phrase might also be used to describe job satisfaction. Some things we can change—but others we must *accept* as pretty well given, fixed and firm for the forseeable future. And so, if we are wise, we learn to live with most aspects of our daily lives, including our job routine. We can't really do much about where our job is located, when the work hours are set, who our boss happens to be, what his or her philosophies are, why our group was organized, or even when the mail arrives. There are hundreds of such "givens" in our life.

Job satisfaction, for most of us, begins with adjusting what we can—and proceeding promptly to *acceptance* of fixed factors, at least for now. Graciously accepting conditions has two important advantages for you: First, you get along much better with your boss and the system—enhancing your near-term future prospects with your company. Second, you simply improve your own working conditions and environment. You make your surroundings and atmosphere far more tolerable, hospitable, enjoyable, and satisfying. Your life itself improves a bit.

Famous ad executive Leo Burnett ran a business of nearly a billion dollars a year—one well-known in the industry as "a happy ship." Said Leo, "I want to enjoy going to work in the morning." He did, so did his people. Some of Leo's secrets and those of other key leaders are summarized in the next few pages.

MESH YOUR GOALS WITH THE COMPANY'S

A vital (and surprising) secret of satisfaction is to mesh your goals with those of the company. Review your company's real objectives. This tells you lots of things—its wants and needs and what game you are in. After all, you can't hope to win much if you don't know where the goal line is located or how to make points with the scorekeeper.

Your company's goals may be sales or market share, growth, profits, or return on investment. Or the goals may be less specific or statistical and instead more qualitative, such as satisfied customers or just maintaining the status quo or the owner's happiness, peace, security, or prestige. Then again, the goals may be neither statistical, stated, nor obvious. If you aren't very sure of company goals, there is usually a reason. It means they are either partly hidden or just possibly ill-defined and maybe nonexistent.

You may need to ask a little and look and listen quite a lot to positively identify the company's goals. But it is well worth doing. When you do, you may want to adopt some of those goals or adjust a few of your own values. Take special note of where your career goals overlap the company's goals. Be particularly careful to be realistic in terms of the size and time frame of your goals (like how rich, how soon).

Plan in Terms of Your Mutual Goals

Make a plan aimed at your mutual objectives—those you share with the company—and adjust your activities accordingly. For example, if a major mutual goal is a peaceful status quo or job security, then you should take very few big risks. Instead build a solid base of satisfied supervisors and satisfactory service to your company. If it's prestige that both you and your organization seek, look to projects that enhance your mutual status. Avoid the negative and mundane. If your mutual goal is to build sales, profits, or the boss's ego, don't waste your time on many other projects.

Get a Kick out of Goals

Deliberately decide that you are going to have fun hitting certain targets. Mount the numbers on a chart on the wall and keep score, perhaps in red, in the form of a rising thermometer. This can seem a bit old-fashioned, but it can also add a little more meaning, fun, and satisfaction to your job.

And then you may find some projects that are basically means to an end—yet they, too, can become fun in and of themselves. The means or methods actually become sources of satisfaction. Your goal might be to increase sales. A means to achieving this target may be developing better advertisements. Yet this might become fun all by itself. Or maybe winning a new account is a means to the same sales increase—but itself becomes an interim goal as well.

Keeping the boss informed may call for a good report—and writing such a report becomes in itself a pleasant goal that you can enjoy while you are doing it. Maybe a team of top-quality achievers is needed by your company to reach its goal of high investment return. Yet simply building the team may become a pleasant, exciting project and goal—an end unto itself. In short, the means become an end.

THE PERSON MAKES THE JOB

While it is not totally true, of course, that the incumbent makes the job, it is partly correct. Every employee brings a unique package of abilities and attitudes to his or her position. That is especially true in a management or executive slot.

Since you know yourself pretty well by now, you know your special strengths. Put those to use. You will gain in three ways: First, you will enjoy your job more, because we almost always like doing the things we do best. Second, by emphasizing the action that is your strength, you are likely to make a maximum contribution to your company. That is not only personally pleasing but rewarding to the organization itself, because a healthy, growing company is usually a more enjoyable workplace than one experiencing sickness, decline, and failure. Third, you will get increased recognition, acclaim, respect, rewards, and possibly promotion. And that's really not too shabby.

To do these things—recheck your talents. Take inventory. Pick two or three strengths and match them up with your job functions. Give these matchups high priority as "things to do" every day. Some of these projects may represent extras, add-ons or new systems, procedures, programs, or methods. But still, these should be things you like to do—yet things that help you reach both your personal goals and company objectives.

Involve the Firm in Outside Activities

Worthwhile outside activities are those that you enjoy and that fit well with your company—or that will help improve the company's image and reputation. Just be very sure to talk the proposed involvement over with your supervisor. Get approval and give him or her time to clear it on up the line. This can be a major policy decision and, surprisingly, a "touchy," or sensitive, subject. Your supervisor may be very supportive and even enthusiastic about the idea—after all, you are enhancing his or her reputation, too.

The outside involvements might be in support of such activities as the local hospital fund drive, the community art fair, the civic symphony orchestra, the university's annual career day, the college sports team, civic service clubs, or handicapped groups.

Volunteerism is coming back to full strength in America. It never really died. About 25 percent of our population does some volunteer work. Becoming involved builds one's reputation and opens new contacts, new friends, new vistas, even new business opportunities—and can add lots of enjoyment to your career.

Beware of Internal Crosscurrents

In-house conflicts or "church fights" are often primarily emotional and pointless intergroup power struggles—long on feelings and short on logic. Drifting firms are particularly vulnerable to such crosswinds. If you get involved, the days can suddenly become mighty long, tedious, and unpleasant. This is what many people mean when they say, "I had a really rotten day at the office!"

To increase your on-the-job enjoyment, just stay out of such clashes. Stay neutral. Pretend to almost ignore the matter. Make mildly positive statements to both groups but no negative remarks against either. Concentrate on your daily chores. Remain friendly with each group, if you possibly can. You never know who will win.

Remember, the whole thing usually blows over in a few

months. People will soon forget what it was all about. But enemies made during such fights can remain bitter foes for many years. Avoiding this sort of thing sometimes requires real effort. But in the end, this diplomacy can greatly enhance your career enjoyment.

Try New Directions

You might consider encouraging the company to strike out in a new direction if—but only if—you enjoy excitement. It can be a lively ride either way—being turned down or taking the trip.

Even quiet, sleepy companies usually have untapped potential or marketing opportunities. Your best approach is to simply outline this situation and recommend action to take advantage of it. Be sure this is in line, or at least not in direct conflict, with company objectives.

To survive in case of trouble, simply propose a harmless test on a very small scale. Be sure you have widely recognized support from higher authorities—and that the program is designed to help the total company and *make the top people look good*. Have a clear understanding about just what will happen to participants (like you) if the program fails. And don't commit all or even most of your energies to the experiment for very long. Keep at least one foot planted firmly on solid ground. Test these new waters with just one toe at a time.

Beware of a Take-Over or Company Failure

Sleepy, drifting, or declining operations are especially vulnerable to take-overs or failures. You can protect yourself, at least somewhat, by doing all you can to build your reputation on every level—with your supervisors, associates, other allied or related organizations (that might play a take-over role), the nearby local community, and any national groups you can contact, impress, or influence.

Watch for signs of danger and be alert to consistent rumors. Know where the lifeboats are, and you will literally sleep better at night.

BRING IN THE PSYCHOSOCIOLOGISTS

There are among us, and for hire, people who specialize in improving human relations. Good sources of these are industrial relations associations or departments at major companies or universities. These people are trained, skilled, and expert at teaching corporate groups and individuals how to improve internal and external personal relations.

The great advantage to employing this outside service (generally for a series of one- or two-hour presentations) is that these people usually get good results. They improve morale and boost the feelings people have toward themselves, their fellow employees, and their customers. This often has the major advantage of increasing company respect, regard, status, sales, and profit.

To make all this happen, be sure to get your supervisor's approval and active support. Then contact several services. Shop around. Check with their customers and ask a few of them to write letters of recommendation to your boss. Then get them to phone him or her, so the chief can ask questions. A key step: When the program is launched, be absolutely sure that the boss and all supervisors *demonstrate their strong endorsement*. Then encourage first-level supervisors to take part in the presentations and later use the methods in their daily activities.

If and when the program succeeds, your job will suddenly become more enjoyable—even in a quiet, conservative company.

Perhaps Use the "Shake 'em Up" Approach

Sometimes the "shake 'em up tactic can lead to personal excitement, enjoyment, and group progress. This action may take the form of an open, constructive, and friendly call to reappraise current methods and consider new policies.

To succeed, this should not be a confrontation. That generates strife, stress, and unpleasantness. Instead, this should be a step made when there is a generally open mind among top people, at least a moderate spirit of receptiveness, and a willingness to consider and try new things.

The "shake 'em up" alternatives should be offered in the best interests of the company in general and the *top people in particular*. If there is a chance that this is *not* the way these suggestions will be taken, don't make them—not if your goal is to increase your job enjoyment.

The Japanese Philosophy of Career Satisfaction

Executives in Japan learn to enjoy the whole package. They believe in their company, their products, their services, their people, and their role in society and the community. Managers believe in the corporate mission and adopt it as their own personal objective. Therefore, company progress becomes personal progress. The managers encourage nonsupervisory employees to feel the same way. *Japanese managers make sure that company success does, in fact, directly benefit all company employees.*

If you can adopt some or most of this philosophy, you will increase your own job satisfaction. In a sense, you simply raise yourself by raising others.

ENJOY YOURSELF

Relax and coast. There is nothing that says you can't get a kick out of your work—or that you must be making maximum effort every minute. No one does, especially in a quiet, nonagressive organization. Learn to pick certain days of the week or just hours of the day when you tune in to some especially easy or fun-type work. This might be visiting friendly associates or reading the trade and professional journals or newsletters.

And there is nothing really wrong with taking another look, making a reappraisal of your own personal goals, values, and lifestyle. Perhaps you set those too high or aimed them in the wrong direction. A midcourse correction might be a wise decision. You may want to tune your goals in a little closer to prevailing conditions and to the goals of your organization. They might know something you don't know or haven't yet recognized.

Millions are very happy in nondynamic firms.

Get Your Jollies Elsewhere

Your career can be a source of great personal satisfaction, but it need not be your whole world, your main purpose in life, and your sole font of enjoyment. In fact, it is just a little unfair to ask that of your company—and a little unrealistic to expect it. It never promised you a rose garden. And even roses have thorns.

You can do a good job, get good pay, enjoy your work to a certain degree and yet look on it as only one element in your life—an important element, to be sure, but still just one.

Your job can provide your support and your income without being your prime source of satisfaction. Instead, it can serve as your base or launching pad to other activities. Many a successful professional gets modest satisfaction from doing a good job, yet the prime source of his or her enjoyment is in some other field—music, art, politics, design, construction, volunteerism, church, farming, teaching, travel, sports, learning, or a hobby. Some of these activities can even be far more productive than their full-time career duties.

To do this, keep an open mind and try things a few times. Keep your options open as the months and years go by. Pick out one or two things you like, especially activities that may relate to or supplement your career.

Learn and Make Contacts Through Your Company

Use your company to learn and to make contacts outside your everyday world of work. Enjoy and benefit from the training and educational opportunities that many, perhaps most, jobs offer. These broaden your horizons—give you new vistas, new chances to expand your scope of duties and try new activities.

This also builds and widens your reputation and increases the number and quality of your contacts. From these, you might very well get new opportunities or offers within your current career or in addition to it—or even in place of it. Broadening your contacts is an activity almost without limits—restricted only by our own time, inclination, and supervisor's approval. If you do wish this to lead to greener pastures, however, move casually, quietly, and cautiously. Don't be obvious. There's really no need to tip your hand.

Burn no bridges if you can possibly avoid it. Have a good opportunity or two lined up in advance and well ahead of the time when your patience runs out or an emergency hits you.

VOTE WITH YOUR FEET

Sometimes the best way to enjoy a job is to leave it! We opened this chapter with a partial quote from famous adman Leo Burnett. Now let's finish it. He said, "I want to enjoy going to work in the morning—and the day that I don't, I'll start looking for another job."

The decision must be yours. Give it more than a fair and extensive effort but recognize when it just isn't your cup of tea. Level with yourself. Bite the bullet. Perhaps you'll feel like the executive who said, "I've enjoyed about as much of this job as I can stand!"

Then it's time for you to vote with your feet. And we have now come full circle—all the way back to the first chapter in this second part of the book, where we said, "This above all, know thyself": know your own mind, your wants, needs, weaknesses, and strengths. Take this package of capabilities down to your friendly neighborhood executive recruiter. You'll probably be glad you did. So will your family, and likely, so will your former employer. You'll all be better off, and you will have an improved career situation that can become truly enjoyable.

SUMMARY

Here are your best approaches to finding job satisfaction, even in a quiet company:

1. Mesh your goals with those of your organization.
2. Make a plan aimed at your mutual objectives.
3. Deliberately get a kick out of some of your goals.
4. Use the person-makes-the-job idea.
5. Involve the firm in outside activities.
6. Avoid destructive internal crosscurrents.
7. Encourage tests of new directions.

8. Beware of a take-over or business failure.
9. Bring in the psychosociologists.
10. Consider the "shake 'em up" tactic.
11. Look at the Japanese philosophy of career satisfaction.
12. Enjoy yourself, coast, and relax.
13. Consider getting your jollies elsewhere.
14. Use your company to learn and make contacts.
15. If it's really not your cup of tea, leave it.

Your OBI (one best idea) for greater job satisfaction is to merge your goals into a plan you like, adjusted to your tastes; look outside for new activities; avoid infighting; enjoy yourself and your job; look elsewhere for your main source of personal fulfillment—or seriously consider finding a new position.

Index

AMACOM Paperbacks

John Fenton	The A To Z Of Sales Management	$ 7.95	07580
Hank Seiden	Advertising Pure And Simple	$ 7.95	07510
Alice G. Sargent	The Androgynous Manager	$ 8.95	07601
John D. Arnold	The Art Of Decision Making	$ 6.95	07537
Oxenfeldt & Miller & Dickinson	A Basic Approach To Executive Decision Making	$ 7.95	07551
Curtis W. Symonds	Basic Financial Management	$ 7.95	07563
William R. Osgood	Basics Of Successful Business Planning	$ 7.95	07579
Dickens & Dickens	The Black Manager	$10.95	07564
Ken Cooper	Bodybusiness	$ 5.95	07545
Richard R. Conarroe	Bravely, Bravely In Business	$ 3.95	07509
Jones & Trentin	Budgeting	$12.95	07528
Adam Starchild	Building Wealth	$ 7.95	07594
Laura Brill	Business Writing Quick And Easy	$ 5.95	07598
Rinella & Robbins	Career Power	$ 7.95	07586
Andrew H. Souerwine	Career Strategies	$ 7.95	07535
Beverly A. Potter	Changing Performance On The Job	$ 9.95	07613
Donna N. Douglass	Choice And Compromise	$ 8.95	07604
Philip R. Lund	Compelling Selling	$ 5.95	07508
Joseph M. Vles	Computer Basics	$ 6.95	07599
Hart & Schleicher	A Conference And Workshop Planner's Manual	$15.95	07003
Leon Wortman	A Deskbook Of Business Management	$14.95	07571
John D. Drake	Effective Interviewing	$ 8.95	07600
James J. Cribbin	Effective Managerial Leadership	$ 6.95	07504
Eugene J. Benge	Elements Of Modern Management	$ 5.95	07519
Edward N. Rausch	Financial Management For Small Business	$ 7.95	07585
Loren B. Belker	The First-Time Manager	$ 6.95	07588
Whitsett & Yorks	From Management Theory to Business Sense	$17.95	07610
Ronald D. Brown	From Selling To Managing	$ 5.95	07500
Murray L. Weidenbaum	The Future Of Business Regulation	$ 5.95	07533
Craig S. Rice	Getting Good People And Keeping Them	$ 8.95	07614
Charles Hughes	Goal Setting	$ 4.95	07520
Richard E. Byrd	A Guide To Personal Risk Taking	$ 7.95	07505
Charles Margerison	How To Assess Your Managerial Style	$ 6.95	07584
S.H. Simmons	How To Be The Life Of The Podium	$ 8.95	07565
D. German & J. German	How To Find A Job When Jobs Are Hard To Find	$ 7.95	07592
W.H. Krause	How To Get Started As A Manufacturer's Representative	$ 8.95	07574
Sal T. Massimino	How To Master The Art Of Closing Sales	$ 5.95	07593

William A. Delaney	How To Run A Growing Company	$ 6.95	07590
J. Douglas Brown	The Human Nature Of Organizations	$ 3.95	07514
G.G. Alpander	Human Resources Management Planning	$ 9.95	07578
George J. Lumsden	Impact Management	$ 6.95	07575
Dean B. Peskin	A Job Loss Survival Manual	$ 5.95	07543
H. Lee Rust	Jobsearch	$ 7.95	07557
Marc J. Lane	Legal Handbook For Small Business	$ 7.95	07612
George T. Vardaman	Making Successful Presentations	$10.95	07616
Norman L. Enger	Management Standards For Developing Information Systems	$ 5.95	07527
Ray A. Killian	Managing Human Resources	$ 6.95	07556
Elam & Paley	Marketing For The Non-Marketing Executive	$ 5.95	07562
Edward S. McKay	The Marketing Mystique	$ 6.95	07522
Donald E. Miller	The Meaningful Interpretation Of Financial Statements	$ 6.95	07513
Robert L. Montgomery	Memory Made Easy	$ 5.95	07548
Summer & Levy	Microcomputers For Business	$ 7.95	07539
Donald P. Kenney	Minicomputers	$ 7.95	07560
Frederick D. Buggie	New Product Development Strategies	$ 8.95	07602
Dale D. McConkey	No-Nonsense Delegation	$ 4.95	07517
Hilton & Knoblauch	On Television	$ 6.95	07581
William C. Waddell	Overcoming Murphy's Law	$ 5.95	07561
Michael Hayes	Pay Yourself First	$ 6.95	07538
Ellis & Pekar	Planning Basics For Managers	$ 6.95	07591
Alfred R. Oxenfeldt	Pricing Strategies	$10.95	07572
Blake & Mouton	Productivity: The Human Side	$ 5.95	07583
Daniels & Barron	The Professional Secretary	$ 7.95	07576
Herman R. Holtz	Profit From Your Money-Making Ideas	$ 8.95	07553
William E. Rothschild	Putting It All Together	$ 7.95	07555
Don Sheehan	Shut Up And Sell!	$ 7.95	07615
Roger W. Seng	The Skills Of Selling	$ 7.95	07547
Hanan & Berrian & Cribbin & Donis	Success Strategies For The New Sales Manager	$ 8.95	07566
Paula I. Robbins	Successful Midlife Career Change	$ 7.95	07536
Leon Wortman	Successful Small Business Management	$ 5.95	07503
D. Bennett	TA And The Manager	$ 4.95	07511
George A. Brakeley, Jr.	Tested Ways To Successful Fund-Raising	$ 8.95	07568
William A. Delaney	Tricks Of The Manager's Trade	$ 6.95	07603
Alec Benn	The 27 Most Common Mistakes In Advertising	$ 5.95	07554
James Gray, Jr.	The Winning Image	$ 6.95	07611
John Applegath	Working Free	$ 6.95	07582
Allen Weiss	Write What You Mean	$ 5.95	07544
Richard J. Dunsing	You And I Have Simply Got To Stop Meeting This Way	$ 5.95	07558